W9-AXJ-758

BATTLESHIPS

BATTLESHIPS

United States Battleships in World War II

BY

ROBERT O. DULIN, JR.

WILLIAM H. GARZKE, JR.

LINE DRAWINGS BY

ROBERT F. SUMRALL

NAVAL INSTITUTE PRESS

ANNAPOLIS, MARYLAND

Library of Congress Catalog Card Number:
74-29128
ISBN: 0-87021-099-8

Printed in the United States of America

PHOTOGRAPHIC CREDITS

Page 30, top: Flying Camera, Inc.; page 31, bottom
right: Seco; page 37, top: courtesy of Robert Sumrall;
page 70: courtesy of Robert Sumrall; page 106:
International News Photo; page 117, top right:
courtesy of Robert Sumrall; page 127, top right:
Wide World Photo; page 127, bottom: Robert de
Gast; page 142: Wes Jefrem; page 152, left: courtesy
of Robert Sumrall; page 156, bottom: courtesy of
Robert Sumrall; page 157, top: Robert de Gast;
page 204: Robert de Gast.

All photographs not otherwise credited are official
U. S. Navy releases. The dust jacket, binding, and
end papers depict various views of the *New Jersey*
as photographed by Robert de Gast.

Preface

Battleships and battlecruisers were, for the first several decades of the twentieth century, regarded by major naval powers as the ultimate weapon and were accorded the compliment of being termed "capital ships." It was axiomatic until World War II that capital ships were considered to be the basic measure of relative naval power. Now they are merely the vanished symbols of a bygone age of sea power.

During most of the first half of the twentieth century, until air power made them obsolete, the number, characteristics, and availability of capital ships fundamentally influenced foreign policy and naval strategy. From the onset of the *Dreadnought* era, government officials, naval officers, civilian engineers and technicians, and laymen debated the complex problems of determining suitable numbers of capital ships, the establishment of the desired characteristics of such ships, and the best means of deploying and operating battle fleets centered on the capital ship.

Two epochal developments during World War I significantly influenced the course of capital ship design. The development of the submarine as an effective combatant type forced designers of capital ships to provide reasonable protection against torpedo detonations. Similarly, the development of aircraft prompted interest in antiaircraft gunnery and in heavier deck armor to resist bombs.

In the years immediately following the end of World War I, advocates of air power insisted, accurately but prematurely, that the primacy of the capital ship was doomed by air power. The success of U. S. Army aviators under the leadership of General William "Billy" Mitchell in sinking a destroyer, a light cruiser, and three obsolete battleships (most notably the ex-German *Ostfriesland*) in rather sensational (and one-sided) ordnance trials in 1921 and 1923 inflamed the controversy. For the next two decades, periodicals and books proliferated which forecast the demise of battleships under air attack, either at sea or in port. Inevitably, these developments influenced the design of new capital ships.

However, the Washington Naval Treaty of 1922 (and the subsequent London Naval Treaty of 1936) had a considerably more profound effect on the design of capital ships. The treaty established two basic limitations on capital ship characteristics—the displacement was limited to a maximum of 35,000 tons "standard" and the maximum bore of the main battery guns was set at 16 inches. These treaty limitations accelerated technological improvements which promised to save weight in warship construction; there was an extreme emphasis on weight control in all aspects of warship design, arrangement, and construction. Even so, *all* navies building capital ships violated the treaty limitations.

The keel-laying of the French battlecruiser *Dunkerque* in 1932 heralded the start of a second great capital-ship building race, similar to that preceding the outbreak of World War I, involving fewer, but much larger, ships. By 1950, when the last battleship (the *Jean Bart*) was finally completed, new capital ships had been built by the United States, Japan, France, Great Britain, Germany, and Italy. Furthermore, capital ships were projected by the Netherlands, the Soviet Union, and Spain.

Even now, an air of fascination surrounds these giant warships, and some of them have been accorded near-legendary places in naval history. The American *Iowa*-class ships and the *South Dakota* (the famed "Battleship X" of World War II communiques) fall into this category, along with such noted foreign ships as the German *Bismarck* and *Tirpitz* and the Japanese *Yamato, Musashi,* and *Shinano.*

This book provides a definitive technical history of all battleships and battlecruisers of the United States Navy since the early 1930s. It covers the design and construction of such ships, including those only projected or not completed, and the operational careers and eventual disposition of all active ships.

Although there is extensive literature describing the histories of the various battleships and battlecruisers, the available data on their technical characteristics have been rather limited and contradictory, with virtually no effort having been made to describe the ships from a technical standpoint, or with emphasis placed on their design, development, and construction.

It is believed that here, for the first time, these noteworthy ships have been given definitive treatment in a study which presents relatively complete plans as well as extensive technical data covering their characteristics and performance. The operational careers of the great ships are chronicled, followed by detailed analyses of outstanding incidents as they pertain to design adequacy, particularly from the standpoint of damage resistance. Research over a period of more than a decade has made extensive use of authoritative (and frequently official) source material, some of which has never before been published.

During the research, writing, and drawing of plans required for this work, many individuals and offices offered valuable assistance. In the preparation of this first volume, the cooperation of various activities within the U. S. Department of the Navy was particularly helpful. The Preliminary Design Branch of the Bureau of Ships—now the Naval Sea Systems Command—made available the design histories of the *North Carolina, South Dakota, Iowa, Montana,* and *Alaska.* In that branch, Messrs. Kenneth R. Lovell, George W. Dankers, and Owen Oakley were of great assistance. Mr. Philip Sims, of the Naval Ship Engineering Center, was particularly helpful in researching the design histories of these ships. Dr. Dean C. Allard of the Operational Archives Branch, Office of Naval History, arranged access to official operational reports and other classified material.

The voluminous source data on the U. S. ships were discussed with key individuals who were knowledgeable about them, including several who had participated in their design: Mr. John C. Niedermeir, Mr. George Sieker, and Rear Admiral Charles C. Wheelock. Among the various shipyards and major engineering firms consulted were the New York Shipbuilding Corporation, Babcock & Wilcox, Foster Wheeler Corporation, Westinghouse, and General Electric Corporation.

Particular thanks are due to Rear Admiral E. C. Holtzworth, who provided invaluable suggestions on the interpretation of battle damage reports and arranged for interviews with former crew members of ships; and to Mr. Robert S. Egan of the Philadelphia Naval Shipyard, who helped to obtain much valuable source data on American ships, as well as suggesting other possible sources of such data.

The illustrations for this study are worthy of special comment. Official plans at times vary in detail from the ships as built, are sometimes poorly preserved, and in some instances have become so illegible as to be considered incomplete. In producing the highly detailed line drawings, Mr. Robert Sumrall, Naval Architect, Curator of Ship Models, U. S. Naval Academy vii Museum, had to research and examine literally scores of photographs of the various ships in order to verify the accuracy of the appearance plans as presented here. The assistance of Alan Chesley and George Sears made possible the completion of a most painstaking and involved drafting job which the authors feel surpasses the work in any contemporary book of this nature.

Still others whose fascination with battleships and interest in this project helped bring it to completion are Rear Admiral A. E. Uehlinger, U. S. Navy (Retired), Captain John R. Burwell, U. S. Navy (Retired), Commander Iler Fairchild, assistant gunnery officer of the USS *Massachusetts*, Messrs. A. D. Baker, III, Kenneth S. Brower, P. C. Coker, III, Richard W. van Hooff, Norman Friedman, Horst Feistel, John S. Rowe, Prof.-Dr. Erwin Strohbusch, John Hastings, and Christopher C. Wright. Various members of the U. S. Naval Institute staff have participated in the development of this study, with the Senior Book Editor, Lieutenant Commander Arnold S. Lott, U. S. Navy (Retired) having spent untold hours reducing many reams of rough manuscript to this final form.

Lastly, special credit goes to two people who, through long years of encouragement and patience, have become battleship experts by marriage, as it were—the co-authors' wives, Joan M. Dulin and Loretta M. Garzke.

Table of Contents

BATTLESHIPS

CHAPTER ONE

Introduction

Heavy-gun battleships and battlecruisers, long considered the ultimate embodiment of naval power, have now disappeared from the oceans of the world, the victims of technological progress. The final evolution of these ships was highly accelerated during World War II and produced fast, powerful, and progressively larger warships. In order to understand their place in naval history, it is necessary to examine their development.

The modern battleship was an evolutionary warship combining, in most respects, the essential characteristics of the dreadnought and battlecruiser of the 1905-22 era. Generally, modern battleships were capable of moderately high speeds without the previously necessary sacrifice of either protection or offensive power. The first ones were designed within the limitations of the Washington Naval Treaty of 1922; later designs were affected only by the naval requirements of the various nations. Despite artificially imposed treaty limitations,* they gradually evolved into massive ships combining high speed and considerable offensive power with the ability to withstand heavy punishment. The primary goal of the designers was to design a ship able to take such punishment, yet still able to deliver destructive blows at an enemy. Such requirements forced considerable growth in size and displacement.

World War I battleship types. Battleships of the World War I era were direct descendents of two notable warships. The Royal Navy's *Dreadnought,* completed in 1906 and the first "all-big-gun" battleship, revolutionized naval warfare by rendering obsolete all existing battle fleets in the world. The U. S. Navy's *Michigan,* whose design antedated that of the *Dreadnought* and featured a much superior centerline-mounted main battery, established a general arrangement that was eventually adopted for subsequent capital-ship designs. The battleships and battlecruisers that followed soon formed the main strength of all battle fleets. As late as 1935, despite the increasing menace of air power and the enthusiasm of all air-power advocates, battleships and battlecruisers were considered first-line warships, and the aircraft carrier was still an untested weapon.

These battleships had large displacement, the best possible armament, massive protection, and the ability to stay at sea in any kind of weather. Their main-battery guns were as large as 16 inches in bore, the largest caliber allowed by the Washington Treaty of 1922, although designs for several ships featured 18-inch guns. The last generation of battleships completed during the World War I era featured either 15-inch guns (the British *Queen Elizabeth* class and the German *Baden* class) or 16-inch guns (the U. S. *Maryland* class and the Japanese

---

*Washington Conference (1921-22), London Conference (1930), and Second London Naval Disarmament Conference (1935-36). For practical purposes, all treaty limitations expired on 31 December 1936.

The battle line of the U. S. fleet, about 1935. These ships were then the pride of the Navy—they were powerful, majestic, yet headed for certain obsolescence. The three Colorado-class ships in the foreground were designed during World War I, fought during World War II, and were scrapped in the years following the end of the war.

Nagato class). Secondary batteries ranged up to 6-inch caliber but lacked antiaircraft capabilities. Antiaircraft defense, typically, was provided by a few guns of about 3-inch caliber, supplemented by machine guns, and emphasized the primary mission of the battleship—destruction of the enemy by massive gunpower—and the current low state of naval air power.

Battleship protection was a matter of paramount concern, frequently leading to severe limitations on maximum speed. Typically, the armor system was designed to withstand attack by guns equivalent to those carried in the main battery. This protective system was of necessity confined to the vitals of the ship (the "all-or-nothing" principle), as weight and stability considerations prohibited adequate protection for the entire structure. There was an increasing emphasis on horizontal protection, because the likelihood of accurate long-range fire increased with improved guns and fire-control systems. In addition, later battleships of the dreadnought era were given side protective systems against torpedo and mine explosions.

Battlecruiser characteristics. Battlecruisers, on the other hand, characteristically were armed similarly to battleships (albeit often with fewer guns) but attained relatively high maximum speeds by sacrificing protection. British practice in this regard was most extreme. The loss of three British battlecruisers during the Battle of Jutland (1916) confirmed the wisdom of the German practice of emphasizing protection and accepting a smaller-caliber main battery (a decision eased by the marked superiority of German naval ordnance at the time) and somewhat lower maximum speeds. The notable effectiveness of the German battlecruisers and the British *Queen Elizabeth* class fast battleships at Jutland foreshadowed and accentuated the trend, leading to the ultimate merging of the battlecruiser and the battleship types in the giant fast battleships of the World War II era.

The tactical and strategic requirements imposed on battlecruisers demanded high speeds. Such speeds required large power outputs, and continuous high-speed operations required considerable fuel capacity. As a consequence, in the case of the *Hood* (the latest battlecruiser of the World War I era), some 20 per cent of the full-load displacement was taken up by machinery and fuel. Among the operational missions assigned to battlecruisers were the following:

- Rapid concentrations and enveloping maneuvers during fleet actions and the pursuit of a retreating enemy.
- Support of heavy and light cruisers.
- Reconnaissance in force involving, perhaps, breaking through a screen of destroyers or light cruisers.
- Independent operations.

By the end of World War I, the fast-battleship concept had been accepted by all major naval powers except the United States. Japan, Italy, Germany, Russia, and Great Britain were all constructing ships that could reasonably be termed fast battleships. Although few of them were completed, they established the trend for the next major naval building program, two decades later, when improved technology facilitated the construction of well-protected fast battleships.

Washington Naval Treaty. The end of World War I found the U. S. Navy just beginning an all-out expansion program so extensive that it threatened the traditional supremacy of the Royal Navy, and forced the United Kingdom to consider the construction of more ships if it intended to maintain this supremacy. The American program also threatened the new position of power established by the Japanese in the Far East. Because of financial strains imposed by this building program, the United States finally proposed a moratorium on capital-ship construction.

On 12 November 1921, representatives of the major naval powers met in Washington, D. C., for the Washington Naval Conference, which resulted in a disarmament treaty that lastingly affected warship design.

In the sometimes bitter sessions, the conferees discussed at length whether a balanced battleship design could be achieved with a standard displacement of 32,500 tons. As four *Maryland*-class battleships with a standard displacement of about 32,500 tons were under construction in the United States, the Americans accompanied this proposed displacement limitation with insistence on an armament of 16-inch guns. The Japanese readily agreed, refusing to scrap the nearly completed *Nagato* and *Mutsu,* which were armed with 16-inch guns. The British argued for a 15-inch-gun limit, claiming that this would provide all the hitting power needed for a 32,500-ton ship, and that such a ship would not be materially inferior to that proposed by the Americans. Of course, most of the British battleships carried 15-inch guns, and their combat effectiveness would have been much greater if "treaty battle-ships" were limited to a similar gun caliber. Japanese and American insistence on the 16-inch gun limit doomed the proposed 32,500-ton displacement limit, as the British insisted on an added 2,500 tons displacement if the limit on gun caliber was set at 16 inches.

It is worthwhile to note those provisions of the Washington Naval Treaty, signed 6 February 1922, which influenced capital-ship design:

- British and American fleets were limited to 580,450 and 500,360 tons respectively, with Japan at 60 per cent of U. S. strength (301,320 tons), France at 221,170 tons, and Italy at 182,000 tons. (This was the famous "5-5-3 ratio" so bitterly resented by the Japanese. All displacements in tons of 2,240 pounds—1,016.05 kilograms*—and the comparative displacements were calculated on the basis of the "standard" displacements, defined later.)

- Capital ships were limited to 35,000 tons standard displacement, with 16-inch guns the largest permissible.

- Capital ships could be replaced by new construction 20 years after completion, with no new construction permitted before that time.

- Reconstruction of capital ships was limited to improvement of protection against air

---

*Metric—English Measurements. The comparison of characteristics of ships built by different nations has long been complicated by the use of diverse measurement systems. In this text, measurements for any ship are given in the system employed by the country that built it; all tabular data is presented in both metric and English measurements. This may at times result in too-precise values, where a general value in one system is converted into the other and the exact conversion is retained in order to best indicate the actual value under discussion.

The evolution of battleship design in the U. S. Navy, from start to finish, covered about half a century during which 73 ships were projected, 66 were laid down, but only 58 were completed and placed in service. The first Texas, and the better known Maine, commissioned in 1895, were called "second class" battleships; they were never assigned hull numbers. The Indiana (BB1) top, also commissioned in 1895, mounted four stubby 13"/35 caliber guns in two turrets on a 350-foot hull, and made 15 knots with the modest 9,000 horsepower produced by triple-expansion reciprocating engines.

In the decade following the Spanish-American War, the Navy commissioned nearly two dozen battleships. The Michigan (BB27) bottom, commissioned in 1910, was the first to mount eight guns (12"/45 caliber) in her main battery. She carried the cage masts typical of the era, and an amazing topside clutter brought on by that new development, radio. Like all her predecessors, she had reciprocating engines. Only three subsequent ships— New York, Texas, and Oklahoma—were so equipped.

4

The New York (BB34) and her sistership Texas (BB35) were the most powerful ships in the world when commissioned in 1914, as they were the first in the Navy to mount 14″ guns. They were still coal burners, with reciprocating engines. They were converted to fuel oil in the middle 20s, at which time they lost one funnel and had cage masts replaced by tripod masts. The New York is shown here as fitted out in December 1916, and in World War II trim in February 1942.

and underwater attack, up to a maximum of 3,000 tons increase in displacement. France and Italy were granted greater latitude in reconstruction because they had been unable to replace any of their older ships during World War I.

- Standard displacement was established as the displacement of the vessel complete, fully manned, equipped and ready for sea, including ammunition, provisions, fresh water for the crew, and miscellaneous stores and implements of every description to be carried in war, but *not including* fuel or reserve feed water.

The displacement and armament restrictions made the introduction of efficient weigh saving techniques mandatory. Designers were forced to devise and develop new concepts procedures, many of which later became fundamental when capital-ship construction resumed before World War II. The Washington Naval Treaty, despite the ten-year "holiday" it enforced, altered the course of capital-ship design and exerted the most pr influence on battleship technology since the *Dreadnought*.

British "treaty" battleships. In view of the new Japanese and American battleshi completion, the Washington Naval Treaty permitted the Royal Navy to complet ships *Nelson* and *Rodney*, which were laid down on 28 December 1922. Th ships built under the restrictions of that treaty, they featured many innovation in later battleships. Essentially, they were a modification of the 1921 batt with displacement reduced from 48,000 tons to 33,950 tons, waterline leng feet, and shaft horsepower slashed from 160,000 to 45,000. The arrangemen forward gave the superstructure the appearance of having been pushed f tional position. Armor protection was concentrated in the citadel, w too-shallow internal main side belt inclined from the vertical f thickness. This concentration left the forward portion of the hull and t deck unprotected. Such efforts to save weight on armor protection displacement-limited, modern battleship designs.

Construction of the *Nelson* and *Rodney* afforded much valuab Accurate weight determination and weight-saving were much Standard fittings used earlier were redesigned to minimize wei employed in critical structural members, and joiner-dividing weight, fire-resistant plywood and aluminum. These effor 35,000-ton limit by more than 1,000 tons, a helpful margin f

The *Nelson* and *Rodney* were not auspicious herald battleship. The arc of fire of the main battery was severe salvo fire caused blast damage problems. The ships har because the bridge was so far aft. The maximum sp pre-treaty battleships, was disappointing. At best, th successes.

Postwar capital-ship design. When France autho 1931, the race was on again. Within a few years, were active in all major navies. The new ships, with the exception of several best defined as battlecruisers, all displaced at least 35,000 tons, and had powerful armament, good protection, and maximum speeds of at least 27 knots. The heavy gun was still considered the most effective naval weapon, although aircraft and submarines had advocates who insisted on claiming their supremacy. Naval authorities in Japan, Germany, Italy, Russia, France, the United Kingdom, and the United States showed their confidence in modern battleships by starting to construct powerful new ships with the best possible combination of armor, long-range guns, improved antiaircraft batteries, good speed, and extensive subdivision and compartmentation.

The new ships represented the culmination of a long trend in capital-ship design by merging the speed of the battlecruiser with the gunpower and protection of the battleship. The new, fast battleships approached the characteristics of the ideal battlecruiser as proposed in 1905 by William Hovgaard.* Despite the high speed, technological advances permitted the incorporation of improved protection and more powerful guns in the new capital ships, which had these tactical and strategic characteristics:

- Higher maximum and cruising speeds, which improved mobility and gave added flexibility to the battle fleet.
- Larger and more powerful guns, concentrating greater relative power in a single ship.
- Better gun platform stability and considerably improved gunfire control systems. The wartime incorporation of radar systems accentuated the contrast.
- Greater displacement, contributing to the ability to absorb more punishment.
- Great cost and large crews, which combined to make the loss of such ships tantamount to a national disaster.

The preceding discussion covers general trends in capital-ship design. There follows a discussion of the more technical aspects of ship characteristics and design necessary to full appreciation of the various ships described in this study.

Armament.
Two basic developments led to the most apparent differences between battleships and battlecruisers of the World War I era and later capital ships: the newer ships had more powerful main-battery guns** with greater maximum ranges (largely the result of increased maximum elevation limits in turrets) capable of penetrating heavier armor at given firing ranges, and their increased antiaircraft batteries emphasized the growing threat of air power that would eventually make the battleship obsolete.

Improvements in heavy naval guns were largely evolutionary in nature, but the cumulative effect was of major consequence. Generally, newer guns fired much heavier projectiles

---

*Transactions of the Society of Naval Architects and Marine Engineers, 1905 edition, New York, N.Y.

**See Appendix C for detailed data on all guns.

The Nevada *(BB36) and sistership* Oklahoma *(BB37) were the first battleships built to burn fuel oil. The* Nevada *had the Navy's first geared turbine propulsion system. Both ships carried ten 14" guns in two twin and two triple turrets. Tripod masts replaced cage masts in 1927-29 modernization. Both views show the* Nevada.

than earlier weapons of the same caliber. Muzzle velocities were often less than for similar earlier weapons; this reduced bore erosion noticeably. Improved turret designs increased maximum elevation, thereby considerably increasing range, while the heavier projectiles gave better armor penetration.

Turrets. Several World War I capital ships carried triple turrets, although twin turrets were more often mounted. For ships designed after the naval "holiday," the effect of the Washington Treaty was such that triple and even quadruple turrets received still greater acceptance, thus permitting more guns in the main batteries for less total weight per barrel.

German rejection of the triple turret in the *Bismarck,* despite its success in the *Scharnhorst* and *Gneisenau,* emphasized a long-time conviction that twin turrets permitted more effective gunnery with greater dispersion of the main battery and relatively little added displacement. All later German battleships had twin turrets despite almost universal adoption of triple or quadruple turrets in other navies. The British battleship *Vanguard,* in her twin turrets, mounted obsolescent 15-inch guns held in reserve for older World War I battleships, but she represented a design and material compromise accepted in an effort to expedite the completion of a battleship before the projected 1944 completion date of the first *Lion*-class ship.

The relative power of heavy guns of similar vintage was generally proportional to their bores, with some exceptions. The U. S. *Iowa*-class ships mounted 16-inch guns that were superb weapons for that caliber, while the Japanese *Yamato* and *Musashi* mounted 18.1-inch guns that were at best of mediocre quality. As a result, for similar battle ranges, the penetrative capabilities of the two guns were essentially equal. This is a classic example of the difficulties inherent in comparing the attributes of different classes of capital ships.

Cartridge and bag ammunition. Although powder charges for small-bore guns had long been contained in metallic cartridges, the use of such cartridges in capital-ship heavy guns was not widely accepted. The German Navy had pioneered the use of such cartridges before World War I. In certain respects the cartridge has considerable advantage. A magazine loaded with powder charges in cartridges instead of bags in lightweight canisters is much less likely to receive severe damage from a shell hit. In addition, the cartridge contributes to the sealing of the gun breech opening, thus making possible the adoption of sliding wedge-type mechanisms and improving the potential for higher rates of fire.

There is less likelihood of flareback-type disasters caused by smoldering remnants from a previous powder charge when cartridges are used. On the other hand, cartridges for heavy guns are, of necessity, heavy and awkward to handle, forcing the adoption of complicated handling equipment if the potentialities of higher rates of fire offered by the simplified breech mechanism are to be realized. Bag ammunition is normally segmented, thus permitting the handling equipment to be much less heavy and complicated. Bag ammunition requires the adoption of complicated interrupted-screw type mechanisms to provide the gastight seal given by the cartridge case.

The United States Navy declined to follow the German lead. (Even in the mid-1970s, the largest caliber naval gun using cartridges for the powder was an 8-inch/55 caliber weapon. This

was a semiautomatic gun in a triple turret—the turret was almost twice the weight of a similar turret with bag ammunition.)

Dual-purpose guns. The United States, the United Kingdom, France, and Japan developed efficient new dual-purpose guns effective against either light surface ships or aircraft. The Germans and the Italians, on the other hand, had not developed such guns and adopted mixed-caliber batteries.

The merits of the dual-purpose battery, as compared to the mixed-caliber battery, can be debated at length. Briefly, the former permitted a more numerous single-caliber battery that would in all likelihood never be needed to engage surface and air targets simultaneously. Dual-purpose mounts were relatively economical of weight and space, while mixed-caliber batteries of necessity required greater weight and space, yet provided fewer barrels to engage either surface or air targets. On the other hand, proponents of the mixed-caliber battery argued that the necessity of a high rate of fire limited dual-purpose batteries to a bore too small to be effective against cruisers and destroyers. Normally, heavier guns in the mixed battery were of about 6-inch caliber, with dual-purpose guns of about 5-inch caliber. The point was a valid one, if in fact surface ships of cruiser and destroyer size were encountered. This was a case where there was no "right" answer—the key was the operational employment of the ships under discussion.

In any event, the heavy antiaircraft fire of such ships generally was sufficient, although more guns would have been desirable. Under World War II combat conditions, prewar conceptions of the need for machine-gun batteries proved to be hopelessly inadequate.

Antiaircraft machine guns. Typically, at the outbreak of World War II a capital ship had perhaps two dozen antiaircraft machine guns of two or three calibers. By the end of the war it was common for such ships to carry as many as a hundred machine gun barrels.

This progressive increase resulted in enormous superstructure clutter and increased vulnerability to bomb and shell damage. The larger crews needed for these batteries caused severe crowding in berthing areas and reduced habitability standards.

Combat experience in general dictated a gradual increase both in number and caliber of machine-gun batteries. In 1939 the typical machine-gun armament on American battleships included .50 caliber and 1.1-inch weapons. At the end of the war, the batteries ranged from 20mm to 40mm; the guns were far more numerous and powerful, and the ships were capable of awesome close-range fire volume.

Of equal importance to the improved ballistic properties of guns was the improvement in fire-control equipment. Even before the advent of radar, such progress had been made that one naval authority commented:

> By the early 1930s, battleships were demonstrating their ability to fire effectively 14- and 16-inch projectiles at unseen, maneuvering targets at ranges greater than 15 miles in salvos of from 8 to 12 guns, remotely controlled and fired from a single key. . . .

Radar. The progressive development of radar and mechanical fire-control computers, particu-

The Arizona (BB39) (original design, top; as converted, bottom) and her sistership Pennsylvania (BB38) were the first U. S. battleships to exceed 600 feet in length, the first to have all triple-gun (14"/45 caliber) turrets and, when converted, the last to be fitted with tripod masts.

The New Mexico *(BB40) top, and her sisterships*
Mississippi *(BB41) and* Idaho *(BB42) featured
clipper bows. The* New Mexico *was the first
battleship with turboelectric drive. When rebuilt, these ships were given tower superstructures and stick masts. Note coincidence range
finder atop No. 3 turret in original configuration, fire-control directors, and added AA batteries in October 1944 view, bottom.*

larly in the U. S. Navy, enormously increased the effective ranges of naval guns against both surface and air targets, and vastly improved accuracy against targets obscured by darkness, fog or smoke.

The proliferation of antiaircraft batteries and the increasing sophistication and complexity of fire-control systems contributed inevitably to the topside clutter on modern capital ships. In addition to various search-radar installations, a typical American battleship had two main-battery fire-control directors, one forward and one aft, plus four secondary battery directors, two on either side. Late in the war, directors were installed for the 40mm batteries. All of this equipment, of course, contributed greatly to gunnery accuracy, but it also made the ships more susceptible to damage.

Antiaircraft VT fuzes. In addition, the development of the proximity or VT (variable time) fuze for antiaircraft guns considerably increased their chances of a "kill," as a direct hit was no longer necessary to damage an aircraft. The mechanical time fuze was used throughout the war, but the VT fuze represented a vast improvement in antiaircraft defense.

Torpedoes. Although no capital ships completed during World War II had torpedo tubes installed owing to weight and space difficulties and the risk of severe damage resulting from hits in the vicinity of the tubes, several German ships after their completion were fitted with deck-mounted tubes for use against merchant ships. The torpedo tubes were never used because of the decline in importance of the surface ship as a commerce raider early in the war. The elimination of torpedoes from capital ships was prudent and understandable.

Armor Protection.

Battleship armor protection, traditionally, was designed to withstand attack by guns equal in caliber to those carried in the main battery. Battlecruisers were given protection on the basis of widely varying standards, ranging from essentially a battleship scale of protection down to the requirement that the citadel be able to withstand shellfire from heavy cruisers.

Side protection. Early in the dreadnought era, side armor thickness was the primary index of adequate protection, because the relatively close ranges anticipated in combat made the likelihood of shells hitting the deck negligible. As ordnance refinements increased the effective gun ranges, there was a growing awareness of the need to provide deck armor systems. Eventually the concept of the immunity zone as a criterion for the adequacy of the armor suit of a ship was widely accepted.

The immunity zone defines the range band, for a specified gun fired from directly on the beam of the target ship, within which the armor system is theoretically immune to penetration. The inner range limit is fixed by the resistance of the belt armor, while the outer limit is established by the resistance of the horizontal armor system. Normally, the immunity zone refers to the armored citadel of the ship, which encompassed essentially the amidships half of the ship below the deck armor system.

Belt armor. Prior to the dreadnought era, belt armor had been fixed vertically on the exterior sides of the hull amidships. A few capital ships at the end of the World War I era were completed with inclined side armor systems, in an effort to improve the armor resistance owing to the increased tendency of projectiles to ricochet harmlessly from the inclined armor. A projectile striking an armor plate obliquely meets a greater thickness of armor, but the effective thickness of the plate increases well beyond this factor. Thus, a plate inclined 15 degrees from the vertical is equivalent to a vertical plate some 30 per cent thicker than the inclined plate. On the other hand, a projectile striking an inclined plate obliquely meets a smaller armored area than if the plate were vertical. The inclined plate must be wider to present the same effective area to an oncoming projectile (the ballistic data following describes the 16-inch gun carried on the Japanese *Nagato):*

Range (yards)	Angle of fall	Vertical plate* target width	Inclined plate (15°) width	
10,936	6° 58'	19.85'	21.4'	+ 7.01%
15,311	11° 39'	19.60'	21.9'	+ 9.56%
21,872	21° 39'	18.40'	23.0'	+14.86%
32,808	43° 57'	14.40'	27.9'	+39.60%

*Vertical plate width 20'

At a firing range of 21,872 yards, an inclined plate (15 degrees from vertical) seems some 30 per cent thicker than a vertical one, yet it must be only about 15 per cent larger than a vertical plate of equivalent effective area. For similar resistance, the inclined plate saves about 10 per cent of the weight required by a vertical belt system. As the firing range increases, the inclined plate gradually loses its advantage, but it was the closer ranges that were of importance to designers. At longer ranges, the horizontal protection is much more likely to be hit than the side protection.

Deck armor. The requirements for deck armor protection increased rapidly during World War II, as aircraft bombs became progressively more powerful. A 1944 German battleship design study stipulated 13.78 inches of deck armor, as compared to 6.93 inches of armor on the *Bismarck,* completed only a few years earlier. Such massive protection could only be provided in giant ships, and the full load displacement planned for *"H-44"* was 141,500 tons, as compared to 50,900 tons for the *Bismarck.*

As is evident from the preceding discussion, the rapid increase in required deck armor protection made the problem nearly insoluble. The only ships that could carry such massive armor systems would have to be enormous, even with respect to those actually built during the World War II era. When willing to forego the chances of near-miss damage (which could be considerable with large, high-explosive bombs), modern aircraft with armor-piercing bombs could defeat any conceivable armor system.

Similarly, although to a somewhat lesser degree, refined fire-control systems greatly increased the chance of long-range shellfire penetrating the deck armor. The possible penetration of deck armor increases with range, as the more nearly normal impact angle of the long-range

The Mississippi *(BB41)* top, as built, and immediately after completing modernization in 1932, when she was given eight new 5"/25AA guns and improved fire-control equipment. The main battery elevation was increased from 15 to 30 degrees for longer range.

14

The Idaho *(EB42) top, as completed (1919) and in 1945. Modernization in 1931-32 replaced cage masts with tower superstructure and stick mast, added 5"/25 AA guns and fire-control gear. The radar installations were completed during 1944-45 overhaul.*

shell is coupled with increasing striking velocities because of the effects of gravity. At very long ranges, the striking velocity actually *increases* as range is increased.

The effect of modern ordnance technology on battleship design was the widespread acceptance of the "all-or-nothing" concept of protection, with the heaviest possible protection concentrated over the most essential areas, and the remainder of the hull and superstructure essentially unprotected. Whatever the details of the armor arrangement, it was evident that much of the ship would remain vulnerable.

As far as resistance to penetration is concerned, it is pertinent to note that a single deck of a given thickness provided considerably more resistance than two decks of the same total thickness. A given deck composed of two layers of plating is intermediate in its resistance. Hence, it was highly desirable to concentrate as much deck armor as possible on one deck.

The problem of providing armor for gunnery positions above the citadel was most difficult. Main battery turrets and barbettes were generally adequately armored, but secondary and machine gun mounts were given only modest protection. Weight penalties prevented heavy armor except for the main battery; for example, 2-inch armor for a 5-inch gun mount totaled some forty tons. Machine gun positions were normally given token protection by a shield of ¼- or ⅛-inch thickness.

A tough yet flexible structure was vital to the effectiveness of the armor systems. The armor was designed to defeat projectiles by breaking them up, deflecting them, or resisting the effects of their detonation. Although a good understanding of explosive phenomena was important to the design of effective armor systems, it was vital in the design and construction of underwater protective systems.

Underwater protection systems. Imperfect knowledge of underwater explosive phenomena hindered the development of efficient side protective systems for capital ships of the World War II era. Frequently, very crude empirical relationships derived from explosion tests were extrapolated to permit the design of new systems. Although even the most massive capital ship could never approach the ideal of the "unsinkable ship," it was possible to develop systems that would withstand several torpedo hits and enable a ship to remain in combat. Battleships generally conformed rather well to this basic requirement, although increased torpedo explosive charges reduced the effectiveness of earlier designs. Battlecruisers, on the other hand, were highly vulnerable to underwater damage, as the weight and volume of effective side protective systems prevented their use in such ships.

Appendix *A* gives a detailed example of the type of experimentation that profoundly influenced capital ship design of the World War II era. The specific example is a series of Japanese tests on the incomplete battleship *Tosa* conducted in June 1924.

An effective side protective system requires the following basic features:

- The exterior shell plating of the hull must detonate the explosive charge with the minimum possible fragmentation.
- The protective layer must allow the initial dissipation of energy by permitting the free expansion of gases resulting from the detonation.

- The protective layer must absorb and contain the remaining explosive energy.
- The inboard boundary (the holding or torpedo protective bulkhead) must remain intact after the explosion of even a large charge.
- Individual bulkheads within the side protective system must have sufficient clearance to permit their maximum elastic and plastic deformation to the point of rupture without contacting the bulkhead inboard.

Implicit in the design of side protective systems is the acknowledgment that it is impossible to protect the ship against the effects of a contact or powerful near-miss detonation. On detonation, the solid explosive converts into a powerful gas bubble that expands in the direction of least resistance. If the detonation is sufficiently close to a ship, that direction is through the shell plating into the hull. Details of various protective systems varied, but the basic required characteristics were always the same.

Damage control features. Conventional side protective systems incorporated a series of longitudinal compartments with dewatering and counterflooding capabilities for effective damage control. Compartments were designed to be kept either liquid loaded or void; specific arrangements varied from design to design. The inboard boundaries of such systems were framed by a protective bulkhead, the "holding bulkhead" or "torpedo protective bulkhead," designed to remain watertight against underwater attack. Although later systems were more sophisticated, the design of World War II-era capital ships did make them resistant to underwater attack.

A typical side protective system such as that in the USS *Maryland*,* completed in 1921, incorporated five elastic bulkheads with the inboard one designed to remain intact and watertight after an underwater explosion. The outboard void compartment permitted unresisted initial expansion of the gas bubble. Inboard were three compartments designed to be kept liquid loaded with fuel oil or water, to permit the inboard-bounding bulkheads to absorb much of the explosive energy as they were deformed and ultimately ruptured. The torpedo bulkhead was located inboard of a void compartment that was carefully kept at such a depth that the next outboard bulkhead would not strike the protective bulkhead before rupturing. A final dissipation of energy was achieved by liquid turbulence in this last compartment. The total depth of the torpedo protective system was a critical factor in its effectiveness, hence the advantage of large beams in protective system design.

Unfortunately, the transverse depth required in an effective torpedo protective system prohibited its installation at the extremities of a ship. Generally, it extended the length of the armored citadel—about 55 per cent of the waterline length. This left the bow and stern, and such vital equipment as rudders and propellers, exposed. Sir Eustace Tennyson d'Eyncourt, the designer of the *Nelson* and *Rodney*, found no practical means of protecting rudders and

---

*Manning and Schumacher, *Principles of Naval Architecture and Warship Construction* (Annapolis, U. S. Naval Institute, 1928), Plate IV.

The Maryland *(BB46) and her sisterships* Colorado *(BB45) and* West Virginia *(BB48) were the last U. S. battleships of the post-World War I building program, and the first to mount 16" guns. Being the newest ships in the fleet, they were relatively unchanged until World War II. The* Maryland *was damaged at Pearl Harbor, but throughout the war retained her forward cage mast. She is pictured here, as of 1927, and after last major overhaul in April 1944, opposite.*

propellers and called them the "Achilles heel" of the battleship. This weakness was dramatically demonstrated during the *Bismarck's* last engagement (26-27 May 1941) with British forces.

Subdivision, although highly important in restricting flooding, is at best an imperfect means of protecting a ship. Normally, fragmentation resulting from a bomb, shell, or torpedo hit is sufficient to riddle numerous watertight bulkheads in the vicinity of the hit. As a consequence, considerable flooding often resulted even when the damaged ship had excellent subdivision. Despite this shortcoming, the subdivision of all warships was a most important factor in their resistance to damage.

Electronics. When most capital ships of the World War II era were designed, the requirements of electronics equipment played a very small role. By the end of the war, however, the efficiency of electronic gear, particularly radar, was a major factor in evaluating a ship's performance.

Search-radar equipment developed rapidly to the point where long-range contacts were commonplace. The classic surface engagement of the Battle of Surigao Strait (25 October 1944) resulted in the near annihilation of the Japanese force in a night action during which American ships tracked them by radar and used radar fire-control equipment.

Air-search radar proved to be of enormous value in antiaircraft defense of surface ships. By often detecting enemy aircraft at ranges in excess of fifty miles, it permitted vectoring fighters to meet the attack and alerted antiaircraft batteries in ample time to put up effective fire.

As used by the U. S. Navy, the combination of radar-directed antiaircraft guns and the VT fuze was highly effective in antiaircraft defense, although by no means a complete defense against determined attack.

The increasing complexity of naval warfare forced a major growth in the communications facilities of all ships, leading to the installation of literally dozens of transmitters and receivers. The net effect was the proliferation of electronics spaces in the superstructures, to the detriment of habitability and battle-worthiness. Ironically, the electronics installations essential to the combat effectiveness of a ship are perhaps the most susceptible to damage of all vital systems on board. Consequently, a ship with electronics gear by necessity located in the superstructure was much more susceptible to crippling damage than a comparable ship of an earlier era.

Propulsion Plant. The generally accepted need for speed markedly influenced modern designs, and all capital ships of the World War II era were designed for speeds of at least 27 knots. Such ships were distinguished by their great length and very fine lines,

designed to attain higher speed by minimizing underwater hull resistance. The relatively fine hull form caused the machinery plant and main armament to be located farther aft than in World War I battleships. Wave-making resistance, created by the generation of waves as a ship moves through the water, depends on the hull form, speed-length ratio,* and similar features. Such resistance—as much as 40 per cent of the total at high speeds—can be minimized by fine bow forms, well-designed stern shapes, and efficient longitudinal distribution of buoyancy. Frictional resistance, on the other hand, is a result of the relative motion of ship and water and varies in proportion to the wetted surface areas of the hull. Hence, there is some contradiction in the desire to reduce the speed-length ratio (i.e., increase length) to lessen wave-making resistance, because the effect of the increased length (greater surface area) results in more frictional resistance. Overall, the advantages of increased length offset the disadvantages of increased frictional resistance, hence the consistent adoption of long hull forms for high speed.

As speed requirements were increased, the demand for more powerful propulsion plants was enormously increased. This trend was particularly serious because of the effect of increased speed on the resistance of displacement hulls—power requirement varies approximately with the cube of the speed. For example, if 32,000 shaft horsepower drives a ship at 20 knots, some 62,500 shaft horsepower would be required for 25 knots, and 108,000 shaft horsepower for 30 knots—a 50 per cent increase in speed requires more than triple the power.

Model-basin tests. As a consequence, extensive model-basin tests were made, seeking the best possible hull form to permit the highest speed with the least possible power. The tests generally indicated that a block coefficient**of from 0.55 to 0.60 should be combined with a speed-length ratio of at least 1.0 in order to minimize power requirements for high-speed operations. At speed-length ratios greater than 1.0, the majority of the total resistance can be attributed to wave, form, and eddy resistance. The greater lengths and finer hull forms resulted in substantial fuel and power savings. Large bulbous bow structures became common, reducing wave-making resistance and the power required for high-speed operations. Although the details of the various hull forms varied, in all cases the hull geometry was the result of careful consideration of all factors involved.

Model-basin tests in the United States and Japan evaluated various forms of twin keels from the standpoint of propulsion efficiency and hull resistance. Interestingly, while American

---

*Ratio of the ship speed in knots to the square root of the waterline length in feet—an index of the effective speed of the ship in terms of resistance. The lower this ratio, the less the resistance per unit area of hull-wetted surface. This is one of the prime reasons that high-speed ships are usually relatively long.

**The ratio of the actual hull displacement volume to the product of the waterline length, maximum waterline beam, and maximum draft. It is another index of the suitability of the hull form to high-speed operations. The lower this ratio (a rectangular form has a value of 1.0), the more fine the hull form, but the less available volume for any given set of dimensions.

Airpower vs seapower was still more of a game than a reality when these carrier aircraft made a mock attack on the Colorado *and* West Virginia *in the middle 1930s. Battleships lacked adequate AA defense to drive off air attack of sufficient intensity to disable a battleship.*

20

The West Virginia (BB48), top, commissioned in 1923, was the newest U. S. battleship in the Pacific when World War II began. The newer North Carolina and Washington were still in the Atlantic at that time. The West Virginia was badly damaged at Pearl Harbor and was completely rebuilt, entering service again in 1944, as pictured in this July 1944 photo, center, with an entirely new superstructure arrangement.

The Wisconsin (BB64), bottom, was the last Iowa-class battleship (in hull number sequence) to be completed, although the Missouri (BB63) went into service about two months after the Wisconsin in 1944. Compared to the 1895-vintage Indiana, she was a giant—887 feet long, displacing 45,000 tons nominal standard. Her propulsion plant produced 212,000 horsepower to drive her at 33 knots, and she mounted nine 16"/50 caliber guns.

tests on twin-skeg models demonstrated such outstanding improvements in propulsive efficiency that all new U. S. battleships were given such a stern form, Japanese tests indicated a 30 per cent *increase* in the required power. Notwithstanding such differences, and despite the complexity of the design problems, model tests were of considerable value to the development of hull forms.

Design effect on power. Although improved hull forms somewhat alleviated the problems confronting the marine engineers, the remaining requirement—compact and powerful main-propulsion plants—was a major design challenge. In general, these problems were met by lighter weight propulsive equipment, higher steam temperatures and increased pressures, improved boiler design, improved mechanical reliability, and electric arc-welding.

The United States and German navies were especially bold in the adoption of steam turbine plants with relatively high pressures and temperatures. All other factors being equal, a steam turbine installation designed for extreme operating conditions can be more compact and efficient than a traditional, conservative design. As might be expected, there are complicated metallurgical problems involved in the adoption of more severe steam conditions, and German ships in particular were plagued by operational casualties caused by equipment failures. Many navies settled for more traditional designs, sacrificing speed for improved operational reliability and durability.

The United States Navy was extremely successful in the adoption of moderately high steam temperatures and pressures. The resultant compact, high-speed steam turbines were combined with new designs of double reduction gears to retain the advantages of high turbine speeds and operating efficiency, while reducing shaft speed sufficiently to permit maximum propeller thrust and minimum cavitation.

Turbo-electric drives, pioneered for capital ships after World War I, offered great operational flexibility and ease of subdivision, but they were heavier and costlier than steam turbine plants with reduction gears. Earlier American capital ships were given cruising endurance of from 8,000 to 10,000 miles at ten knots in the normal condition. These designs featured substantial emergency tank capacity. In the new ships, with specified endurance of at least 15,000 miles at 15 knots, design allowed for necessary fuel capacity without appreciable added emergency capacity; many new ships carried three or four times the amount of fuel carried by earlier types.

Electrical installations. The increased electrical requirements of modern capital ships demanded powerful generator installations. Normally, electrical plants were separated into several compartments, in an effort to improve combat effectiveness after damage. Although there was no consistent trend toward either steam turbine or diesel drive and there were variations between different classes of ships in the same navy, all navies with the exception of the United States and German navies, used DC almost exclusively. The U. S. Navy had pioneered with alternating current and all American ships featured AC installations. There are numerous advantages in using AC as compared to DC power—weight, efficiency, compactness, and reliability. The larger capital ships had a maximum generating capacity of about 10,000 kilowatts.

Ship Construction.
In an era of treaty displacement limitations and emphasis on high speed, the efficient use of structural weights was of paramount importance. Careful analysis of structural design arrangements and construction techniques became of particular consequence and resulted in considerable progress.

The conventional riveted construction of steel ships, requiring the overlapping of plates and additional material to insure structural strength in areas of heavy loading, involved excess weight, and riveted joints were known to be weak points in the overall structure. Welded joints compared in strength to the base metal.

Welding. Unfortunately, welding technology was insufficiently developed when modern capital ships were designed and built, and there were not enough skilled welders. There was, however, a constant increase of welded joints in nonvital structural members.

As a consequence of the enormous advantages of structural welding, considerable experimental and developmental work was devoted to improvements in welding techniques and materials. The mass production of auxiliary and escort vessels was considerably facilitated by extensive welding. Capital ships, on the other hand, relied on riveted structure for vital armor systems and major structural members, as the integrity of welded members under explosive loadings was suspect. In the long run, the trend was decidedly in favor of welding.

Framing systems. Two basic structural systems were used in capital-ship construction. The transverse framing system consisted of closely spaced continuous frames with widely spaced deep longitudinal members connecting adjacent frames. Such a system is relatively rigid and heavy. The longitudinal framing system is characterized by widely spaced transverse frames joined by numerous closely spaced shallow longitudinal members. This system is more flexible and considerably lighter for a given designed stress level. Normally, transverse framing arrangements were necessary amidships to help support the massive turret structures as well as the deck and side armor systems, while longitudinal systems at the extremities helped to conserve vital structural weight.

Political Effects.
Domestic and international political considerations often played major roles in capital-ship design and construction. The enormous expense and industrial effort required to build even one capital ship often made the construction of such ships a matter of considerable domestic controversy. Construction was often delayed owing to political considerations, and at times such concerns led to the cancellation of major projects.

The most obvious international factors were the treaties establishing displacement and armament limitations. Of somewhat lesser consequence was any one government's concern as to the reaction of another to the construction of new capital ships—for example, the German decision to retain 283mm guns in the *Scharnhorst* and *Gneisenau* in an effort to allay concern in the British government.

All navies, of course, can be strongly influenced by a powerful chief of state. A classic example of such influence was the construction of the *Alaska*-class battlecruisers by the U. S. Navy—it is but a slight exaggeration to comment that the only individual at all enthusiastic about such "white elephants" was the President of the United States, Franklin D. Roosevelt. Adolf Hitler's preoccupation with heavy guns in massive capital ships was a major factor in the German design studies of the *H*-class ships, which would have been such monsters that they could not have been berthed in any existing German harbor. The German ships were, of course, never built. The United States completed two of the *Alaska*-class battlecruisers late in World War II, but despite their being very nearly new when the war ended, they were decommissioned with less than three years of active service each, while other older but more useful ships were kept on for decades of service.

CHAPTER TWO

The North Carolina class

T he Navy's first new battleships in two decades entered service in 1942. They gave a good account of themselves in combat, although seldom in the traditional roles for which they had been designed. Eventually, the Navy ordered 17 new battleships and six battlecruisers, in five classes. Ten battleships (two *North Carolina* class, four *South Dakota* class, four *Iowa* class) and two *Alaska*-class battlecruisers entered service. Two *Iowa*-class ships were begun but not completed; five *Montana*-class battleships were projected but never laid down. Four additional *Alaska*-class battlecruisers were authorized; only the *Hawaii* was laid down and she was never completed.

In 1929, as the Navy seriously contemplated the problem of building treaty battleships, the Secretary of the Navy approved outline characteristics for new ships with 35,000-ton standard displacement, 100-foot beam, nine 16-inch guns, maximum speed of 22-23 knots, a conventional 5-bulkhead side protective system, 13.5-inch vertical side belt armor, and 4.5-inch side armor.

During 1934, the Bureau of Construction and Repair was directed to design the largest practicable battleship, carrying 20-inch guns, that could transit the Panama Canal. Two outline designs were produced—one of 60,000-ton standard displacement with 25-knot speed and one of 72,000-ton standard displacement with 30-knot speed. In 1935 the General Board outlined the characteristics of new ships for further study in a letter to the Bureau of Construction and Repair dated 11 July. On 21 August, the Chief of Naval Operations asked for the evaluation of ships "designed for defensive use upon minimum displacements." The range of the characteristics studied as a result of these efforts is presented in Table 2-1.

TABLE 2-1

Basic Design Characteristics

Standard displacement	23,500 to 40,500 tons (23,877-41,150mt)
Main battery	8-12"/50 to 9-16"/50 (305mm-406mm)
Maximum speed	20.0 to 30.5 knots
Main side belt armor	9.0" to 17.0" (223mm-432mm)

The five resulting studies, known as the "Defensive Series," were characterized by a main battery so weak that the ships could not possibly be considered as offensive, and they would have been hard pressed to defend themselves against likely opponents.

A summary of these studies follows:

* *Scheme 1*—Designed to illustrate the lower limit for capital ships, but with negligible protection (Table 2-2). Considered definitely inferior to nearly all possible opponents; characterized by the Navy as a "death trap for her personnel."

* *Scheme 2*—Scheme 1, speed 30 knots instead of 23 knots. The Navy felt "she might escape destruction under favorable circumstances."

Salvo! Number 1 turret of the North Carolina *(BB55) fires all three guns at near extreme elevation and directly over the bow. Total weight of such a three-gun salvo—about 8,100 pounds.*

TABLE 2-2

Design Studies, 1935 Series

Design series Design scheme	Defensive 1935-1		General Board 1935 D		General Board 1935 E		General Board 1935 F	
Standard displacement	23,500	(23,877)	40,500	(41,150)	40,500	(41,150)	31,750	(32,259)
Waterline length	542'	(165.202)	750'	(228.600)	750'	(228.600)	680'	(207.264)
Maximum beam	99'	(30.175)	106'	(32.309)	106'	(32.309)	101'	(30.785)
Draft	26.5'	(8.077)	32'	(9.754)	32'	(9.754)	28.8'	(8.778)
Main battery	8 [1]-12"/50	(305)	9 [2]-16"/45	(406)	8 [1]-16"/45	(406)	8 [3]-14"/50	(356)
5"/38 (127)	12		12		12		12	
1.1"/75 (28)	8		8		8		8	
0.50 cal. (12.7)	16		16		16		16	
Main side belt	10.5"	(267)	17.0"	(432)	17.0"	(432)	13.5"	(343)
Turret face plate	10.0"	(254)	15.5"	(394)	15.5"	(394)	13.0"	(330)
Turret tops	4.0"	(102)	6.25"	(159)	6.25"	(159)	5.25"	(133)
Barbettes	10.5"	(267)	17.0"	(432)	17.0"	(432)	13.5"	(343)
Uptake protection	1.5"	(38)	2.0"	(51)	2.0"	(51)	2.0"	(51)
Protective deck	3.25"	(83)	6.25"	(159)	6.25"	(159)	4.5"	(114)
Splinter deck	1.0"	(25)	1.25"	(32)	1.25"	(32)	1.25"	(32)
Gun standard [4]	12"/50	(305)	16"/45	(406)	16"/45	(406)	14"/50	(356)
AP shell wt. [5]	870	(395)	2,240	(1,016)	2,240	(1,016)	1,500	(680)
Immunity zone								
inner limit	19,000	(17,374)	19,000	(17,374)	19,000	(17,374)	22,000	(20,117)
outer limit	24,700	(22,586)	30,000	(27,432)	30,000	(27,432)	27,000	(24,689)
Torpedo bulkheads	4		4		4		4	
Type bottom	triple		triple		triple		triple	
Shaft horsepower	57,500	(58,298)	185,000	(187,566)	185,000	(187,566)	160,000	(162,219)
Maximum speed	23 knots		30.5 knots		30.5 knots		30 knots	
Endurance @ 15 knots	10,000		15,000		15,000		15,000	
Aircraft (catapults)	3 (2)		3 (2)		3 (2)		8-13(3)	

[1] 2 twin turrets forward, 2 aft
[2] 3 triple turrets forward, none aft
[3] 2 quadruple turrets aft
[4] caliber on which immunity zone calculations based
[5] theoretical range band for armored citadel immunity:
  inner limit determined by side armor resistance,
  outer limit determined by horizontal protection.

- *Scheme 3*—Similar to Scheme 1 in armament and speed, but with better protection (versus the new 14″/50 gun). Classed as "ineffective."
- *Scheme 4*—Scheme 3, with speed increased to 30 knots. While unable to threaten a potential enemy, her speed might permit such a ship to escape.
- *Scheme 5*—Minimum design capable of meeting the defensive needs of an important nation—32,500-ton standard displacement with six 14″/50 guns and a speed of 30 knots. Armament, speed, and protection offered at least a fair chance of engaging a modern enemy with success, but modest offensive capabilities would discourage offensive action against such an opponent.

The "Defensive Series" designs were thoroughly inferior; only Scheme 5 approached adequacy. As increased armament and protection would have duplicated the "General Board Series," this series was abandoned while the latter was refined. The General Board Series represented much more conventional ships, ranging from 31,500 to 40,500 tons displacement, armament ranging from eight 14″/50 to nine 16″/45 guns, and speeds of 30 to 30.5 knots (Schemes A through F) or 23 knots (Schemes G and H). Protection was generally adequate. Detailed characteristics of the two most powerful designs, Schemes D and E, are shown in Table 2-2.

Design studies of 40,000-ton class ships demonstrated the weight price to be paid for adequate armament and protection with 30-knot speed. As a result, there was skepticism of the 35,000-ton standard displacement attributed to the German *Bismarck* and *Tirpitz*.

Design Characteristics.
The new ships, termed as "Battleship 1937," were to have 35,000-ton standard displacement and maximum beam of 108 feet (as limited by the Panama Canal). Full load draft was set at 38 feet in order to allow use of as many anchorages and navy yards as possible. These limitations complicated the design development by limiting the range of technical compromises available.

Armament studies. In the desired characteristics specified by the General Board, armament was given primary consideration. The new 14-inch 50 caliber gun, Mark 11, was specified, with an allowable maximum of 12 barrels. All possible combinations of twin, triple, and quadruple turrets were to be studied. Dual-purpose guns, although caliber was not initially specified, were to comprise the secondary battery. Light antiaircraft protection was to be provided by 1.1-inch and .50 caliber machine guns. The *North Carolina* and the *Washington* were unique in modern battleship history in that the main battery armament was changed late in the design evolution after construction had actually commenced.

Protection. The Navy desired, as a secondary consideration, that complete immunity be provided against the most powerful projectiles then used by any possible enemy, or those which might be developed within the life of the ships. Practical considerations forced modifi-

With shakedown and underway training completed, the North Carolina lies at Norfolk on 3 June 1942, before sailing to the Pacific war zone.

Nearly 20 years after she sailed on her first combat mission, the North Carolina was hauled out of mothballs and towed to Wilmington, North Carolina, where she became a war memorial. Contrast the empty decks with crowded scene in previous photo. Note cocoon coverings over AA mounts, in photo at bottom, left.

Details of fantail catapult installation, with Kingfisher observation planes warming up on the catapults. "Cat" shots were always witnessed by an eager crowd of fantail sightseers, and a plane guard destroyer stood ready to pick the crew out of the water in case the plane splashed on takeoff.

30

Soon after commissioning at New York, the North Carolina is shown in the East River, with topmast lowered to clear the Brooklyn Bridge. Aircraft complement was not yet aboard, and the topsides were relatively clear; extensive light AA batteries were added later.

On 11 October 1945, the North Carolina cleared the Panama Canal, en route to Boston, Massachusetts. The object slanting down from the top of the mainmast to the fantail is a homeward bound pennant. (Bottom, left.)

The North Carolina was formally dedicated as a war memorial at Wilmington, North Carolina, on 3 October 1961, after a small problem of maneuvering her into her permanent slip. (Bottom, right.)

Scheme XVI

cations of this goal, with the stipulation that the armored citadel was to provide an adequate immunity zone against a 1,500-pound 14-inch shell, while the side protective system was designed to withstand explosive effects equivalent to that of 700 pounds of TNT. Adequate splinter protection was desired for otherwise unprotected critical areas in the superstructure. Furthermore, turrets were to be spaced so that a damaging hit on the one would not derange a second.

Propulsion systems. A speed of up to 30 knots was desired, to be provided by either turbo-electric or geared-turbine drive. It was accepted that maximum speed might have to be reduced in favor of an acceptable combination of armament and protection. The type of propulsion system and details of the machinery arrangement were studied extensively. Good steaming endurance was necessitated by the lack of a strong U. S. naval base in the western Pacific.

Habitability. Liberal habitability requirements specified by the Navy called for more living space than was usual in foreign vessels. The LaFollette Law of 1926, governing living accommodations on American-flag merchant ships, was voluntarily extended to warship designs. These requirements contributed to large superstructure volumes and greatly complicated ventilation and air-conditioning systems. The price paid for this comfort was considered justified by improved crew efficiency and higher morale.

Design evolution. A total of 77 designs were developed during the period 1935-37, when the characteristics for the *North Carolina* were established. This total includes the "Defensive Series" and the "General Board Series," discussed earlier. The final sequence of studies, starting with "Battleship 1937—Scheme I" in October of 1935, is too large to merit discussing individually, but pertinent highlights of particularly interesting designs are worthy of note:

- *Scheme I*—Standard displacement was 35,000 tons (as was the case for all the design studies in the Battleship 1937 series). The ship had 165,000 shaft horsepower, good for a speed of 30 knots. Waterline length was 710 feet, with a beam of 106 feet 6 inches. Armament featured nine 14"/50 guns in three triple turrets, concentrated forward. Secondary armament was twelve 5"/58 guns. Protection was adequate against the new 14"/50 gun.
- *Scheme III*—Conventional main battery arrangement with two triple 14" turrets forward, one aft. Beam was increased by one foot, and the scale of armor protection was increased.
- *Scheme V*—In response to vehement objections from senior admirals in the Bureau of Ordnance, this study was outlined. It featured the new 16"/45 gun in two triple turrets forward, with a single twin turret aft. Length was reduced to 660 feet on the waterline, with a beam of 107 feet 6 inches, to offset the added weight of the armament. The shaft horsepower was reduced to 130,000, adequate for a speed of about 27 knots. In many respects, this design was the precursor to the later *South Dakota*-class battleships.
- *Scheme VIII*—Waterline length was 690 feet, with a beam of 107 feet 9 inches. Armament was ten 14"/50 and sixteen 5"/38 guns, plus assorted machine guns. The shaft

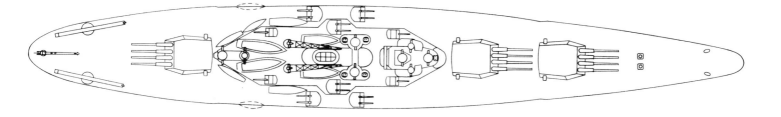

horsepower was reduced to 116,000, good for a speed of 26.5 knots. The Navy felt this design provided good protection and armament with moderate speed. Six of the ten 14″ guns were mounted forward.

- *Scheme XVI*—This study, dated August 1936 (Table 2-3) was one of the last design versions prepared before contract plans were issued. Three quadruple turrets, two forward and one aft, and a large, prominent single funnel well aft of the forward superstructure tower were the two most apparent features of the design. The propulsion plant was located in four compartments, with two boiler rooms and two engine rooms.

TABLE 2-3

Preliminary Design Characteristics (Scheme XVI)

Standard displacement	35,000 (35,562mt)
Waterline length	714′ (217.627m)
Waterline beam	105′ (32.004m)
Draft	32′4.8″ (9.876m)
Armament	12-14″/50 quadrupled (356mm)
	12-5″/38 paired (127mm)
	4-5″/38 single (127mm)
	16-1.1″ quadrupled (28mm)
Shaft horsepower	115,000 (116,595 mhp)
Maximum speed	27 knots
Endurance	15,000 nautical miles at 15 knots
Main side belt	12.4″ (315mm) sloped 15°
Turret face plates	16.0″ (406mm)
Turret tops	8.0″ (203mm)
Barbettes	15.0″ (381mm)
Protective deck	5.1″ (130mm)
Splinter deck	0.625″; 0.25″ (16mm; 6mm)

The contract design version of the *North Carolina* (Table 2-4) differed in several major respects from Scheme XVI. An altered machinery arrangement located two boilers and one set of geared turbines in each of the four major spaces, thereby reducing the number of openings in watertight bulkheads bounding these spaces. This change led to the use of a two-funnel arrangement for the uptakes. The secondary battery was increased to ten twin 5″/38 caliber gun mounts, adding four barrels at a very modest weight increase. The contract design plans and specifications were issued for bids on 4 May 1937.

Trends in battleship construction programs, as announced by foreign navies, and particularly Japan's formally announced intention not to sign the 1936 London Naval Treaty, led to a reconsideration of the main battery arrangement. It was apparent that 15-inch guns were being mounted on new German, French, and Italian battleships, and the best available intelligence data indicated that the Japanese intended to mount 16-inch guns on their new battleships. The Navy recommended on 21 June 1937 that the main battery be changed to nine 16-inch guns in three triple turrets.

TABLE 2-4

Contract Design Characteristics

Standard displacement	35,000 (35,562)
Full load displacement	42,330 (43,009)
Waterline length	714' (217.627)
Waterline beam	104'3" (31.776)
Draft	31'6" (10.973)
Shaft horsepower	115,000 (116,595)
Maximum speed	27.5 knots
Endurance	17,450 nautical miles at 15 knots
Armament	12-14"/50 quadrupled (356mm)
	20-5"/38 paired (127mm)
	16-1.1" quadrupled (28mm)
Main side belt	11.7" sloped 15° (297mm)
Turret face plates	16.0" (406mm)
Turret tops	7.8" (198mm)
Barbettes	15.0" (381mm)
Protective decks	6.3" over magazines (160mm)
	5.3" over machinery (135mm)

The Navy received permission to modify the *North Carolina's* armament in November of 1937, after the keel of the *North Carolina* had been laid. When the final contract plans for the *North Carolina* and the *Washington* were completed, all the necessary changes had been made to allow 16-inch guns. In a tacit confirmation of the existence of a renewed naval building race, the State Department announced in July of 1938, that "there is not a universal acceptance of the limit of gun power at 14-inches."

Fortunately, the turrets for the heavier guns were almost the same size and weight as the quadruple 14-inch turrets, so that only relatively minor alterations to barbette structures and turret fittings were required. Total weights for the different turrets, in each case with the same armor protection, are shown in Table 2-5. This change slightly increased standard displacement to 35,021 tons. Minor changes to the armor protection in March 1938 increased it to 35,095 tons.

TABLE 2-5

Turret Weights

Battery	Barbette diameter	Tons*	Metric tons*
3-14"/50 quad	37'3" (11.354 m)	6,720	6,828
3-16"/45 triple	37'3" (11.354 m)	6,768.	6,877
3-16"/45 triple	35'10" (10.992 m)	6,675	6,782

*Total weight including ammunition and supporting hull structure.

Construction.
Construction was delayed by several factors, including a large number of design alternations, and was further compounded by the late delivery of some materials. The necessity to extend and strengthen the building ways at the New York and Philadelphia Navy Yards also contributed to the delays.

To save weight and improve the structural design efficiency, extensive welded construction was proposed. However, welding would have introduced numerous technical complications affecting construction speed, erection cost, and shipyard procedures. A great increase in the estimated cost and time of construction dictated a drastic curtailment of welding, despite the fact that welding would have saved about 10 per cent in structural weight. Primary structural components were riveted and part of the secondary structure was welded. The ships were about 30 per cent welded, and the potential weight savings were only partially realized.

This policy was maintained for succeeding battleships, with a gradual acceptance of more welding in each class. Deck plating, the side shell, and main divisional bulkheads were riveted; in general, welding was limited to components considered unessential in the longitudinal strength of the hull structure.

The sweeping flush deck and streamlined superstructure made ships of this class more graceful than their predecessors. The elaborate bridgework, heavy mainmast and secondary battery casemates that had characterized earlier American battleships had been replaced by a modern, efficient look that emphasized their improved capabilities as capital ships.

The keel of the *North Carolina*, the first U. S. battleship built in more than a decade, was laid at the New York Navy Yard on Navy Day, 27 October 1937. The ship was launched on 13 June 1940 and commissioned on 9 April 1941.

Serious vibration problems prolonged her shakedown and training period; she was seen so often in New York Harbor that she was nicknamed "the Showboat." Training was accelerated after the Japanese attack on Pearl Harbor (7 December 1941) and the ship finally entered the Pacific on 10 June 1942.

North Carolina—Operational History.
When U. S. forces invaded Guadalcanal on 7 August 1942, the *North Carolina* was the only battleship accompanying the carriers *Saratoga*, *Wasp*, and *Enterprise*. Late in August, the carrier *Hornet* and the battleships *Washington* and *South Dakota* joined in the Guadalcanal operation.

In the Battle of the Eastern Solomons, on 24-25 August, the *North Carolina* put up such an intense antiaircraft barrage that observers thought she was on fire. In that engagement, she shot down at least seven enemy aircraft and had one man killed in a strafing attack.

Guadalcanal campaign. During the first stages of the Guadalcanal campaign, U. S. naval forces were seriously weakened by attrition. The carrier *Enterprise* was hit by bombs and temporarily put out of action during the Battle of the Eastern Solomons, on 24 August. The

Tremendous energy is released in the firing of
16" guns; the discharge of incandescent gas
leaps hundreds of feet out of the gun muzzles.

36

Wartime camouflage was not intended to make a ship invisible, but merely to break up her normal profile and make it difficult for an enemy to judge her target angle. Note radio antenna array between main and foretopmast.

A typical wartime cruising scene, the North Carolina *with screening destroyers. Main battery guns are trained in, but note that all the dual purpose 5" mounts are ready for action.*

Saratoga was disabled for three months by the submarine *1-26* on 31 August. September 15 was a particularly grim day, as submarines sank the *Wasp* and destroyer *O'Brien,* and damaged the *North Carolina.* As the *South Dakota* had been damaged by grounding on 21 August, this meant that the carrier *Hornet* and the battleship *Washington* were the only undamaged American capital ships in the Pacific.

On the afternoon of 15 September 1942 two carrier task forces were operating off Guadalcanal—the *Wasp* with ten cruisers and destroyers and the *Hornet* with the *North Carolina* and another ten cruisers and destroyers. They were in waters known to be patrolled by Japanese submarines—a calculated risk that proved costly.

Torpedo damage. When the Japanese submarine *I-15* attacked the *Hornet* force, the carrier evaded the torpedoes but the *North Carolina* was hit once. She was making 19 knots in an evasive turn to starboard when the detonation occurred on the port side at frames 45-46 in way of the forward main-battery turret. The 21-inch, oxygen-propelled torpedo carried a charge equal to 900 pounds of TNT. The explosion shook the ship and sent a column of oil and water as high as the funnel. Heavy, acrid smoke came up through the open forecastle hatches and the forward magazines were flooded. There was no serious fire and only minor shock damage. In less than six minutes the original port list of some 5.5 degrees was removed in a remarkable demonstration of effective damage control. The explosion killed five men and wounded twenty.

The ship immediately changed course and increased speed to 25 knots but remained in formation until dusk, when she sailed for Tongatabu, escorted by the destroyers *Anderson* and *Dale.* She anchored at Tongatabu on the morning of 19 September for emergency repairs, which were completed on 21 September with the assistance of the repair ship *Vestal.* The extent of the damage was:

- A rectangular hole some 32 feet long and 18 feet high in the shell plating, with its top about 16 inches below the lower edge of the armor shelf. Hull indentation extended from frames 42-55, a distance of 44 feet.

- Severe local structural damage, including three cracked sections of armor belt, a damaged roller plate support for the forward turret, and the second and third decks buckled and ruptured. The holding bulkhead failed, and about 970 tons of water flooded numerous magazines and other spaces; this was offset by some 480 tons of counter-flooding. (See Torpedo damage, page 68.)

- Shock effects were not serious. The search-radar antenna was out of use due to rupture of its coaxial line and the failure of numerous weld joints in its structure. Damage to electrical equipment was negligible.

The nature of the damage and the fact that the flash from the torpedo explosion penetrated the forward turret-handling room revealed the failure of the side protective system. This was the only combat test of a post-treaty U. S. battleship side protective system. Of course, the hit was in the most vulnerable part of the citadel. Evaluation of the overall performance of the ship shows the value of excellent damage-control organization and training.

Torpedo damage effects on operational characteristics were:

- Maximum sustained speed was reduced to 18 knots. For short period of time, 24 knots could be maintained. These limitations were imposed by shoring in the damaged structure.
- Number 1 turret could be fired only in extreme necessity, which reduced main battery strength to 6 guns.
- Armor protection between frames 37-59 port side was seriously reduced.
- About 15 per cent of the port side protection system was ineffective.
- About 528 tons—8 per cent—of fuel capacity was lost.
- The search radar was put out of commission.

On 21 September 1942 the *North Carolina* sailed to Pearl Harbor for permanent repairs, completed on 7 December, which included drydocking for hull work, and additional antiaircraft machine-gun armament.

Solomon Islands. Late in December the ship was based at Noumea, New Caledonia, for several months. She made numerous sorties into the Solomons area but was not in combat. In March 1943, she withdrew to Pearl Harbor for dry dock availability and installation of more antiaircraft machine-gun batteries and improved radar equipment. She returned to Noumea in mid-April and for the next two months carried out routine patrols and training exercises.

On 1 June 1943, she began supporting operations in the central Solomon Islands and along the north coast of New Guinea and served as a screen unit with a fast carrier task force during the invasions of New Georgia (30 June), Vella Lavella (15 August), and Bougainville (1 November). In late November she left the South Pacific and joined Task Force 50 for the 20 November invasion of the Gilbert Islands. She served as a screening ship during that operation, and from 1 to 8 December 1943, bombarded the island of Nauru. She then made a futile search for Japanese surface units in the Kavieng and Rabaul areas.

In January 1944, at Funafuti, the *North Carolina* joined Task Force 58 for the Marshall Islands campaign. On 29-30 January she participated in the bombardment of Roi and Namur Islands. After their occupation in early February, she sailed to Majuro Atoll to replenish. Following further operations with Task Force 58, she left Majuro on 14 May, en route to Pearl Harbor for rudder repairs which were completed by 24 May. She returned to Majuro and on 6 June sortied with Task Force 58 for the Marianas campaign. She took part in the bombardment of Saipan and Tinian on 13 June and the Battle of the Philippine Sea from 19 to 24 June, and on 25 June began operations in support of carrier attacks on Guam. This assignment terminated on 28 June, when she returned to Eniwetok.

Shaft trouble on 6 July forced a return to the Puget Sound Naval Shipyard at Bremerton, Washington, for repairs and overhaul, which were completed on 30 September. The ship resumed task force operations on 7 November 1944. When the Third Fleet completed its mission of supporting the invasion of the Philippines she returned to Ulithi on 25 January 1945.

Okinawa operations. On 10 February she sortied with the Fifth Fleet for the assault on Iwo Jima, where she arrived on 19 February. In four days of intensive bombardment her ammunition supply was exhausted and she returned to Ulithi. She sortied again on 14 March with a carrier force that launched preliminary air attacks on Okinawa on 23 March. On 24 March the *North Carolina* carried out a diversionary bombardment along the southeastern coast, followed by sustained operations providing gunnery support for assault forces on Okinawa.

Gunfire damage. On the afternoon of 6 April, during an enemy air attack, a projectile hit the foundation of number 2 secondary battery gunfire control director (frame 99) on the port side. The detonation killed three men and wounded 44 others. The director was disabled. The detonation occurred about three feet below the director roller path, tore a 10-inch hole in the foundation, severed 16 cables from the director, and damaged equipment within the director. Investigation of the damage showed that it was caused by "friendly fire," an American 5-inch/38 AA Common shell. Such accidents were not uncommon during the latter part of the war, especially when formation screens were firing on many high-speed targets, and at low angles.

The *North Carolina* was in Pearl Harbor for battle damage repairs and general operational overhaul from 9 May until 28 June, when she sailed for Eniwetok to join the Third Fleet for air strikes and pre-invasion bombardment of the Japanese home islands. This began on 17 July when, with the *Wisconsin, Missouri, Alabama,* HMS *King George V,* and numerous smaller ships, she bombarded the Hitachi industrial area about 65 miles from Tokyo. All offensive action against Japan ceased on 15 August 1945, and the *North Carolina* anchored in Tokyo Bay for the 2 September surrender ceremony. She then sailed for Okinawa, en route to the United States, and on 17 October 1945 arrived at Boston, Massachusetts.

Final Disposition. During her combat career, the *North Carolina* steamed more than 307,000 nautical miles, took part in nine shore bombardment operations, and shot down twenty-four enemy aircraft. The ship was placed out of commission in reserve at Bayonne, New Jersey, on 27 June 1947.

On 26 July 1954, the Chairman of the Ship Characteristics Board requested a preliminary design study of BB-55 (and BB-57) class conversions to increase speed in order to better suit the ships for modern fleet operations. Evaluation of fast task force operations indicated that the *North Carolina* class was still well suited for fleet use in every regard but speed. As the main battery armament was considered greatly in excess of requirements, it was proposed to remove the after turret, thereby providing hull volume for added machinery. It was desired to increase the maximum speed to approximately 31 knots.

The Bureau of Ships reported on its investigations of the proposed conversions of BB-55 and BB-56 on 14 September 1954. It was calculated that 240,000 shaft horsepower would be necessary to attain a speed of 31 knots. If the ships were lightened by removing their main armor belt, this power requirement was reduced somewhat to a total of 216,000 shaft horsepower. In either case, the installation of a plant with a greatly improved steam cycle or a plant with gas turbine boosters, using the existing 115,000 SHP plant for base load power, would be required if no space other than that in way of the after 16-inch turret would be available.

The added power would necessitate larger propellers, which would require the relocation and modification of shaft bearings, skegs, struts, stern tubes, rudders, and steering gear. Similarly, the entire hull form of the stern would need to be modified in order to provide proper water flow to the propellers for satisfactory propulsive efficiencies, and to prevent vibration that would be induced by the skegs.

Although in a broad sense the conversion was technically feasible, it was not very practical. In view of this consideration, and the estimated conversion cost of $40,000,000 per ship, the project was abandoned.

The *North Carolina* was formally stricken from the Navy List on 1 June 1960. Purchased by the State of North Carolina for $250,000, the battleship was formally dedicated as a war memorial at Wilmington, North Carolina, on 3 October 1961.

Washington—Operational History. The keel of the *Washington*
was laid at the Philadelphia Navy Yard on 14 June 1938. The ship was launched on 1 June 1940, commissioned on 15 May 1941, and joined the fleet as flagship of Battleship Division Six for operations on the East Coast and in the Caribbean.

Atlantic operations. On 26 March 1942 the *Washington* was designated flagship of Task Force 39, which on the same day was detached from the U. S. Atlantic Fleet for duty under the operational control of the Commander in Chief, British Home Fleet, based at Scapa Flow. The task force reached Scapa Flow on 4 April 1942 and joined the British Home Fleet, which was commanded by Admiral Sir John C. Tovey in the *King George V.*

On 28 April, after several weeks of maneuvers and battle practice, the *Washington* sortied with units of the Home Fleet for operations covering convoys between Iceland and Murmansk. On 1 May, while steaming at 18 knots in a dense fog, the British battleship *King George V* collided with the destroyer *Punjabi* and cut her in two. The *Washington,* in column astern of the *King George V,* passed through the wreckage of the destroyer as depth charges were exploding, resulting in some serious damage and numerous derangements. Hull damage was slight—only one diesel fuel tank sprang a leak. There was minor damage to all main-battery range finders, including those in the turrets. Shock caused numerous motors to start up. Three large circuit breakers in machinery spaces 1 and 2 tripped, causing interruption of about one-fourth of the power supplied by the forward switchboard and cutting out the emergency power supply to the forward half of the ship. The search radar and three fire-control radars were disabled by the shock damage. This demonstrated the importance of the consideration of shock loadings in the design of warships and their equipment.

The *King George V,* under destroyer escort, returned to port for repairs. On 5 May the American ships left the formation to rendezvous with the supply ship *Mizar* at Hvalfjord,

The Washington *(BB56), the only other ship of the* North Carolina *class. The massive super-structure of these ships is most apparent in bow views such as this, top.*

Prior to World War II, the Navy perfected the technique of fueling and provisioning major combatant ships while underway. This enabled them to remain in forward areas, constantly operating, for as long as 60 days. Here, in stormy seas off Okinawa in the last days of World War II, the Washington *fuels from the* Kaskaskia, *(AO27), bottom.*

42

Viewed broadside on, the 729-foot North Car-
olina-*class ships appeared graceful, but from
head on their 108-foot beam gave them the appearance of floating tubs. This and the photo at
top of preceding page were made in Puget
Sound in April 1944.*

Iceland. They sortied on 15 May to rejoin the Home Fleet, returning to Scapa Flow on 3 June. The *Washington* continued operations in support of the Home Fleet until 14 July when, with four destroyers, she was detached at Hvalfjord to return to the United States. She then entered the New York Navy Yard for overhaul. She departed New York on 23 August 1942, in company with three destroyers, cleared the Panama Canal on 28 August, and reached Tongatabu on 14 September. The following day she joined Task Force 17, centered on the carrier *Hornet*, and until November of 1942 operated in support of the Solomons campaign.

On 11 November 1942, the *Washington* sailed from Noumea, New Caledonia, for Guadalcanal. Two days later the *South Dakota* and *Washington* and four destroyers were directed to operate off Savo Island with the *Enterprise* to intercept a Japanese force approaching Guadalcanal.

Naval Battle of Guadalcanal. The Naval Battle of Guadalcanal, 12-15 November, had two distinct phases. In the first, the cruiser night action, a Japanese bombardment force of the old battleships *Hiei* and *Kirishima*, the light cruiser *Nagara*, and 11 destroyers, attempted to shell U. S. air defenses on Henderson Field. At 0124 on 13 November—a Friday—the Japanese were detected by an American group of five cruisers and eight destroyers. In the fierce battle that followed, the U. S. Navy lost the cruisers *Atlanta* and *Juneau* and the destroyers *Cushing*, *Monssen*, *Laffey*, and *Barton*. The Japanese lost the destroyers *Akatsuki* and *Yudachi*, and the *Hiei* was so badly damaged that U. S. aircraft finished her off the next day.

On the evening of 13 November, the Japanese heavy cruisers *Suzuya* and *Maya*, the light cruiser *Tenryu*, and four destroyers shelled Guadalcanal unopposed. The *Washington*, the *South Dakota*, and four destroyers left the *Enterprise* off Savo but failed to reach Guadalcanal in time, although they took part in another violent engagement the next day when a strong Japanese force, detected north of Guadalcanal by the U. S. submarine *Trout*, moved in to disable the chief obstacle to victory at Guadalcanal, the American air strip at Henderson Field. The Japanese knew they had been detected, but planned to eliminate American interference and carry out the bombardment thwarted by the cruiser night action on the morning of 13 November. The action did not go as planned.

The Japanese bombardment force—the battleship *Kirishima*, the heavy cruisers *Takao* and *Atago*, the light cruisers *Sendai* and *Nagara*, and nine destroyers—was no match for the two new radar-equipped U. S. battleships, although the violent night engagement began disastrously for the Americans.

At 2316 the U. S. battleships opened fire on the *Sendai* at 16,000 yards, but she made smoke and opened the range at high speed. The four U. S. destroyers engaged enemy cruisers and destroyers, but within 20 minutes all were out of action without having fired a single torpedo, the result of a combined torpedo and gunfire attack by the Japanese cruisers and destroyers. The *Preston* and *Walke* were sunk, the *Benham* was damaged and sank the next morning, and the *Gwin* was badly damaged. The *South Dakota* had a series of power failures, lost contact with the *Washington*, and inadvertently closed the Japanese main body, where she was silhouetted by the burning U. S. destroyers. She was then illuminated by Japanese searchlights at a range of only 5,000 yards, subjected to concentrated fire, and repeatedly hit, with severe damage to the superstructure. The *Washington* was not detected by the enemy.

A 16″/45 gun barrel is 720 inches (16x45) long, but the overall length of the gun is 736 inches, a meaningless figure except when compared with a regulation Navy seaman. Note the shiny band on the gun, indicating the 4-foot recoil.

With the *South Dakota* and the destroyers out of action, the *Washington* was confronted by the entire Japanese force, but took advantage of their concentration on the *South Dakota* to approach to within 8,400 yards (point-blank range for 16-inch guns) of the *Kirishima*. In only seven minutes of radar-directed fire, the *Washington* hit the *Kirishima* with nine out of seventy-five 16-inch shells and about forty 5-inch shells, wrecking her steering gear and setting the topsides aflame. The wreck was scuttled the next day by the Japanese. During the entire engagement the *Washington* fired 117 16-inch shells and 522 5-inch shells, and was never hit. She continued in support of the Guadalcanal campaign, with Task Forces 11 and 16, until 30 April, when she sailed for Pearl Harbor.

The ship arrived in Pearl Harbor on 8 May and began an overhaul period on 28 May. After completion, and a training period, she departed on 27 July for Efate, New Hebrides, where she trained until 31 October. She joined the invasion fleet for the Gilbert Islands campaign on 15 November and screened a carrier task group throughout the campaign, which ended 6 December 1943. The island of Nauru was shelled on 8 December; carrier air raids supplemented the gunfire. The task group returned to Efate on 12 December.

On 18 January 1944, the *Washington, Massachusetts, Indiana,* and several destroyers joined the carriers *Bunker Hill* and *Monterey* and five destroyers and sailed for Funafuti. They left there on 23 January and on 29 January launched air strikes against Japanese positions in the Marshall Islands. During the next two days Kwajalein Atoll was bombed and bombarded.

Collision damage. At 0428 on 1 February, with the formation zigzagging at 19 knots, the *Indiana* signalled that she was clearing the formation to refuel destroyers. Invisible in darken-ship condition, she turned across the bow of the *Washington,* which sighted her when only a thousand yards separated them. Collision was inevitable, although the *Washington* used emergency backing power and was almost dead in the water when she hit the *Indiana* on the starboard side abreast of number 3 turret.

The *Washington's* bow was demolished, smashed in and pushed to port from the keel up to within about ten feet from the main deck, and from the stem aft to frame 15. The structure above collapsed on the wreckage and the deck buckled along a diagonal line from frame 14 on the port to frame 21 on the starboard side. The collapsed structure was supported by the anchor chains and the damaged structure below. The ship was watertight and apparently undamaged aft of frame 26. The watertight bulkhead at frame 16 was ruptured. Shell plating on the starboard side was missing from frame 21 on the main deck level down to frame 15 below the third deck. On the port side, shell plating was missing forward of frame 15. There was considerable flooding below the second deck between frames 16 and 26. Three officers were killed.

Both ships, escorted by four destroyers, sailed to Majuro at six knots, arriving on 2 February. Temporary repairs to the *Washington* were completed by 11 February. She then sailed to Pearl Harbor for a temporary bow and to Puget Sound Navy Yard for permanent repairs. She was back at Majuro, ready for service, on 30 May 1944.

Pacific operations. The *Washington* sortied on 7 June 1944 for the Marianas campaign. On

13-14 June she shelled enemy installations on Saipan and Tinian, and from 19 to 24 June took part in the Battle of the Philippine Sea. She then continued operations in support of carrier strikes off the Marianas until 6 August.

On 11 August the task group replenished at Eniwetok, then sortied on 30 August to support the capture of Peleliu and Angaur. Covering operations included support of carrier srikes on Okinawa, northern Luzon and Formosa, and the Visayas. From 5 November 1944 through 17 February 1945, the *Washington* supported widespread carrier raids from Hong Kong to Tokyo.

During 19-22 February 1945, the *Washington* bombarded Japanese installations on Iwo Jima, and until 16 March she supported operations coincident with the landings there, including a 25 February carrier raid on Tokyo. She shelled Okinawa on 24 March and 19 April.

Final Disposition. The *Washington* left the Western Pacific on 6 June and reached the Puget Sound Navy Yard on 23 June. After overhaul, she sailed to Philadelphia, where she arrived on 17 October for conversion to troop transport duty. On 15 November, with a reduced complement of only 84 officers and 835 men and the addition of 145 bunks, she sailed for Southampton, England, to begin returning American troops from Europe. With that duty completed, the ship was placed out of commission in reserve at Bayonne, New Jersey, on 27 June 1947. She was stricken from the Navy List on 1 June 1960 and sold for scrap on 24 May 1961.

Armament. Characteristics of guns mounted on these ships, as well as the 14-inch/50 caliber guns initially projected for the *North Carolina,* are shown in Table 2-6.

The most notable feature of the original design concept was the unprecedented acceptance

TABLE 2-6
Gun Characteristics

Gun	16"/45 (406mm)	14"/50 (356mm)
Shell weight (lb.)	2,700 (1,225 kg)	1,500 (680 kg)
Muzzle velocity (fps)	2,300 (701 m/s)	2,700 (823 m/s)
Maximum range (yd.)	36,900 (33,741 m)	43,200 (39,502 m)
Maximum Elevation	45°	45°

Gun	5"/38 (127mm)	40mm/56 (1.57")
Shell weight (lb.)	53.85 (24.43 kg)	1.98 (0.898 kg)
Muzzle velocity (fps)	2,600 (792 m/s)	2,890 (881 m/s)
Maximum range (yd.)	17,575 (16,070 m)	11,000 (10,058 m) [1]
Maximum Elevation	85°	90°

[1] Fuzes were self-destructive, at range of 5000 yards (4,572 m)

Superheated steam at 850 degrees powered turbines at 6,000 rpm to produce 121,000 horsepower which drove the four propellers that
propelled the Washington. With such power,
even under light breeze conditions in the placid
Pacific, she sometimes plowed into the sea with
immense bow disturbance.

48

of quadruple main-battery turrets, a choice based on the need to save weight without reducing offensive power. The projected use of 14-inch guns apparently conflicted with the desire for improved firepower, but the General Board was convinced that the 14-inch shell would have sufficient destructive effects once it penetrated any armor. Since most navies seemed to favor 14- or 15-inch guns and the U. S. Navy had an improved 14-inch gun then ready for installation, its use appeared to be logical, and its performance was considered adequate for assigned tasks.

The 14-inch gun, Mark 11, was an improved version of a similar gun mounted on the *New Mexico* and *California*-class battleships. The new 14-inch guns, which were progressively mounted on the old battleships, fired a heavier shell. The development of loose barrel liners simplified the replacement of worn barrels. By comparison, the new guns were considerably more powerful than the older guns, as shown in Table 2-7.

TABLE 2-7

Comparison, Mark 4 vs Mark 11 Guns

Gun	14"/50 Mark 4	14"/50 Mark 11
Shell weight (lb.)	1,400 (635 kg)	1,500 (680 kg)
Muzzle velocity (fps)	2,800 (853 m/s)	2,700 (823 m/s)
Penetration	13.8" (351mm) @ 13,000 yd (11,887 m)	14.0" (356mm) @ 20,700 yd (18,928 m) 16.0" (406mm) @ 17,600 yd (16,093 m)

The development of semiautomatic breech mechanisms and power rammers improved the effectiveness of main-battery guns by increasing rates of fire, while separate sleeves permitted them to be individually elevated and fired. The training rate of the quadruple turrets was 1.67 degrees per second; the elevation rate was 15 degrees per second.

Quadruple turrets were extremely undesirable if they limited a battleship to two turrets, and especially if both turrets were either forward or aft. The loss of one turret on such a ship would reduce its effective battery by half. With three turrets, however, the *North Carolina* would have had eight guns operational if any one turret was disabled. But despite all considerations, the quadruple turrets and 14-inch guns were never fitted.

Main battery. The 16-inch gun actually mounted fired a 2,700-pound shell at relatively low muzzle velocity. Although it had only mediocre penetrative capabilities, it represented a major improvement over the 14-inch gun. In terms of the traditional measure of battleship firepower, the weight of a broadside, the 16-inch guns fired a salvo of 24,300 pounds, compared to the 18,000 pounds possible with the 14-inch guns.

The decision to adopt the remarkably heavy armor-piercing shell with its reduced muzzle velocity somewhat diminished the maximum range, although it improved armor penetration at long ranges. The 16-inch/50 caliber gun mounted in the later *Iowa*-class ships finally attained adequate maximum range capabilities, but was not available when the *North Carolina* was designed. Calculated values of armor penetration (Table 2-8) show the relative

TABLE 2-8

Armor Penetration Comparison, 14″ vs 16″ Gun

Gun	14″/50 [1] (356mm)		16″/45 (406mm)	
Shell weight (lb.)	1,500	(680 kg)	2,700	(1,225 kg)
Muzzle velocity (fps)	2,700	(823 m/s)	2,300	(701 m/s)
Belt Penetration				
Inches @ muzzle	27.17		29.74	
(mm @ muzzle)		(690)		(775)
Inches @ 10,000 yd.	20.12		23.51	
(mm @ 9,144 m)		(511)		(597)
Inches @ 20,000 yd.	13.75		17.62	
(mm @ 18,288 m)		(412)		(447)
Inches @ 30,000 yd.	9.29		12.77	
(mm @ 27,432 m)		(297)		(324)
Deck Penetration				
Inches @ 10,000 yd.	1.27		1.87	
(mm @ 9,144 m)		(32)		(47)
Inches @ 20,000 yd.	3.02		4.29	
(mm @ 18,288 m)		(76)		(109)
Inches @ 30,000 yd.	5.31		7.62	
(mm @ 27,432 m)		(135)		(194)

[1] Based on muzzle velocity of 14-inch gun of 2,625 feet per second
(800 m/s), average for life of gun. The 2,300 feet per second for the
16-inch is a new-gun velocity.

merits of the two guns considered for the *North Carolina,* although values stated are not necessarily precise representations of actual performance.

The rotating weight of the turrets, exclusive of projectiles, varied from 1,403 to 1,437 tons. The maximum training rate was 4 degrees per second; the elevation rate was 12 degrees per second. The length of recoil was 4 feet. The outside diameter of the roller path was 34 feet 5 inches.

Secondary battery. The Navy was fortunate in having developed the 5-inch/38 caliber dual-purpose gun, first mounted on *Farragut*-class destroyers in 1934, and tested and refined over several years of operation. The armored closed mount was ready for installation on battleships by 1937. The development of fuzed, explosive antiaircraft projectiles greatly increased the effectiveness of these guns, and the later proximity fuze made them especially useful against air attack, although they were considered capable of firing a shell heavy enough to damage surface ships. Further improvements came with more efficient fire-control systems and radar equipment.

These ships were designed to mount twenty 5-inch/38 caliber dual-purpose guns, Mark 12, in ten twin-armored mounts, five on each side. Six mounts were on the main deck; the rest were on the superstructure deck. This secondary battery, destined to prove its value in combat, soon became typical for almost all American battleships; its flexibility, with adequate range and an antiaircraft ceiling of 31,680 feet, was of great value to the *North Carolina* and her successors.

Machine gun battery. A light machine gun capable of rapid train and elevation was necessary for close-in protection against low-flying aircraft. During the design of "Battleship 1937," quadruple-mounted 1.1-inch and single-mounted .50 caliber machine guns comprised the light antiaircraft batteries. The 1.1-inch gun mount proved as difficult to position as a 5-inch mount, and only four were fitted on each ship, owing to space limitations in the superstructure. That gun, plagued by numerous "bugs," was too heavy to serve as a last-ditch free mount and not heavy enough to span the gap between light machine guns and the secondary battery. It also had open sights and a rather primitive target-designation system. Wartime operations showed the .50 caliber machine gun, the standard Navy close-in antiaircraft weapon, to be ineffective against high-speed aircraft. By January of 1941, naval ordnance experts recognized that a serious weakness existed in the close-in protection carried by new battleships and that none of the original machine guns were equal to the demands made on them.

In 1941 the Bureau of Ordnance, after a study of available weapons, contracted for U. S. production of the Swedish 40mm Bofors and the Swiss 20mm Oerlikon machine guns. First shipboard installations were made in the summer of 1942. The light antiaircraft batteries were finally converted to 40mm and 20mm machine guns in much greater numbers than had been initially planned (Table 2-9).

The 40mm Bofors antiaircraft shell was normally self-destructive at a range of about 5,000 yards. Maximum rate of fire was about 120 rounds per barrel per minute. In the last months of the war, defense against Japanese suicide planes required heavier guns, but this shell was still of great value.

The 20mm Oerlikon, which replaced the .50 caliber guns, had a .27-pound explosive projectile, half again as heavy as the .50 caliber, and fired 450 rounds per minute at a muzzle velocity of 2,740 feet per second with a maximum range of 4,800 yards. It needed no power supply, thus permitting great flexibility in installation and operation.

By the end of World War II, the combination of 5-inch dual-purpose guns and the 40mm and 20mm machine guns was a proven defensive armament, with effectiveness increased by superior fire control.

TABLE 2-9

Light AA Batteries

	As Commissioned	*1945*
North Carolina	16-1.1" quad. 12-0.50 cal.	60-40mm quad. 36-20mm single
Washington	16-1.1" quad. 12-0.50 cal.	60-40mm quad. 83-20mm single

Aircraft. Air spotting of gunfire at extreme ranges was considered essential when these ships were designed. All new battleships carried three seaplanes, one stowed on each catapult and one on deck. There was insufficient space in the stern for a below-decks hangar. Shipboard aircraft were a serious problem; it was dangerous to reduce speed in enemy waters to recover them, and gasoline was a fire hazard. Radar reduced and eventually eliminated the need for aircraft spotting.

Protection.
The armor protection provided for the *North Carolina* and the *Washington* was designed to withstand 14-inch 1,500-pound projectiles. Against 14-inch guns, the armor could provide immunity to the citadel for ranges between 19,000 and 30,000 yards. Against the 16-inch/45 caliber 2,240-pound projectile, the immunity zone was about 21,300 to 27,800 yards. The armor was only marginally capable of satisfying the traditional standard of resisting the equivalent of the main battery guns. This protection was improved in later designs.

The armored citadel was protected by a main side belt of 12-inch plates on .75-inch STS backing plates, inclined 15 degrees with the lower edge inboard, which increased effective resistance to about that of 16-inch vertical armor. The vertical extent of this armor was partly dictated by concern for adequate protection against shells falling short but not sufficiently slowed by the water due to wave profile, especially at high speed. The lower side belt tapered from 12 to 6.6 inches with the same inclination; this reduction was considered justified in view of the slowing effect of the water. Its lower edge, nine feet below the waterline, rested on top of the blister, which was designed to contribute to its vertical support. Supplementary protection, compensating for the reduction in thickness fore-and-aft over the main battery magazines, was provided by a particularly heavy torpedo bulkhead, which varied from 2.05 inches to 3.75 inches in thickness at a 10-degree slope from the vertical. The side protection was never tested by shellfire.

The armored citadel required heavier horizontal protection than in previous ships, a consequence of emphasis on long-range shellfire and air attack. The capability of penetrating horizontal armor increases as the range increases, as shown in Table 2-10.

TABLE 2-10

Effect of Range on Horizontal Armor Penetration

Gun/cal.	US 14"/50 (356mm)	Japanese 18.1"/45 cal. (460mm)
Shell weight	1,500 (680 kg)	3,230 (1,465 kg)
Muzzle velocity (fps)	2,700 (823 m/s)	2,559 (780 m/s)
Penetration, inches	5.0 (127mm)	6.6 (168mm)
Range, yards	29,400 (26,883 m)	21,872 (20,000 m)
	6.0 (152mm)	9.1 (231mm)
	32,900 (30,084 m)	32,808 (30,000 m)

TABLE 2-11

Deck/Armor Thicknesses

| | Amidships | |
	Centerline	Outboard
Main deck	1.45" (37mm)	1.45" (37mm)
Second deck	5.0" (127mm)	5.5" (140mm)
Third deck	0.62" (16mm)	0.75" (19mm)
Total	7.07" (179mm)	7.70" (196mm)

Deck armor. The *Maryland*-class ships, completed in 1921-23, carried good deck-armor protection for that time—3.5-inch upper armor deck, and 2.5-inch lower armor deck. Protection was markedly increased in the *North Carolina* class, as shown in Table 2-11.

Battleship deck armor was designed on a simple premise: the uppermost deck activated fuzed projectiles while the lower deck protected vital areas from the resulting explosion. These ships had a third armor deck for splinter protection. They had very good deck-armor protection for such displacement-limited ships.

Citadel. The armor decks and the side armor belt formed a box like structure—the "raft body"—which extended longitudinally from forward of number 1 turret to aft of number 3 turret. The lower armor deck extended aft, shielding access to the steering engine rooms, with 6-inch plates directly over the steering gear itself. The raft-body concept of battleship protection was standard doctrine in the U. S. Navy; it was accepted that this left the extremities of a ship unprotected. The ends of the armored citadel were shielded by 11.1-inch transverse armor bulkheads, and equally heavy armor protected the steering engine rooms. Side armor 14.9 inches thick and inclined 45 degrees protected the steering gear, with heavy but somewhat lighter armor shielding access to the steering gear from the citadel. Battle stations, except for ship control positions, gunnery installations, and the like, were located within or below the raft body and were relatively well shielded.

Turrets, gun mounts, magazines. The main battery was rather well protected, but this was augmented in later designs. The turret had 16-inch face plates, with 9.9-inch sides, 11.8-inch backs, and 7-inch tops. Barbette armor was similarly heavy, ranging in thickness from 14.7 inches forward to 16 inches on the sides to 11.5 inches on the centerline aft. Armor protection below the armor deck was provided by plates with a total thickness of 4.42 inches. This protection, already superior to that of most foreign battleships, was increased in later turret designs.

The face plate thickness was limited to 16 inches by production facilities. By 1939, 18-inch plates could be manufactured, but the *North Carolina* protection was not upgraded because such a modification was estimated to necessitate delaying completion by six to eight months.

The 5-inch gun mounts and magazines were protected against fragmentation damage and

strafing by 1.95-inch STS plates. Later designs provided slightly improved protection, but completely adequate protection was never obtained.

Conning tower. The conning tower was a double-level structure, connected to the armored citadel by a communications tube of 14-inch armor. Side armor thicknesses varied from 16 inches on the beam to 14.7 inches on the centerline, with 7-inch top armor and 3.9-inch plating on the bottom. Although some navies discarded heavily armored conning towers, the U. S. Navy remained convinced of the need for them.

Side protection. The side protective system, with a designed resistance of 700 pounds of TNT, featured a prominent blister which increased the beam. Amidships, the side protective system comprised five compartments. The outboard two, including the blister, were to be kept void, while the next two were to be kept liquid loaded. The compartment adjacent to the holding bulkhead was a void. At the extremities of the system, over the main battery turrets, there were only four compartments—an outboard void, two liquid-loaded compartments, and an inboard void. The holding bulkhead over the magazines was built of armor plates up to 3.75 inches thick, to at least partly compensate for the reduced width of the side protective system. This was a tough system, although it was defeated the only time it was tested, when the *North Carolina* was hit by a single Japanese torpedo with a charge equivalent to 900 pounds of TNT, in a section where unavoidable hull volume reduction appreciably diminished its capabilities.

Many battleships of the World War I era were lost because of capsizing caused by off-center flooding, rather than by bodily sinkage. Lists reduce the transverse stability of ships and hinder damage control, as well as interfering with the normal operation of shipboard equipment. To be effective, counterflooding had to be done rapidly; the capability for rapid dewatering of counterflooded spaces was also a necessity. The *North Carolina* and *Washington* were given improved counterflooding capabilities as compared to earlier American battleships.

The results of the effect of a single torpedo hit amidships are shown in Table 2-12. Inclining experiments on the *Washington* on 2 February 1941 indicated that the actual metacentric height at the full load displacement of 44,377 tons was 8.70 feet.

TABLE 2-12

Torpedo Hit Effect, Calculations

Uncorrected list due to one torpedo hit	7°	
Armor freeboard after one torpedo hit	0.1′	(0.030 m)
Counterflooding water to right the ship	644 tons	(654 mt)
Reduction in the metacentric height	1.57′-1.81′	(0.490-0.552 m)
Increase in draft after counterflooding	10.6″	(0.269 m)

The Washington *at the Navy Yard, Philadelphia, just after commissioning. Her profile is fairly clean; the wartime complement of radar, added communications equipment, and augmented light AA batteries were still to come.*

Underbottom protection. Some insight into American thought with respect to the bottom protection of battleships is offered in the following quotation:

> There is little probability of an explosion occurring under the flat bottom of the ship. An aerial bomb cannot attain such a position for its motion is vertical and it must pass the side of the ship. Although a contact mine may theoretically explode under the flat bottom, experiments have shown that in practice it cannot be made to attain this position. The usual form of torpedo must strike the ship's side, which precludes its exploding under the flat bottom.
>
> The usual form of protective layer cannot be constructed along the flat bottom because its depth (a vertical dimension for the flat bottom) would be such as to force the vitals of the ship up above the waterline or to make the draft and other characteristics impracticable.
>
> Even though the protective layer were extended down under the flat bottom of the ship, it would not be effective against an explosion of even moderate force. As noted above, the usual explosion against surface craft is partly vented to the air above and partly vented into the ship. With an explosion under the flat bottom, these two venting actions coincide; that is, the full force of the explosion is directed upward into the ship. *No protective layer practicable will withstand such action.* [Emphasis added.]
>
> Any attempt to protect a ship against an explosion under its flat bottom is therefore impracticable because no such explosion will probably ever occur, the usual protective layer cannot be built under the flat bottom, and even if such a protective layer could be constructed and an explosion occurred against it no effective protection would be obtained.*

The *North Carolina*-class ships were given limited underbottom protection by a triple bottom structure 5 feet 9 inches deep. The lower layer, 3 feet deep, was designed to be kept liquid loaded; the upper 2-foot 9-inch layer was to be kept void at all times. This triple bottom was extensively subdivided and the volume of the compartments above was kept to the least possible value, to minimize damage from an underbottom detonation. Unquestionably, this was at best an imperfect system of protection, but it was better than nothing at all.

---

*George C. Manning and T. L. Schumacher, *Principles of Naval Architecture* (Annapolis, Md.: U. S. Naval Institute, 1924).

Radar.

Radar systems were not included in the basic design of the *North Carolina*, but the ships were given progressively better systems as the war progressed. By the end of the war, the *North Carolina* mounted the following radar systems:

Surface-search radar	SP
Air-search radar	SK-2
Main-battery GFCS (2)	Mark 38
	Mark 27 radar (conn. tower)
	Mark 13 radar (directors)
Secondary battery GFCS (4)	Mark 37
	Mark 12/22/32 radars
MG battery GFCS	Mark 57
(40mm)	Mark 34 radar

Propulsion Plant.

The *North Carolina*-class battleships were the first American capital ships to combine moderately high speeds with powerful armament and strong protection. They benefitted from rapid advances in marine engineering technology that contributed to high maximum speeds.

After World War I, the design of boilers and steam turbines for land power plants had progressed until in 1926 operating conditions of 600 pounds per square inch and 850 degrees Fahrenheit were commonplace. Turbines were characterized by their high speeds, small size, and small number of parts. This rapid development of the high-pressure, high-temperature steam cycle influenced the decision of the Bureau of Engineering to give the *Mahan*-class destroyers of 1933 propulsion plants operating at 400 pounds per square inch and 700 degrees. They were the first warships to have high-speed turbines with double reduction gears and direct-coupled cruising turbines. Turbine speeds were much higher than in land installations, as there were fewer restrictions on maximum revolutions per minute.

Boilers. A new two-furnace, double-uptake type of boiler with a convection superheater located in one of the boiler-tube banks was first introduced in the *Somers*-class destroyers, commencing in 1935. They were the first warship boilers with superheat control. Accurate control was necessary to avoid damage to the steam turbines and to better respond to the varying demands of naval operations. Superheat control permitted such rapid and exact variations (within one degree) that the changes had to be recorded by thermocouples instead of mercury thermometers. Weight and space were saved by providing direct steam temperature control without dampers, without a separately fired superheater, and by using fusion-welded steam drums.

Another important advance in marine boiler technology was the introduction of the double-cased boiler, which was somewhat insulated by air en route to the furnace. This eliminated the cumbersome and vulnerable closed fire-room system and permitted preheating the air before it entered the furnace, improved thermodynamic efficiency in the propulsion plant, made it possible to operate the fire rooms at normal atmospheric pressure, and greatly reduced the noise level. With open fire rooms, gas-contaminated air was fed into the firebox without the fire-room crew having to breathe it. The first such installations were made in the heavy cruisers *Minneapolis, Astoria,* and *New Orleans.*

Compact, light, and efficient boilers and high-speed, compact, and efficient steam turbines (operating at 6,000 rpm for HP and 5,000 rpm for LP turbines) were available, and rapid development in the power plants of new-construction destroyers prompted the decision to install such improved plants in ships of the *North Carolina* class.

Reduction gears. Turbo-electric, single-reduction gear and double-reduction gear drives were evaluated as possible components of the 115,000-shaft-horsepower propulsion plants. Each system offered advantages and disadvantages.

The single-reduction gear drive first considered would have featured a low gear ratio resulting in considerable turbine simplicity and reliability. A cruising speed of 15 knots was attainable but with poor fuel economy. High turbine speeds desired for better efficiency would have necessitated a very large reduction gear, difficult to arrange in the raft body. Installation, replacement, and maintenance of such a gear also promised to be expensive.

Early in the design synthesis, the very successful and highly efficient turbo-electric drive installations in the aircraft carriers *Saratoga* and *Lexington* were evaluated. Turbo-electric systems offered outstanding advantages in reliability, operation, and compartmentation. Each turbo-alternator, main motor, and boiler could be installed in a separate compartment, thus allowing extremely good subdivision of the machinery spaces. A turbo-electric drive would have resulted in longer propulsion units, but would have eliminated reduction gears. However, additional space was needed to allow withdrawal of the alternator rotors, making the machinery space larger than for geared turbine installations of similar power.

The extensive subdivision of machinery spaces, a design concept common in U. S. capital ship design of the World War I era, was later discarded as a result of stability considerations. Longitudinal subdivision was eliminated in order to avoid asymmetrical flooding. To minimize the effects of damage, self-contained propulsion units were desired for each shaft. Thus, derangement of any one shaft might well leave the others operational. This would be impossible if the boilers were concentrated in one or two fire rooms.

The turbo-electric system was much more vulnerable to shock damage than steam turbine plants with conventional reduction gears and, if the motor rooms flooded, the motor windings would have to be replaced, an extremely expensive and time-consuming operation.

However, the primary objection to a turbo-electric drive was its great weight as compared to conventional steam turbine plants. The ships were severely weight-limited, and weight conservation was essential. A double-reduction gear steam turbine installation was 180 tons lighter than a turbo-electric installation of the same power.

Double-reduction gears had been used in American warship design in 1917, but operational failures indicated that the manufacturing methods and metallurgy of the period were

not adequate for such high-speed gears. As a consequence, single-reduction gears were fitted in later destroyers and cruisers with the turbo-electric drive used in aircraft carriers and battleships. Subsequent technical progress permitted the installation of double-reduction gears in new construction destroyers in 1933. Such gears proved to be efficient and reliable.

A comparison of the *Lexington* (1927) with the *North Carolina* (1941) shows the weight economies inherent in the decision to use a double-reduction gear installation (Table 2-13). Part of the tabulated weight advantage is due to the later period of the *North Carolina* design.

The double-reduction gear drive offered more flexibility in the arrangement of the gears and turbine units. Because the compact locked-train, double-reduction gear permitted higher, more efficient turbine speeds, the specified horsepower could be obtained with smaller turbines than for a single reduction gear drive. This was most desirable from the standpoints of engineering reliability and design, especially with the higher pressure and temperature steam cycles contemplated.

TABLE 2-13

Weight Savings, Double Reduction Gear

Ship	Lexington	North Carolina
Year completed	1927	1941
Type drive	Turbo-electric	Double red. gear
Shaft horsepower	180,000 (182,497 mhp)	121,000 (122,678 mhp)
Weight (tons)	6,335 (6437 mt)	3,286 (3339 mt)
Pounds/hp (Kg/mhp)	78.3 (35.03)	60.83 (27.21)

Note: Shafting runs for the *Lexington* were much shorter, partially offsetting the weight savings of the double reduction gear drive.

Initial design studies indicated that the boilers might have to project above the splinter deck; but the boilers developed were sufficiently powerful and low enough to avoid this. With the long shafts and the increased power to be transmitted by them, there was a distinct possibility of developing serious vibration problems. The four propellers were statically and dynamically balanced, with the best possible tip clearances. Nevertheless both ships were subject to serious vibrations at high speeds.

Steam conditions. The steam installation was initially designed to operate at 600 pounds per square inch and 700 degrees Fahrenheit. Early in the design of the power plant for the *North Carolina*, Vice Admiral Harold G. Bowen, Chief of the Bureau of Engineering, ordered operating temperatures increased to 850 degrees. All the potential economies of this change could not be obtained, as turbine nozzles and steam piping had already been completed, but it did improve operating efficiency and fuel economy. An important gain in fuel economy had been realized with the introduction of the new type of machinery in the destroyers of the *Mahan* and *Somers* classes.

The steam conditions specified aroused considerable controversy. Line officers objected to high pressures and temperatures as experimental and unproven. The Bureau of Engineering

Even in a moderate sea, high speed operations meant a wet forecastle. Here the Washington *shows a long wake as she keeps company with the carrier* Hancock (CV19) *during flight operations.*

was interested in the better efficiency possible with the proposed new steam conditions, but the Bethlehem Steel Company, Newport News Shipbuilding and Dry Dock Company, and the New York Shipbuilding Corporation opposed the change, as they were licensed to manufacture Parsons turbines which were not suited to such conditions. Secretary of the Navy Charles Edison finally directed adoption of the 600-pound, 850-degree steam cycle, a major factor in the excellent performance of these and many other combat and merchant ships.

During 1936-37, new destroyers experienced accelerated oxygen pittage in the economizers and other boiler components, the result of difficulties in obtaining an accurate analysis of feedwater oxygen content. A portable-type continuous reading apparatus that could indicate the oxygen content was perfected by the Naval Research Laboratory. The problem was further alleviated by the introduction of a closed feed-heating system in one stage of a triple-purpose combined de-aerating feed heater and surge tank, especially at high speeds.

Machinery arrangement. In the design of the *North Carolina* and *Washington,* both six- and eight-boiler schemes were studied. The six-boiler scheme would have reduced the length of the main propulsion spaces by six feet and saved about one hundred tons in weight. The eight-boiler plan permitted a more flexible machinery arrangement and the use of smaller boilers, and provided two boilers for each shaft. Scheme XVI for "Battleship 1937" featured the six-boiler arrangement, with three boilers in each boiler room. The final eight-boiler arrangement—two boilers in each of four spaces—permitted full power operation on any shaft, entirely independent of the others.

Power output. Four sets of geared turbines delivered a normal maximum of 115,000 shaft horsepower, good for a designed maximum speed of 27.5 knots at 199 rpm. The three-drum express boilers had a designed maximum working pressure of 618 pounds per square inch, with the capability of generating steam for two hours to permit a maximum overload shaft horsepower of 121,000. In service, the maximum speed known to have been attained was 27.3 knots, with a nominal endurance of 16,230 miles at 15 knots. In four months of operations in 1942 under war conditions, the *Washington* actually performed as follows:

	Normal Fuel* 5,550 tons	Emergency Fuel* 7,554 tons
Endurance @ 15 knots	13,500 miles	18,375 miles
Endurance @ 20 knots	8,640 miles	11,800 miles
Endurance @ 25 knots	4,925 miles	6,700 miles
Endurance @ 27 knots	3,456 miles	4,698 miles

*Fuel tonnage includes diesel oil.

This performance, combined with efficient under-way refueling and replenishment techniques perfected during World War II, gave these and succeeding battleships outstanding endurance.

In the 20 years between the completion of the *Maryland* and the *North Carolina,* battleship displacement had increased only 10 per cent while power had increased by 300 per cent.

Improved fuel economy contributed to their better performance. The London Treaty restrictions on displacement did not permit the complete development of power plant potential. Only in the *Iowa* class was the advantage of the high-pressure-temperature plant and the double-reduction gear drive fully demonstrated.

Hull Characteristics.

The *North Carolina* and *Washington* had a rather daring stern design, a twin-skeg arrangement that approximated the advantageous flow conditions of a single propeller ship for two of the four shafts. The skeg extended along a considerable part of the afterbody, reaching all the way down to keel level, and enclosed and supported the two inboard shafts and improved propeller efficiency. Model basin tests, comparing this arrangement with conventional hull forms, were so convincing that no comparative studies were made in the design of the *South Dakota* and *Iowa* classes, although a normal stern form was again tested in the design of the *Montana*-class battleships. Test results are shown in Table 2-14. Analysis of the tests showed that the improved performance resulted from a lower appendage resistance and improved propeller efficiency.

TABLE 2-14
Test Results, Twin Skeg

Speed	Per cent change in resistance
15 knots	5.0 reduction
22 knots	1.0 increase
28 knots	5.0 reduction

Twin skegs, despite their many advantageous features, created some operational problems, and severe vibrations experienced in the *North Carolina* during trials were ultimately traced to them. The vibration was never completely eliminated, but was reduced to acceptable levels, partly by changing to four-bladed propellers. The twin skegs gave improved maneuvering qualities and better protection of the inboard shafts against underwater explosions, and served as excellent docking supports for the overhanging stern, eliminating the need of special skegs and docking keels. Additionally, they stiffened the after portion of the hull structure by acting as deep girders which extended from the keel level to the main deck. The skegs were an extension of the torpedo bulkhead, which arrangement increased the effectiveness of the skegs in contributing to the overall longitudinal strength of the ships. There were other improvements, but these were the most important.

These ships were fitted with balanced, streamlined twin rudders located in the races of the inboard propellers, with their centers about 10 feet off the centerline. The zero helm setting for each rudder was slightly more than a degree from the centerline, with the trailing edges inboard to correct for the horizontal rake of the inboard propeller shafts. Positive stops for each rudder were located on the upper part of the rudder hub, limiting rudder traverse to a maximum of 36.5 degrees port or starboard.

Summary. Both ships of the *North Carolina* class served with distinction throughout World War II. The *Washington* had perhaps the best combat record of any new U. S. battleship, yet failed to gain the fame and acclaim given others. The combat records of both ships were excellent; few other capital ships performed assigned tasks so well.

The armament of these ships was to become typical of modern American battleships. The primary importance of the 16-inch guns was frequently overshadowed by the antiaircraft batteries, as the battleship was gradually relegated to a subordinate role in which its ability to deliver a great volume of accurate antiaircraft fire was of paramount importance.

The armor protection, designed to resist the 14-inch gun, was never tested in combat. Although the ships had adequate protection against 14-inch fire, a primary concern in the design of later battleships was the improvement of the armor protection against heavy shellfire.

In describing the torpedo damage to the *North Carolina* on 15 September 1942, the commanding officer stated that he never had ". . . considered the underwater protection of this ship adequate against a modern torpedo. It was expected that the third deck would be ruptured. A total of 165 bunks were relocated to avoid major combat crew losses due to a torpedo hit . . ."

Despite this natural concern, resulting from the progressive increase in enemy torpedo explosive charges, the underwater protective system was good. Later designs incorporated the following improvements: the blister structure was supplanted by a wall-sided hull form which gave improved stability when heeled over, the side armor system was carried down within the side protective system, and the liquid-loading scheme, much the same as that of World War I U. S. battleships, was completely changed in the *South Dakota*-class ships. All in all, it is apparent that U. S. Navy experts in the design of ship protective systems saw fit to radically alter the arrangements of the underwater protective systems of capital ships subsequent to the *North Carolina* class.

Both ships had vibration problems, partly alleviated but never completely corrected by propeller changes. The propulsion systems were efficient and trouble-free, and served well, especially in view of their extensive under-way operations under wartime conditions.

When the carrier *Franklin*, with the same type of boilers as those in the *North Carolina* and *Washington*, was bombed off Kyushu in March 1945, four boilers, hot from high-speed steaming, were flooded with cold sea water. They remained in nearly perfect condition and later operated satisfactorily with salt concentrations far in excess of designed values. That performance established their reliability beyond all question.

Both the *North Carolina* and the *Washington* served effectively and well; their records and characteristics proved them to be extremely good examples of the modern battleship as designed under treaty displacement limitations. Later ships surpassed their capabilities, but few surpassed their records.

North Carolina Class

Name & hull number	*North Carolina* (BB-55)	*Washington* (BB-56)
Builder	New York Navy Yard, Brooklyn, N.Y.	Philadelphia Navy Yard, Philadelphia, Pa.
Laid down	27 October 1937	14 June 1938
Launched	13 June 1940	1 June 1940
Commissioned	9 April 1941	15 May 1941
Operational*	4 June 1942	27 March 1942
Disposition	Dedicated as a war memorial at Wilmington, N.C., on 3 October 1961.	Purchased on 24 May 1961 by Lipsett Div., Luria Brothers, for $757,000. Scrapped.

*Based on first sortie on an operational mission.

Displacement

North Carolina
(1942) 36,600 tons (37,188 m.t.) Standard
44,800 tons (45,519 m.t.) Full load
(1945) 46,700 tons (47,520 m.t.) Full load

Washington
(2 Feb. 1941)　34,708 tons (35,265 m.t.) Light ship
43,288 tons (43,983 m.t.) Optimum battle
44,377 tons (45,089 m.t.) Full load
46,796 tons (47,547 m.t.) Emergency load
(1942) 36,600 tons (37,188 m.t.) Standard
44,800 tons (45,519 m.t.) Full load
(20 Aug. 1945) 35,668 tons (36,241 m.t.) Light ship
45,370 tons (46,098 m.t.) Full load

Dimensions

North Carolina
728' 8.625" (222.113m) Length overall
713' 5.250" (217.513 m) Waterline length
108' 3.875" (33.025 m) Maximum beam
104' 6.000" (31.852 m) Waterline beam
31' 7.313" (9.635 m) Mean draft @ 42,329 tons
35' 6.000" (10.820 m) Maximum draft

Washington
728' 11.625" (222.246 m) Length overall
713' 8.000" (217.526 m) Waterline length
108' 3.875" (33.025 m) Maximum beam
104' 6.000" (31.852 m) Waterline beam
31' 8.625" (9.668 m) Mean draft @ 42,329 tons
32' 11.500" (10.046 m) Mean draft @ 44,377 tons
34' 6.500" (10.528 m) Mean draft @ 46,796 tons
34' 9.000" (10.592 m) Maximum draft

Hull Characteristics at D.W.L.

Displacement	42,329 tons (43,008 m.t.)
Mean draft	31' 7.313" (9.635 m) *North Carolina*
	31' 8.625" (9.668 m) *Washington*
Hull depth amidships	49' 2.125" (14.989 m)
Freeboard at bow	29' 4.000" (8.941 m)
Freeboard at stern	19' 4.000'' (5.893 m)
Block coefficient	0.628
Prismatic coefficient	0.629
Waterplane coefficient	0.704
Midship section coefficient	0.999
Tons per inch immersion	124.93 (49.976 m.t./cm.)
Moment to trim one inch	4,600 foot-tons (one cm: 560.86 m-m.t.)
(GM) metacentric height	8.31' (2.533 m.)
Wetted surface	94,300 sq. ft. (8,760.8 sq.m.)

Actual GM *Washington*—2 February 1941

> 3.91' (1.192 m.) @ 34,708 tons (35,265 m.t.)
> 8.06' (2.457 m.) @ 43,288 tons (43,983 m.t.)
> 8.70' (2.652 m.) @ 44,377 tons (45,089 m.t.)
> 9.53' (2.905 m.) @ 46,796 tons (47,547 m.t.)

> *Washington*—20 August 1945
> 3.69' (1.125 m.) @ 35,668 tons (36,241 m.t.)

Armament

Nine 16-inch/45 caliber guns (Mark 6) (406mm)

Twenty 5-inch/38 caliber guns (Mark 12) (127mm)

Antiaircraft machine guns

	40mm/56	1.1"/75 (28mm)	20mm/70	.50 cal. (12.7mm)
North Carolina				
(Apr. 1941)	none	16	none	12
(Dec. 1941)	none	16	40	12
(June 1942)	none	16	40	28
(Dec. 1944)	60	none	48	none
(June 1945)	60	none	36	none
Washington				
(Apr. 1941)	none	16	none	12
(Dec. 1941)	none	16	20	12
(June 1942)	none	16	20	28
(Dec. 1944)	60	none	67	none
(Aug. 1945)	60	none	83	none
(Nov. 1945)	60	none	63	none

Armor Protection (Refer to plans for arrangement details)

Immunity zone from 21,000 to 26,000 yards (19,202-23,774 m)
> (Citadel) U. S. 16"/45 gun (406mm) firing 2,240 lb.
> (2,204.6 kg) shell

Midship Section

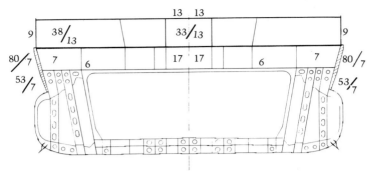

from 19,000 to 30,000 yards
(17,374-27,432 m) (Citadel) U. S. 14″/50 gun
(356mm) firing 1,500 lb. (1,476.3 kg) shell

Amidships

Belt armor 12.0″ on 0.75″ STS, inclined 15° (305mm on 19mm)
        Tapered to 6.6″ on 0.75″ STS at lower edge (168mm on 19mm)
        No lower side belt armor

Deck armor	Centerline	
main	1.45″	(37mm)
second	1.4″ + 3.6″	(36mm + 91mm)
third	0.62″	(16mm)
Total	7.07″	(180mm)
	Outboard	
main	1.45″	(37mm)
second	1.4″ + 4.1″	(36mm + 104mm)
third	0.75″	(19mm)
Total	7.70″	(196mm)

Barbette armor
    centerline forward 14.7″ (373mm)
    sides 16.0″ (406mm)
centerline aft 11.5″ (292mm)

Turret armor
    face plates 16.0″ (406mm)
    sides 9.8″ (249mm)
    back plates 11.8″ (300mm)
    roof plates 7.0″ (178mm)

Secondary gun armor
    gun mounts 1.95″ (50mm)
    magazines 1.95″ (50mm)

Conning tower armor
    centerline sides 14.7″ (373mm)
    beam sides 16.0″ (406mm)
    roof plates 7.0″ (178mm)
    bottom plates 3.9″ (99mm)
    comm. tube 14.0″ (356mm)

Underwater Protection

Designed resistance 700 pounds TNT (317 kg)
Side protective system depth . . .′ @ half draft amidships
S.P.S. designed loading (shell) void-liquid-liquid-liquid-void
Total bulkhead thickness . . .″
Bottom protective system depth 5′ 9″ (1.753 m) amidships
Upper layer 2′ 9″ (0.838 m) (void)
Lower layer 3′ 0″ (0.914 m) (liquid loaded)

Machinery Schematic

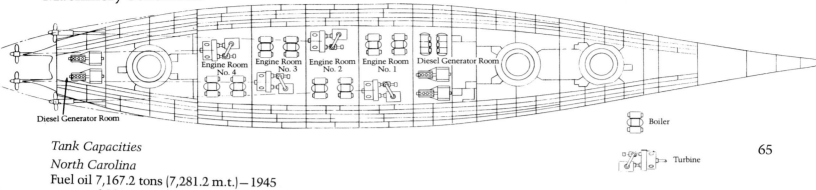

Engine Room No. 4 | Engine Room No. 3 | Engine Room No. 2 | Engine Room No. 1 | Diesel Generator Room

Diesel Generator Room

Boiler

Turbine

Diesel Generator

Evaporator

Tank Capacities

North Carolina
Fuel oil 7,167.2 tons (7,281.2 m.t.) — 1945
   6,589.9 tons (6,695.4 m.t.) — 1947 (normal)
Diesel oil 677.1 tons (688.0 m.t.)
Gasoline 22.1 tons (22.5 m.t.)
Reserve feed water 410.7 tons (417.3 m.t.) — 1947
Potable water 607.9 tons (617.7 m.t.) — 1947

Washington
Fuel oil 6,259.9 tons (6,360.4 m.t.) — 1942
   6,399.0 tons (6,501.7 m.t.) — 1945
   6,584.5 tons (6,690.2 m.t.) — 1947 (normal)
   7,553.5 (7,646.7 m.t.) — 1947 (emergency)
Diesel oil 686.2 tons (697.2 m.t.) — 1945
   677.1 tons (688.0 m.t.) — 1947
Gasoline 22.1 tons (22.5 m.t.)
Reserve feed water 343.5 tons (349.0 m.t.) — 1942
   410.7 tons (417.3 m.t.) — 1947
Potable water 607.9 tons (617.7 m.t.) — 1947

Machinery

Boilers	eight Babcock & Wilcox three drum express type boilers fitted with two furnaces and double uptakes. pressure: 575 psi (40.43 kg/cm²) temperature: 850°F. (454.4°C.)
Turbines	four sets General Electric geared turbines high pressure impulse turbines — 12 stages, 5,904 rpm maximum low pressure impulse turbines — 6 stages, 4,937 rpm maximum astern impulse turbines — 3 stages, 3,299 rpm maximum
Shaft horsepower	121,000 (122,678 mhp) 32,000 (32,444 mhp) astern
Maximum speed	28.0 knots @ 199 rpm and 121,000 shp — 1941 26.8 knots — 1945
Nominal endurance	17,450 nautical miles @ 15 knots — 1941 16,320 nautical miles @ 15 knots — 1945 5,740 nautical miles @ 25 knots — 1945
Generators	four ship's service turbogenerators (1.250 kw) four ship's service diesel generators (850 kw) two emergency diesel generators (200 kw) total ship's service capacity: 8,400 kw, 450 Volts, AC
Propellers	two four-bladed 15' 4" (4.674 m.) diameter propellers — inboard two four-bladed 16' 7.5" (5.067 m.) diameter propellers — outboard
Rudders	two balanced streamlined type rudders with a projected area of the profile of each of 302.5 sq. ft. (28.1 sq. m.). Train limits 36.5 degrees to port and starboard.

Frames

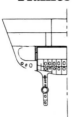

Frame 162
Steering

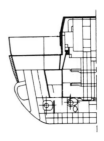

Frame 138
Turret No. 3

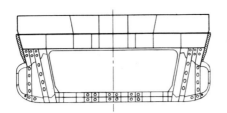

Frame 87
Midships

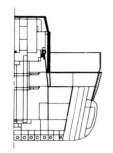

Frame 63
Turret No. 2

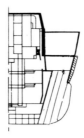

Frame 45
Turret No. 1

Frame 11

66

Miscellaneous

Complement 1,880 (108 off./1,772 enl.)—design
2,339 (144 off./2,195 enl.)—1945 accommodations
1,774 (135 off./1,639 enl.)—1947 *North Carolina*
1,989 (146 off./1,843 enl.)—1947 *Washington*

Frame spacing 4.0′ (1.219 m)

Washington (BB-56)
Weight Summary
1941

	Tons	*Metric tons*	*Percent of total*
Hull structure (excl. armor)	12,213.133	(12,409.553)	34.82
Armor	14,849.062	(15,087.687)	42.34
Propulsion	2,579.890	(2,621.272)	37.36
Electric plant	706.477	(717.811)	2.02
Communications and control	30.433	(30.921)	0.01
Auxiliary systems	981.176	(996.984)	2.79
Outfit and furnishings	1,013.175	(853.838)	2.87
Armament	2,729.029	(2,772.795)	7.79
Light Ship Displacement	35,102.375	(35,666.018)	100%
Ammunition	1,788.486	(1,817.206)	
Complement	192.264	(195.350)	
Supplies and stores	869.030	(882.975)	
Aeronautics	52.503	(53.345)	
Standard Displacement	38,004.658	(38,614.733)	
Fuel oil	6,259.900	(6,360.361)	
Reserve feed water	343.500	(349.016)	
Full Load Displacement	44,608.058	(45,396.973)	

Deck Plans

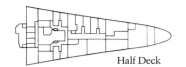

Half Deck

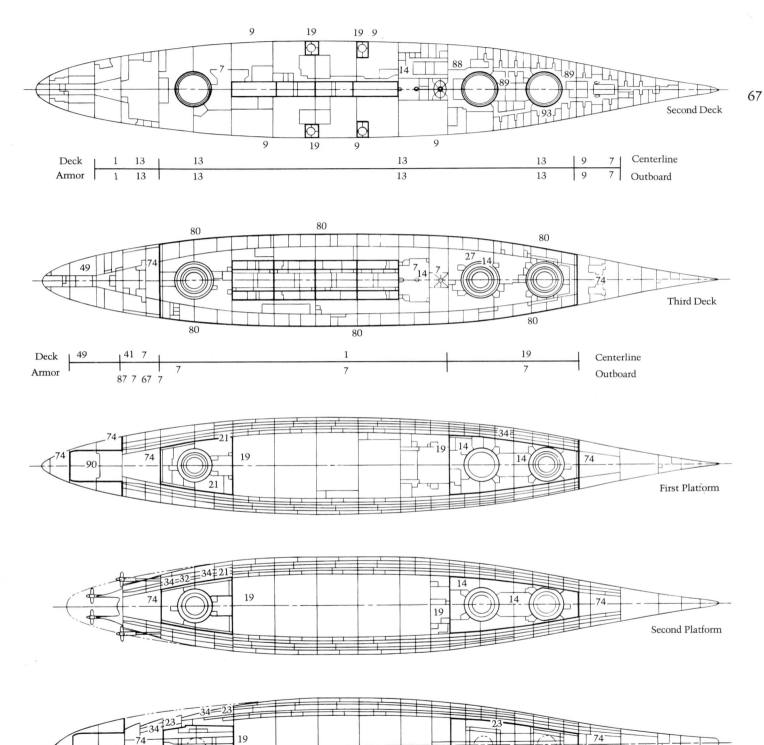

Second Deck

| Deck | 1 | 13 | 13 | 13 | 13 | 9 | 7 | Centerline |
| Armor | 1 | 13 | 13 | 13 | 13 | 9 | 7 | Outboard |

Third Deck

| Deck | 49 | 41 7 | | 1 | 19 | Centerline |
| Armor | | 87 7 67 7 | 7 | 7 | 7 | Outboard |

First Platform

Second Platform

Innerbottom

Body Plan

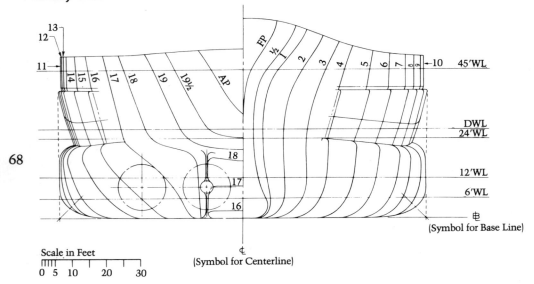

68

Scale in Feet

0 5 10   20   30

(Symbol for Centerline)

(Symbol for Base Line)

Torpedo Damage

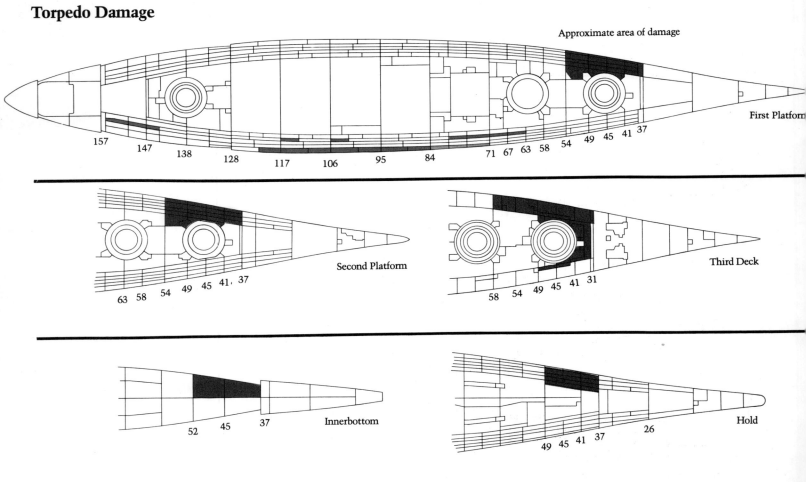

Flooded Spaces

Counter Flooding

Deballasted within one hour

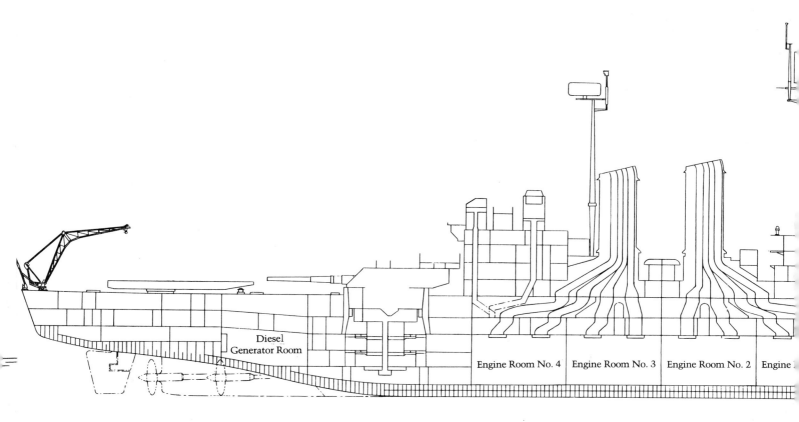

board Profile

Diesel Generator Room

Engine Room No. 4 Engine Room No. 3 Engine Room No. 2 Engine

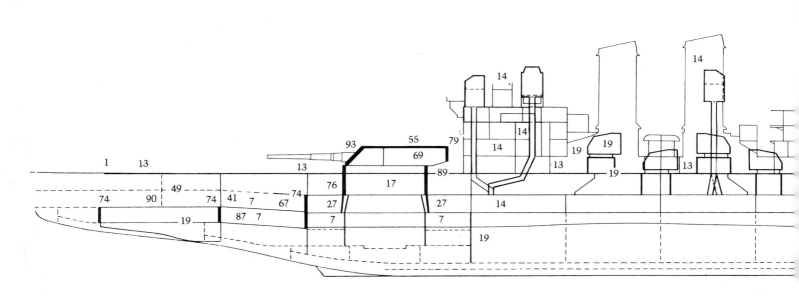

Profile

1   13   13

49

74   90   74   41   7   67   74

19   87   7

93   55

76   17   69   79

27   89

7   27

7   7

14

19

14   14

14   14   13   19   19

14   19   13

19

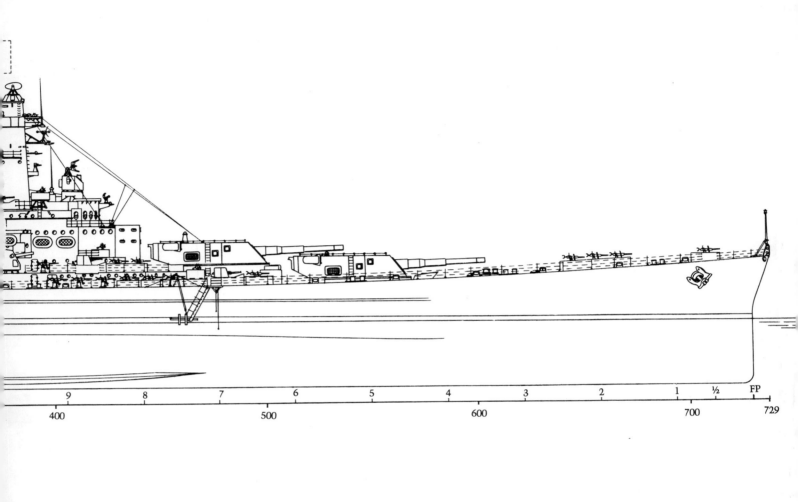

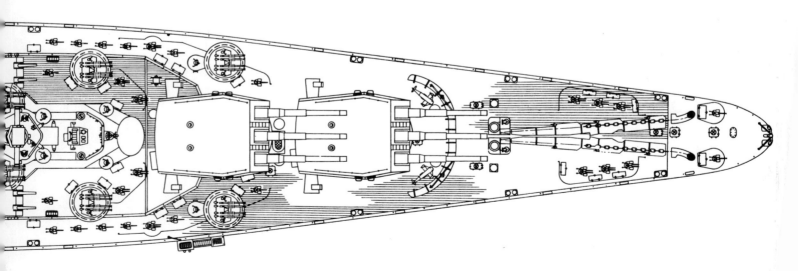

North Carolina

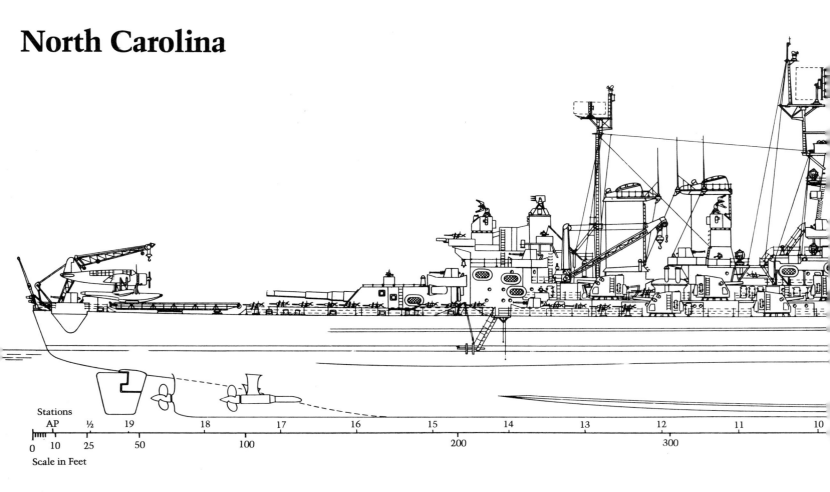

Stations

AP   ½   19   18   17   16   15   14   13   12   11   10

0   10   25   50   100   200   300

Scale in Feet

Outboard Profile

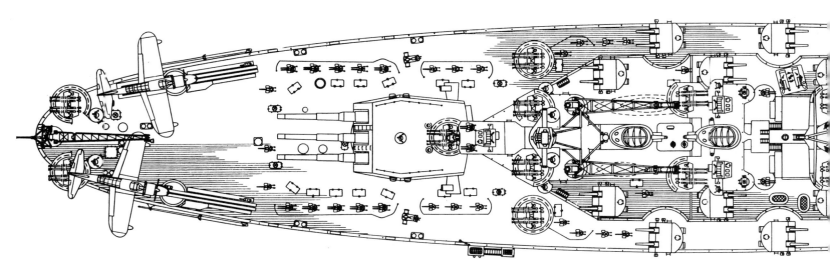

Overhead View

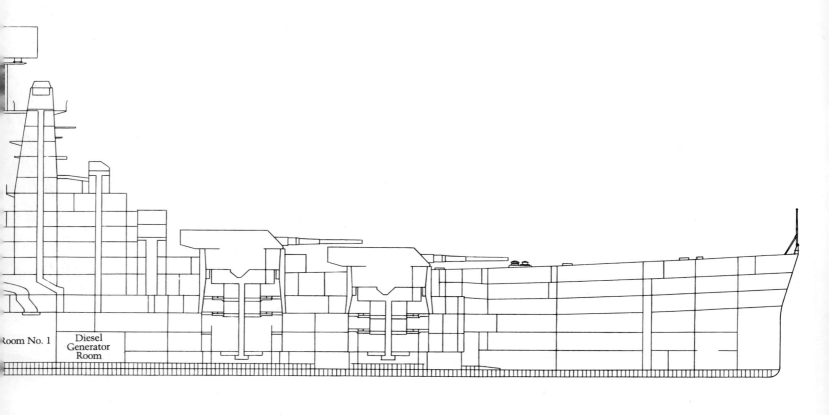

Room No. 1

Diesel
Generator
Room

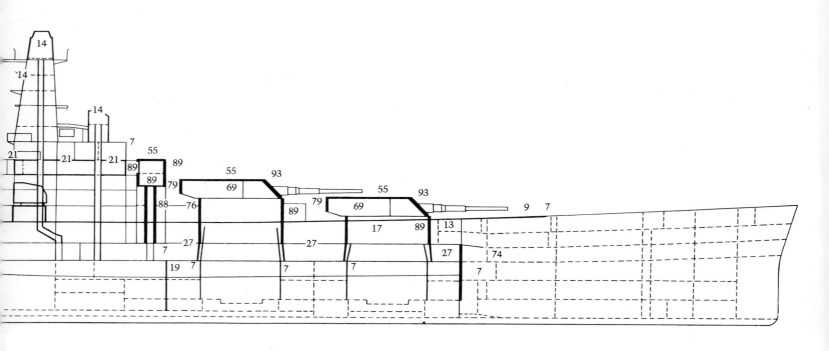

14

`14

14

21

21   21   21

7

55

89   89

89

79

55

69

93

88

76

89

79

27

55

69

93

9   7

17

89

13

7

27

74

19   7

7

7

7

Armor Thickness

Key No.	Inches	Millimeters	Key No.	Inches	Millimeters
1	.25	6	51	6.20	157
2	.30	8	52	6.30	160
3	.375	10	53	6.60	168
4	.45	11	54	6.80	173
5	.50	13	55	7.00	178
6	.625	16	56	7.125	181
7	.750	19	57	7.20	183
8	.875	22	58	7.25	184
9	1.00	25	59	7.40	188
10	1.125	29	60	7.75	197
11	1.25	32	61	7.80	198
12	1.40	35	62	7.85	199
13	1.425	36	63	8.17	208
14	1.47	37	64	8.50	216
15	1.50	38	65	9.00	229
16	1.625	41	66	9.15	232
17	1.71	43	67	9.30	236
18	1.90	48	68	9.50	241
19	1.91	49	69	9.80	249
20	1.95	50	70	10.00	254
21	2.00	51	71	10.20	259
22	2.05	52	72	10.60	260
23	2.20	56	73	11.00	279
24	2.50	64	74	11.10	282
25	2.70	67	75	11.30	287
26	2.80	71	76	11.50	292
27	2.870	73	77	11.60	295
28	2.925	74	78	11.70	297
29	3.00	76	79	11.80	300
30	3.20	81	80	12.00	305
31	3.25	83	81	12.10	307
32	3.30	84	82	12.20	310
33	3.60	91	83	12.75	324
34	3.75	95	84	12.80	325
35	3.82	97	85	13.00	330
36	3.90	99	86	13.50	343
37	4.00	102	87	13.70	348
38	4.10	104	88	14.00	356
39	4.50	114	89	14.70	373
40	4.75	121	90	14.90	378
41	4.80	122	91	15.00	381
42	5.00	127	92	15.25	387
43	5.26	133	93	16.00	406
44	5.30	135	94	16.10	409
45	5.50	140	95	16.70	424
46	5.60	142	96	17.00	432
47	5.625	143	97	17.30	439
48	5.80	147	98	17.50	444
49	6.00	152	99	18.00	457
50	6.10	155	100	19.50	495
			101	21.30	541

CHAPTER THREE

The South Dakota class

The four *South Dakota*-class ships, the best of all those designed under the limitations of the Washington Treaty, shared a common ancestry with the two *North Carolina*-class ships, the first American battleships of the post-treaty era. Specifications for the "Battleship 1937" design series (which culminated in the *North Carolina*) called for the new 14-inch/50 caliber gun. This fundamental design decision was opposed by the Bureau of Ordnance, which favored the new 16-inch/45 caliber gun. As a result, Scheme V of the series was given 16-inch guns. This study was the direct ancestor of the *South Dakota* design.

Scheme V projected ten guns in two triple turrets forward and two twin turrets aft. The waterline length was reduced to 660 feet in order to offset the added weight of armament and protection. A speed of 27 knots was projected, with 130,000 shaft horsepower. The basic *South Dakota* design evolved on the basis of this study, in parallel with the *North Carolina* design. The follow-on ships were known as "Battleship 1939" during the design phase.

The earlier *North Carolina* and *Washington* were considered to represent the best possible 35,000-ton battleships following conventional design practice, and it was accepted that novel changes would be necessary to produce improved ships of the same displacement. The short-hull, 35,000-ton "Battleship 1939" was intended to serve in a homogenous squadron with earlier ships of the *North Carolina* class, and evolved under the basic design criteria shown in Table 3-1. Contract design for the *South Dakota* was completed less than two months after that for the *North Carolina*.

TABLE 3-1
Preliminary Design Characteristics

Standard displacement	35,000 tons (35,562 m.t.)
Armament	9-16"/45 tripled (406mm)
	16-5"/38 paired (127mm)
	16-1.1"/75 quad. (28mm)
	8-0.50-cal. (12.7mm)
Protection	To resist 16" shells (406mm)
Maximum speed	27.5 knots
Endurance	15,000 n.m. @ 15 knots

Design Characteristics. The required improvements in characteristics dictated reductions in the weight of nonessential components in order to provide increased protection without a net increase in displacement. The waterline length was reduced to save

Spotting aircraft were carried by all battleships during World War II, but were seldom used for that purpose, as radar proved far more effective. Floatplanes did carry out some lifeguard missions. These Kingfishers *are carried by the* Massachusetts *(BB59).*

structural weight, although the shorter hull form required increased shaft horsepower if the maximum speed was to equal that of the *North Carolina.* Maximum beam remained the same as in earlier battleships, but the amidships hull form was wall-sided, an improvement that somewhat bettered stability characteristics. Further weight economies resulted from the reduced overall length of the armored citadel, largely a consequence of the shorter propulsion plant. This permitted increased protection against underwater damage, gunfire, and bomb attack, while keeping the same displacement as that of the *North Carolina* class. Consequently, the *South Dakota*-class ships were more potent adversaries than the *North Carolina* class.

The reduced hull length greatly complicated the design of the propulsion machinery because it demanded increased power while all other considerations demanded a shorter engineering plant. The solution of this difficult problem was a major factor in the successful completion of the design, which provided the desired maximum speed of 27.5 knots with a normal maximum of 130,000 shaft horsepower. The reduced hull length resulted in a 7 per cent reduction in the vulnerable areas exposed to damage, as compared with the *North Carolina* class, and with better protection of the citadel, improved resistance to attack.

The contract design requirements, established on 29 June 1937 and slightly modified on 3 August 1937, are shown in Table 3-2. The armor protection then specified was slightly modified later. Minor changes and design modifications in all four ships increased their standard displacement to 35,350 tons, with full-load tonnage of 43,681. Actual full-load displacement of the *South Dakota* in 1942 was 44,519 tons.

TABLE 3-2
Contract Design Characteristics

Displacement (standard)	35,000 tons (35,562 m.t.)
(full load)	42,500 tons (43,182 m.t.)
Waterline length	666'0" (202.997 m)
Maximum beam	108'3" (33.680 m)
Maximum draft	34'4" (10.465 m)
Armament	9-16"/45 tripled (406mm)
	20-5"/38 paired* (127mm)
	12-1.1"/75 quad. (28mm)
Maximum speed	27 knots
Armor protection (29 June 1937)	
Main side belt	11.5"-13" inc. 19° (292-330mm)
Turrets	16" face, 10" side, 12" back (406-254-305mm)
Barbettes, conning tower	16" (406mm)

South Dakota—16

Habitability Characteristics.

Three of the ships were designed as division flagships, while the reduced secondary armament of the *South Dakota* provided the added living and working space required for a force flagship. The suites provided for the admiral and commanding officer, although smaller than in previous ships, were considered more than adequate. Officer accommodations were also slightly smaller than in earlier battleships. Crew accommodations, while considered adequate and well above foreign standards, were unequal to the standards desired. The sick bay was smaller than in the *North Carolina* — in that ship it was deemed larger than necessary.

Construction.

The keel of the *South Dakota* was laid at the New York Shipbuilding Corporation's yard in Camden, New Jersey, on 5 July 1939. The ship was launched on 7 June 1941 and commissioned on 20 March 1942, although she was not ready for sea trials until 4 June because of uncompleted work on the main battery turrets and light antiaircraft armament.

South Dakota — Operational History.

The *South Dakota* commenced her first Pacific war cruise in August 1942. She soon became generally known to the fleet as "Sodak," as "Battleship X" because she was so termed in official news releases, and to her crew as "Big Bastard." She also became one of the Navy's most famous fighting ships of World War II.

During operations in the Solomons, the ship grounded on a coral head at Tongatabu on 21 August 1942 and sliced open part of the bow section. She was repaired at the Pearl Harbor Navy Yard, where she received sixteen 40mm Bofors and at least twenty 20mm Oerlikon machine guns. Two quadruple 1.1-inch machine gun mounts were removed. Repairs and alterations were completed by 9 October, in time for the ship to take part in the Battle of Santa Cruz Island.

Antiaircraft defense. Her first combat came on 26 October, while she was steaming in company with the carrier *Enterprise*. A second carrier group including the *Hornet* was in sight. Both groups were searching for a Japanese carrier force reported moving toward Guadalcanal. The *Hornet* group was first sighted by the Japanese, who attacked with torpedo- and dive-bombers. About an hour later 43 Japanese aircraft made a coordinated dive-bombing and torpedo attack on the *Enterprise* group. The *South Dakota* put up highly effective antiaircraft fire with the new 40mm Bofors guns, which were capable of terrific destruction at intermediate ranges. In this engagement, the radar-directed 5-inch guns fired the proximity-fuzed (VT) antiaircraft ammunition for the first time. This combination greatly augmented the shorter-ranged 40mm guns. She proved the worth of the battleship in antiaircraft defense by downing 26 aircraft — a record never equalled by any other battleship. Enemy aircraft attempted to hit the *South Dakota* but scored only two hits and one near miss out of 23 bombs dropped. Shortly thereafter, 14 torpedo-bombers attacked, but only seven launched torpedoes, all of which missed. Some 40 minutes later 29 dive-bombers attacked and were repulsed. One 500-pound bomb dropped at low altitude hit the *South Dakota* on number 1 turret but failed to penetrate the roof and had so little effect within the turret that only one officer at the periscope was aware of the hit. The explosion wounded 50 men, including the captain, and one man later died. The guns in turret 2, trained over turret 1, were severely gouged. One barrel was too badly scored to be used in the Battle of Guadalcanal and, according to the executive officer, later failed a proving ground test.

During the night of 26-27 October, en route to Noumea, the *South Dakota* collided with the destroyer *Mahan* while maneuvering to avoid a submarine contact. There was no major damage to the battleship other than holes in five fuel oil tanks. The damage was repaired in two days by personnel of the repair ship *Vestal.*

Naval Battle of Guadalcanal. The next major action in the Solomons was a sustained large-scale Japanese assault on Guadalcanal from 12 to 15 November, which resulted in heavy losses on both sides. This series of engagements was climaxed by the night action of 14-15 November, in which the *South Dakota, Washington,* and a screen of four destroyers met a Japanese force of the battleship *Kirishima,* four cruisers, and nine destroyers. Within 20 minutes after the opening gun, all four American destroyers were disabled by enemy torpedoes and gunfire.

The *South Dakota*'s role in that night action was rather ignominious, as she was bedeviled by a series of power failures, starting some 17 minutes after the action commenced. Gunfire had caused a short circuit on the feeder cable to number 4 secondary fire control director. The circuit breaker was locked in, and the overload resulting from the short was transmitted to the main circuit supplying half the power to the forward part of the ship. The breaker on that line tripped, causing power to be interrupted. A switch to the alternate power supply had the same result, as the circuit breaker causing the problem was still locked in. All power was lost aft, gyros and fire-control equipment went out, and for three minutes all power was off in all turrets. The trouble was soon isolated and power was restored to all but two secondary gun mounts. Electrical failures continued, but not to the extent later caused by enemy hits.

At the same time power was restored, a course change was ordered to clear the burning U. S. destroyers. The *South Dakota* started to follow the *Washington,* but had to turn to avoid one destroyer and was silhouetted by two others. Then she resumed fire, but a minute later the SG radar went out for about five minutes. Muzzle blast from number 3 turret set fire to two planes on the fantail; the next salvo blew them overboard and put out most of the fires. The *South Dakota*'s turn to avoid the destroyers put her on a closing course with the Japanese, and with the SG radar inoperative she lost track of the *Washington.* With no accurate radar plot of the tactical situation, she continued to close the Japanese force.

Eight minutes after she resumed fire, Japanese searchlights illuminated her and within half a minute she was under fire from the *Kirishima, Takao,* and *Atago* at a range of about 5,800 yards. Both U. S. battleships shot out the Japanese searchlights, but not before the *South Dakota* took numerous hits, ranging from 5-inch to 14-inch caliber (Table 3-3). While the Japa-

TABLE 3-3
Battle Damage—South Dakota* 14-15 November 1942

Hit No.	Projectile	Description of Damage
1	6"	Penetrated starboard 20mm gun shield at top.
2	8" AP	Projectile detonated on starboard .75" (19mm) sheer strake at frame 30, blowing 5' x 4' (1.524 x 1.219 m) hole in shell, and 6' x 8' (1.829 x 2.438 m) hole in bulkhead 31. Main deck bulged up 2.5" (.064 m) over 5' x 4' (1.524 x 1.219 m) area; half deck dished down 4" (.102 m) over 6' x 6' (1.829 x 1.829 m) area.
3	6" AP	Glancing hit on turret 1, damaged starboard sight port.
4	8" AP	Ricochet detonated against 12.2" (310mm) main side belt armor, frame 46 starboard. Armor not dented; third deck blown down 3.5" (.089 m) over 15" x 30" (.381 x .762 m) area. Compartments A-11-F, A-21-F, A-23-F, A-27-V, A-33-F, A-39-F flooded by this hit and subsequent damage.
5	8"	Projectile detonated on spray shield, 40mm director; director extensively damaged by fragments.
6	8" AP	Projectile passed through starboard splinter shield, 5" secondary battery director foundation, director center column and port splinter shield without detonating.
7	8" AP	Projectile passed through 1.1" clipping room and detonated over no. 4-1.1" mount; mount badly damaged, 75-1.1" clips destroyed or exploded.
8	8"	Projectile passed through 1.1" gun director.
9	8"	Projectile hit wind and spray shield, cap head broke off and made second hole in port wind and spray shield. No detonation.
10	8"	Projectile passed through superstructure without detonating, cap head broke off, making second hole.
11	8"	Projectile detonated on impact with shell, tearing a 3' x 2' (.914 x .610 m) hole. Rivets popped or loosened. Compartments B-23-F, B-31-F, B-39-F flooded.
12	8"	Projectile passed through two 1.5" (38mm) bulkheads without detonating.
13, 14, 15	8"	Projectiles passed through superstructure, no detonation.
16	6"	Projectile passed through superstructure, no detonation.
17	8"	Projectile passed through superstructure, no detonation, stopped by mount 52.
18	6"	Projectile passed through superstructure, no detonation.
19	8"	Projectile passed through no. 3 searchlight.
20	6"	Projectile passed through tank top and armor backing bulkhead before detonating, starting small fire in supply office.
21	8"	Glancing blow made 6" (152mm) dent in 1.5" (38mm) STS plate.
22	5"	Projectile passed through superstructure including foremast housing, no detonation.
23	8"	Projectile damaged radars on secondary gun directors no. 52, 53, passed through stack hood.

Hit No.	Projectile	Description of Damage
24	6″(?)	Projectile detonated against starboard side mount 55; STS plating sprung but not penetrated; both guns on mount 57 were gouged by fragments.
25	8″ AP	Projectile penetrated shell plating, above waterline at seam between .625″ (16mm) and 1.25″ (32mm) plates, pierced another .25″ (6mm) plate, imbedded itself about 8″ (203mm) in 12.2″ (310mm) main side belt armor. Transverse frames 109, 110, 111, 112, were penetrated, third deck was pierced; tanks B-71-F, B-75-V, B-77-F, B-79-F flooded.
26	14″	Projectile penetrated both sides of hatch coaming, detonated on impact with barbette, blew 3′ x 10′ (.914 m x 3.048 m) hole in main deck, gouged sleeves of right and center gun of turret 3, destroyed gas seal and water shed for 30′ (9.144 m) around barbette. Armor deck deflected all fragments. Several 20mm mounts, 20mm ready service lockers, and starboard catapult were damaged.
27	unknown	SC-1 radar antenna shot away and platform riddled by fragments from a projectile detonating on contact with platform.

*Extract from *War Damage Report No. 57.* Refer to Battle Damage, page 105.

nese concentrated fire on the *South Dakota*, the *Washington* engaged the *Kirishima* at a range of only 8,400 yards and pounded her so severely that she had to be scuttled the next day.

Battle Damage. The *South Dakota* had 38 men killed and 60 wounded in this engagement. Damage, while extensive, was superficial in nature and was generally confined to the superstructure and poorly protected parts of the ship. Hits were sustained between 2342 and 0005, the majority subsequent to the searchlight illumination at 2343. Only one radar system was left operational. Fire-control directors, fire-control equipment, and interior communications components were put out of action. Many small fires in the superstructure were quickly put out when the ship withdrew from the battle at 8 minutes past midnight. Contact with the *Washington* was not regained, so she withdrew to a prearranged rendezvous. In her damaged condition, the *South Dakota* was particularly incapable of conducting an effective night action.

Despite 27 shell hits, the ship's hull strength, buoyancy, and general stability were not materially affected. The most serious damage involved the relatively unprotected electrical, radio and radar systems. The location of ship control, fire control, and flag plot spaces within the heavily armored conning tower proved wise, as casualties and damage there were light and did not reduce combat efficiency.

Only slight flooding resulted from several hits in the hull. A list of three-quarters of a degree was corrected quickly by shifting fuel oil. Concerning the loss of the search radar, the commanding officer commented:

The trust and faith in search radar equipment is amazing. After this ship had lost both her SG and SC equipment, the psychological impact on the officers and crew was most depressing. The absence of this gear gave all hands a feeling of being blindfolded.

The *South Dakota* steamed to the New York Navy Yard for repairs and an overhaul that took 62 days of round-the-clock work. One 16-inch gun in turret 2 was replaced, the remaining 1.1-inch guns were removed, and numerous 20mm and 40mm machine guns were added. Small superstructure modifications facilitated operation of the new mounts. The ship could mount more light antiaircraft machine guns than others in her class because of her lighter secondary armament.

Combat Operations. The *South Dakota* served with the British Home Fleet in the North Atlantic during June and July of 1943, screening northern convoys against German heavy surface units. She then returned to the Pacific to serve as an antiaircraft support and bombardment ship. On 19 June 1944, during the Battle of the Philippine Sea, a Japanese bomber made a direct hit on the first superstructure deck with a 550-pound bomb which damaged wiring and piping, wrecked the admiral's and captain's quarters and adjoining wardrooms, and damaged a 40mm mount. The explosion killed 27 and wounded 23 men, but combat efficiency was not impaired. Two minutes later, two Japanese aircraft were shot down by the 5-inch guns, using an improved VT antiaircraft shell. The ship continued combat operations until the war ended, participating in the occupation of the Philippine Islands, the invasions of Iwo Jima and Okinawa, and the bombardments of the Japanese home islands. On 6 May, while operating off Okinawa, the ship was taking on ammunition from the ammunition ship *Wrangell* when a 16-inch powder can exploded as it was being moved into one of the magazines. Two officers and 22 enlisted men suffered injuries or smoke inhalation, and 11 men died, mostly from asphyxiation.

During the war the *South Dakota* steamed 247,000 miles and participated in nine major shore bombardments. The usefullness of a dual-purpose armament reinforced by heavy machine-gun batteries was demonstrated by the total of 64 enemy aircraft shot down.

The ship was placed out of commission in reserve in January 1947.

Conversion design study. On 26 July 1954, the Chairman of the Ship Characteristics Board requested a preliminary design study of BB-57 (and BB-55) class conversions to increase speed. Examination of fast task force operations indicated that the *South Dakota* class was admirably suited for such major fleet service in every regard but speed. As the main-battery armament was considered greatly in excess of requirements, it was proposed to remove the after turret, thereby providing hull volume for added machinery. It was desired to increase the maximum speed to approximately 31 knots.

The Bureau of Ships reported on its investigations of the proposed conversions of the *South Dakota* class on 14 September 1954. It was calculated that 256,000 shaft horsepower would be necessary for a speed of 31 knots (greater than in the *North Carolina* with similar displacement due to shorter hull). The internal location of the main side belt armor precluded the removal of the side armor on *South Dakota*, as had been contemplated for BB-55 and BB-56. In order to obtain this massive increase in power, it would have been necessary to install a vastly improved steam propulsion plant or to utilize a plant with gas turbines for boost power, using the existing 130,000 SHP plant for normal operations.

Such added power would have forced a redesign of the after hull form, in order to obtain reasonable water flow to the propellers for satisfactory propulsive efficiency, as well as to prevent vibration induced by the skegs. Furthermore, larger propellers would have been required, along with the relocation and modification of shaft bearings, skegs, struts, stern tubes, rudders, and the steering gear.

Such major conversions were estimated to cost some $40,000,000 per ship, exclusive of activation expenses and expenses related to the upgrading or repair of electronics and combat systems. The proposed conversions were abandoned.

Final Disposition. The *South Dakota* was formally stricken from the Navy List on 1 June 1962. The ship was sold as scrap to the Lipsett Division, Luria Brothers, on 25 October 1962, for $466,425. Parts of the ship were purchased by the state of South Dakota for incorporation in a war memorial at Sioux Falls.

Indiana — Operational History. The keel for the *Indiana*, second ship of the class, was laid at the Newport News Shipbuilding and Drydock Company, Newport News, Virginia, on 20 November 1939. The ship was launched on 21 November 1941 and commissioned on 30 April 1942. The *Kearsarge*, originally Battleship No. 5, and converted and reclassified *Crane Ship No. 1*, was used to place the 16-inch guns in the turrets.

The *Indiana* began combat operations on 9 November 1942. She replaced the *South Dakota* at Guadalcanal after topside damage sent that ship to the U. S. for repairs. Operations in the Guadalcanal area were confined to gunfire support missions. During the bombardment of Tarawa in November 1943, she destroyed her first enemy aircraft.

Collision damage. The only serious damage to the *Indiana* during lengthy operations with the fast carrier task force resulted from a collision with the *Washington* during the Marshall Islands campaign, when the *Indiana* turned in front of the *Washington* during darken-ship conditions. At 0429 on 1 February 1944, the *Washington* hit the *Indiana* on the starboard quarter at frame 107 at an angle of about 26 degrees. Damage to the *Indiana* extended down from the main deck to the turn of the bilge through the three outer shells, aft to frame 142, and on the main deck from frame 103 to frame 165. A total of 14 voids were flooded and 13 fuel tanks damaged. The starboard outboard shaft was damaged beyond repair and the inboard screw on the starboard side was damaged. Power and degaussing cables were severed, and severe structural damage to interior longitudinal bulkheads within the side protective system extended from frame 106 to 130. Shell plating was dished in between the second and third decks and severely ruptured above the second deck. The starboard range-finder hood and the range finder on the after main-battery turret were damaged, two 40mm quadruple mounts and

The Indiana (BB58) underway off Norfolk on 15 August 1942. This detailed view, top, clearly shows main battery, secondary battery, light AA mounts at bow and stern, fire-control radar, and a coincidence rangefinder.

This aerial view of the Indiana shows her great beam and highly concentrated super-structure arrangement. Note life rafts nested atop turrets 2 and 3, 40mm mounts in gun tubs at stern, fact that main battery guns could be individually elevated (turret 3), and the recess at ship's side for access to fuel oil tanks.

The hull of the South Dakota *(BB57), right, just after launching on 7 June 1941. The traditional rainbow of signal flags was rigged from bow to stern, and the topsides were still cluttered with construction scaffolding.*

80

Completely outfitted and equipped, the South Dakota *now rides about 25 feet deeper in the water than she did on launching.*

In this starboard quarter view of the South Dakota, *her stack is nearly lost in the compact superstructure arrangement.*

The South Dakota, *bow on, in full load condition. Bow and forecastle 40mm gun tubs are visible.*

In fighting trim, the South Dakota is pictured below just after she entered the Pacific in August 1942. The AA batteries which downed 26 aircraft in a single engagement off Guadalcanal are visible here.

fourteen 20mm single mounts were destroyed, and two 20mm mounts were damaged. The starboard catapult and an OS2U-3 seaplane were lost. The resulting starboard list was corrected by flooding port voids. Three men were killed and one was injured. The ship went to Majuro Lagoon for temporary repairs and to Pearl Harbor for permanent repairs. With the exception of ships damaged on 7 December 1941, she was the biggest single repair job handled there during World War II.

The damage sustained by the *Indiana* occurred at the most vulnerable location within the armored citadel length. Indeed, a detailed vulnerability study conducted early in 1945 concluded that, if the unprotected stern area were riddled, flooding the third deck area between bulkheads 113 and 128½ would probably result in a *South Dakota*-class battleship sinking by the stern. This is precisely the area where the *Indiana* was hit by the *Washington*. In this instance, the *Indiana's* holding bulkhead remained intact and the ship's longitudinal stability was not jeopardized. However, it appears that a very similar collision, involving damage to the stern as well as to this critical compartment, possibly would have been sufficient to cause the ship to sink.

After repairs, the *Indiana* took part in the Hollandia campaign, the bombardment of Truk, and the Marianas campaign. On 19 June 1944, during the Battle of the Philippine Sea, a Japanese torpedo bomber launched a torpedo at the ship, but both plane and torpedo were destroyed by gunfire. Another plane was shot down soon afterward, but one Japanese aircraft did succeed in crashing into the battleship's side, scattering debris over the deck. Five men were wounded, but the only visible damage was a small dent in the shell plating.

After two years of operations, the *Indiana* was thoroughly overhauled at the Puget Sound Navy Yard, Bremerton, Washington. Returning to service on 24 January 1945, she conducted bombardment operations against Iwo Jima and the Japanese home islands. Then the ship joined the opening phase of the Okinawa operation, providing shore bombardment support, commencing on 24 March. Kamikaze attacks were almost a daily occurrence; the ship once destroyed three aircraft making a simultaneous attack on her.

On 5 June the U. S. fleet off Okinawa was hit by a typhoon that damaged 33 ships, including battleships, carriers, cruisers, and destroyers. The *Indiana* lost steering control and one main engine lost power, but she rode out the storm with only minor topside structural damage and continued operations.

From July through August the ship bombarded Japanese shore targets and provided fleet air defense. On 30 August she assisted in landing U. S. occupation forces at Yokosuka Naval Base, where the Japanese formal surrender took place on 2 September. When the *Indiana* returned to the United States at the end of September, she had steamed 234,888 miles since her departure from Newport News in June 1942.

Final Disposition. In 1947, the *Indiana* was put in reserve at the Puget Sound Naval Shipyard. She was stricken from the Navy List on 1 June 1962, sold for $418,387 on 6 September 1963, and scrapped in 1964.

The Massachusetts *(BB59) at time of commissioning in May 1942, when her radar installation was not yet complete (top). Ship fully outfitted for sea, after 1943 overhaul at Boston (center), and with added AA defense, after overhaul at Puget Sound Navy Yard, July 1944 (bottom).*

Massachusetts — Operational History.

The *Massachusetts*, third ship of the class, was built in the Fore River Yard of the Bethlehem Steel Corporation, at Quincy, Massachusetts. The keel was laid on 20 July 1939, the ship was launched on 23 September 1941, and she was commissioned on 12 May 1942. She was urgently needed for the Allied invasion of North Africa, in which her participation served as the ship's shakedown cruise. She sailed from Casco Bay, Maine, late in October 1942, as flagship for the Western Naval Task Force, which was assigned to invade French Morocco. Landings were scheduled for the morning of 8 November. The *Massachusetts*, accompanied by the heavy cruisers *Tuscaloosa* and *Wichita*, and four destroyers, arrived off Casablanca the evening of 7-8 November. The French battleship *Jean Bart* was in the harbor, incomplete and only partly armed, but still a formidable foe. The ships took battle stations at 0630 on 8 November; 12 minutes later an "action" signal was made, as American planes had been fired on and two French submarines were sighted leaving port. The *Massachusetts* was then taking station 24,000 yards west of Casablanca.

At 0703 five shells from Batterie El Hank fell to starboard of the *Massachusetts*. One minute later she took the *Jean Bart* under fire on the assumption the shells came from that ship. Actually, the *Jean Bart* did not open fire until 0708, when she fired two shots at one of the cruisers accompanying the *Massachusetts*. The latter ship continued salvo fire at ranges varying from 24,000 to 29,000 yards until 0740 and then ceased fire to reverse course. Fire was resumed at 0747 and a temporary cease fire order was given at 0833, after 47 salvos had been fired. The blast and shock from these first salvos temporarily disabled all radars on the ship.

Action at Casablanca. The *Massachusetts* did enormous damage to the port of Casablanca. The *Jean Bart* was hit five times and damaged by several near-misses. As two of the five shells failed to detonate, there was an impression that the projectiles were somewhat defective. Detailed analysis of the damage to the *Jean Bart* indicated that the two duds both struck the ship at oblique angles, which caused them to lose their base plugs, fuzes, and filler charges. Final evaluation was that the ammunition was not faulty. In any event, the *Massachusetts* did succeed in silencing the single operational main-battery turret on the French battleship for several hours. This was caused by one of the duds, which ricocheted off the heavy armor on the port side of the turret onto the edge of the horizontal armor at the top of the barbette. The deformation of this horizontal plating jammed the turret in train until the plating could be cut away with torches.

One shell detonated in an empty powder magazine for the after 152mm turret. A second shell exploded under the after control station, completely wrecking that space and holing the side of the ship, causing her to flood by the stern. A third hit the funnel aft, penetrating the side of the ship above the waterline before detonating in the water. The final hit was against the side of number 2 barbette (turret 2 had no guns); the dud ricocheted within the ship for 50 yards before coming to rest. The destroyer *Le Malin*, berthed astern of the *Jean Bart*, was severely damaged by a 16-inch shell that exploded in her engine room and caused extensive flooding; the ship eventually capsized against the quay. A floating drydock and four merchant ships were sunk. While the *Massachusetts, Wichita,* and *Tuscaloosa* were firing on the *Jean Bart* and Batterie El Hank, seven French destroyers left Casablanca and headed toward the landing beaches at Fedhala. The cruisers *Augusta* and *Brooklyn* were the only major warships between them and the vulnerable transports. At 0855 the *Massachusetts* increased speed to 27 knots to engage the destroyers. At that time one shot from El Hank hit her main gaff, holing her battle ensign.

The *Massachusetts* resumed main battery fire at 0918, but stopped again at 0940 because of a casualty to the SG radar and smoke obscuring the destroyers. Three minutes later she was straddled by shots from El Hank, and at 1000 a 7.6-inch shell hit the port side between turrets 1 and 2 at frame 48, penetrated the deck armor, and detonated in compartment A-208-L, causing a small fire which was quickly extinguished.

About the same time the French light cruiser *Primaguet* and two more destroyers got under way to assist the other destroyers. The *Fougeaux*, in the van of the destroyer force, was sunk by several 8-inch shells from the *Tuscaloosa* and one 16-inch shell from the *Massachusetts*. At 1005 the *Massachusetts* maneuvered to avoid four torpedoes, presumably launched by a French submarine, one of which missed by 15 feet. Fire was resumed at 1035 and a 16-inch shell hit the destroyer *Milan*, which had already taken four smaller caliber hits, and her forward section was completely wrecked. At 1100 the *Massachusetts* was hit by a 5.1-inch shell from the destroyer *Boulonnais*. The shell struck on the starboard quarter at frame 185, near a 20mm machine gun group, ricocheted, exploded, and started a small fire which was quickly extinguished. That destroyer, in turn, was hit by eight shells from the *Brooklyn* and a salvo from the *Massachusetts*, and rolled over and sank. The *Massachusetts* then made a 16-inch hit on the *Primaguet*, which also took two 8-inch hits from the *Augusta* and several 6-inch hits from the *Brooklyn*, and then broke off the action.

By 1104 the *Massachusetts* had expended 59.2 per cent of her main battery ammunition. The remainder had to be conserved in case the battleship *Richelieu* and cruisers *Montcalm* and *Gloire* sortied from Dakar to oppose the landings, but this threat failed to materialize.

During the early afternoon, the *Massachusetts* fired on the French gunboat *La Grandiere* and two coastal minesweepers heading toward Fedhala. Two minutes later El Hank resumed fire. The *Massachusetts* shifted fire to the shore battery, while the U. S. cruisers engaged the French ships. At 1355 she ceased fire to conserve ammunition. Later that afternoon she fired a nine-gun salvo at El Hank in order to "unload through the muzzles." During the entire engagement, her 16-inch guns fired 786 shells in 134 salvos and her 5-inch guns fired 221 rounds.

Pacific Operations. After a thorough overhaul at the Boston Navy Yard, the *Massachusetts* reached the Pacific in February 1943. During this period, the ex-shipyard workers in the crew relocated the SG radar from the forward to the after superstructure, a change indicated by the battle damage sustained by the *South Dakota* at Guadalcanal. Her first action was at Russell Island in April. During the Gilbert Islands operation on 24 November 1943, the ship downed two aircraft. She served in the Pacific theater for the duration of the war and participated in the bombardment of Nauru, Kwajalein, Truk, the Carolines, Okinawa, the China coast, and

Japan, the Battle of the Philippine Sea, and the Battle of Leyte Gulf. On 17 July 1945, in company with several other battleships and a strong force of cruisers and destroyers, she shelled the steel works at Kamaishi. In that action she fired 55 main battery salvos at an average rate of one per minute, at ranges from 27,000 down to 17,000 yards.

During her combat career, the *Massachusetts* steamed some 225,000 nautical miles, took part in 35 engagements, sank or damaged 5 enemy ships, and destroyed 18 Japanese aircraft.

Final Disposition. In March 1947, the *Massachusetts* was placed in reserve at the Norfolk Naval Shipyard, Portsmouth, Virginia. She was stricken from the Navy List on 1 June 1962 and was formally transferred to the Massachusetts Memorial Committee on 4 June 1965, to become a war memorial at Fall River, Massachusetts.

Alabama — Operational History. The keel of the *Alabama*, last ship of the *South Dakota* class, was laid at the Norfolk Navy Yard on 1 February 1940. The ship was launched on 16 February 1942 and commissioned on 16 August 1942. On 11 November she began her shakedown cruise in Chesapeake Bay and completed it at Casco Bay, Maine. After postshakedown repairs in Norfolk, she returned to Casco Bay for tactical maneuvers with the *South Dakota*.

From March through July 1943, the *Alabama* served with the British Home Fleet, protecting convoys to and from Russia. In August she returned to Norfolk for limited overhaul and repairs and left the shipyard that same month for duty with the U. S. Third Fleet, which began with the Gilbert Islands operation in November and December. She made gunnery strikes on Kwajalein and Majuro in early 1944.

During the evening of 21-22 February 1944, while screening a carrier task force proceeding to station for an air strike against the Marianas Islands, one of the *Alabama*'s 5-inch gun mounts accidentally fired into another 5-inch mount, killing 5 men and wounding 11 others. The accident occurred when the 5-inch mounts on the starboard side were tracking and firing at enemy aircraft on the beam. The ship turned towards the aircraft, causing the line of fire to move towards the bow. Eventually, the aftermost 5-inch mount, number 59, was masked by mount 55 (the amidships mount). The firing cut-out cam mechanism specifically designed to prevent such incidents functioned properly, breaking the firing circuits. At that time, inexplicably, the experienced sight setter in mount 59 inadvertently overrode the safety mechanism, causing both guns to fire into mount 55.

The right gun of mount 59 fired an AA Common projectile, which pierced the rear plate of mount 55 and detonated within the gun compartment, against the face plate between the two guns. The left gun fired a projectile which nicked the rear left edge of the shield and detonated outside.

Investigation showed that part of the mechanism for the firing cut-out system was ex-

The *Alabama* (BB60) on the ways at Portsmouth, Virginia, the day before she was launched on 16 February 1942. Note that outboard screws are aft of inboard screws, twin skegs are outboard with shafts faired in. The stub screws are fitted for dock trials, then replaced by standard-sized screw. Bottom view, ready for sea, November 1942.

posed and subject to inadvertent release. The problem was corrected by providing a metal cover to prevent such tragedies in the future.

The *Alabama* downed her first enemy plane in March. After the Battle of the Philippine Sea, she resumed support operations in the Marianas and then participated in the Battle for Leyte Gulf.

Early in 1945 the ship was overhauled and repaired at the Puget Sound Navy Yard, Bremerton, Washington. She rejoined the fleet at Ulithi early in May. Her first assignment was to screen carriers launching raids on Kyushu. On 14 May five suicide planes penetrated the combat air patrol; one crashed the carrier *Enterprise,* the others were shot down, two of them by the *Alabama.*

On 17 July 1945 the *Alabama* shelled mills and factories about fifty miles north of Tokyo, firing 1,500 rounds in a night bombardment. She helped land occupation forces in Japan when the war ended, and within two weeks was en route to the United States.

Final Disposition.
The *Alabama* went into reserve at Bremerton, Washington, on 9 January 1947 and was stricken from the Navy List on 1 June 1962. She was sold to the State of Alabama, to become a war memorial, and left Bremerton under tow on 2 July 1964 en route to Mobile, where she is now located. Her turbines were removed, and the gun barrels were plugged with concrete.

Armament.
The battleships were designed to mount the new 16-inch/45 caliber guns, Mark 6, in three triple turrets, each of which weighed some 1,437 tons. Each gun was mounted in a separate sleeve, thus permitting individual elevation and depression. These guns were identical to those eventually given the *North Carolina* and *Washington.* Armament characteristics are shown in Table 3-4.

TABLE 3-4

Gun Characteristics

Gun	16"/45	(406mm)	5"/38	(127mm)	1.57"/60	(40mm)
Shell wt. (lb)	2,700	(1,225 kg)	53.85	(24.43 kg)	1.98	(0.898 kg)
Muzzle velocity (FPS)	2,300	(701 m/s)	2,600	(792 m/s)	2,890	(881 m/s)
Maximum range (yds)	36,900	(33,741 m)	17,575	(16,070 m)	11,000*	(10,058 m)
Maximum elevation (degrees)	45		85		90	

*Fuze self-destructive at 5,000 yards (4,572 m).

Main battery. The main battery turrets were identical to those of the *North Carolina*-class ships, except for armor thickness. The maximum training gear rate was 4 degrees per second, the elevation rate was 12 degrees per second.

The 5-inch guns mounted on these ships were identical in all major respects to those on the *North Carolina*-class ships. Space limitations on the *South Dakota* allowed only four twin mounts on each side, while the other ships had five on each side; the mounts in the *South Dakota* class were located one deck higher than in the *North Carolina* for more efficient operation, especially in heavy weather. The secondary batteries served these ships well throughout their combat careers.

Antiaircraft battery. When the *South Dakota* was designed, close-in protection by antiaircraft machine guns was of little concern. Studies in 1940 determined that the lack of adequate short-range antiaircraft batteries constituted the most serious weakness in air defense. Eventually, a combination of 40mm and 20mm antiaircraft machine guns was adopted, and such armament was mounted on the last three ships of the class before their first war cruises. The *South Dakota* was fully converted to the new armament at the New York Navy Yard in 1943. The evolution in the light machine-gun protection of U.S. battleships is shown by the changes in the *South Dakota*'s antiaircraft battery (Table 3-5).

TABLE 3-5
Modifications to Machine Gun Armament

date	0.5"	1.1"	20mm	40mm	total
Aug. '37	12	12			24
Mar. '42	8	28	16		52
Sep. '42		20	36+	16	72
Feb. '43			35	68	103
Dec. '44			72	68	140
Mar. '45			77	68	145

Armor Protection.
The armor was designed to withstand 16-inch shellfire. Against the 2,240-pound shell fired by the 16-inch/45 caliber guns of the old *Maryland* class, the immunity zone was calculated to be from 17,700 to 30,900 yards. This zone was 20,500 to 26,400 yards for the newer 16-inch/45 caliber guns firing the 2,700-pound AP shell.

The designers of the *South Dakota*, at no sacrifice of other important military characteristics and with no net increase in displacement relative to that of the *North Carolina*, had effectively improved her armor protection.

Side belt armor. Side belt armor resistance was also improved; inclination from the vertical was increased from 15 to 19 degrees and thickness was increased to 12.2 inches on 0.875-inch STS backing plates, providing protection equivalent to that of about 17.3-inch vertical plates. The lower side belt extended down through the underwater protective system, tapering from 12.2 inches at the top to one inch at the bottom. This lower side belt armor was installed to provide protection against major caliber projectiles hitting the side of the ship below the water line. In contrast to that on the *North Carolina*, the side belt armor was internally located, which caused some concern. This arrangement left the shell plating relatively unprotected, although it increased the resistance of the overall side protective system to attack. It was accepted that minor damage could cause loss of fuel, which was concentrated outboard of the lower side belt armor. The location of the fuel bunkers near the shell of the ship greatly decreased the possible lists resulting from underwater damage, while the similar densities of fuel oil and sea water were expected to minimize the loss of fuel after damage, although the fuel in damaged tanks would be seriously contaminated by sea water. The apparent advantages were sufficient to merit the modification of the liquid-loading scheme of the *South Dakota* relative to that employed in the *North Carolina*.

The change to an internal side armor system resulted from the decision to increase the angle of inclination of the armor. Hull form considerations limited the feasible outslope of external belt armor to approximately 15 degrees.

Careful analysis of alternative side armor arrangements convincingly demonstrated the weight economies inherent in the 19-degree outslope armor arrangement:

(All schemes give 20,000- to 30,000-yard immunity zone
16"/45 gun, 2,240 lb. shell)

Arrangement	Max. belt thickness	Deck/belt armor weight per foot length
19° outslope internal	12.2"	18.2 tons
15° outslope external	13.3"	19.7 tons
vertical external	16.0"	20.9 tons
15° inslope internal	17.6"	21.4 tons
60° inslope internal	12.4"	20.0 tons

Deck armor. Deck armor followed the same basic arrangement developed for the *North Carolina*, with only minor modifications (Table 3-6). Despite its slightly reduced overall thickness, the deck armor system in the *South Dakota* was more effective than that given the *North Carolina*. This was a result of the fact that a greater proportion of the total thickness was concentrated in one heavy armor deck. A single armor plate of a given thickness has appreciably greater resistance than two thinner plates of the same total thickness.

Very heavy protection for the steering gear was typical of all U. S. battleships. The third deck armor over the steering gear was 6.2 inches thick; over the propeller shafts and the access to the steering engine rooms there were two strakes with a total thickness of 6.35 inches. The sides of these spaces were protected by 13.5-inch plates inclined 19 degrees from the vertical, equivalent to 19-inch vertical armor. The armor bulkhead at the after end was only 11.3 inches thick, while that at the forward end was 0.625-inches thick, a consequence of the shielding by deck and side armor between those spaces and the citadel. Despite heavy armor shielding for the steering gear, the rudders, as in all ships, remained vulnerable to underwater damage.

The Indiana *(BB58), commissioned 30 April 1942, is pictured at Hampton Roads, Virginia, on 8 September 1942.*

TABLE 3-6

Deck Armor Thickness

	North Carolina*	South Dakota**	
Main deck	1.45"(37mm)	1.50"(38mm)	1.50"(38mm)
Second deck	5.0" (127mm)	5.75"(146mm)	6.05"(154mm)
Splinter deck		0.625"(16mm)	
Third deck	1.95"(50mm)	0.30"(8mm)	0.30"(8mm)
Total	8.40"(214mm)	8.175"(208mm)	7.85"(200mm)

*Magazines at centerline
**Magazines and machinery, at centerline and outboard

Turrets, gun mounts, magazines. Main-battery protection was slightly improved over that of the *North Carolina*-class battleships: turrets had 18-inch face plates, 9.5-inch sides, 12-inch backs, and 7.25-inch tops. Barbette armor above the second deck was similarly heavy, ranging from 17.3 inches on the sides to 11.6 inches on the centerline. There was only an inconsequential increase in the armor on the secondary mounts and magazines.

Conning tower. The armored conning tower was characteristic of all U. S. battleships. The designers were convinced that heavy armor on the conning tower and communication tube was necessary, despite the slight probability of hits on such a small target. The sides of the tower and the communications tube were of 16-inch armor. The roof was 7.25 inches thick, and the floor was 4 inches thick.

Side Protection. The side protective system was developed from explosive tests on caissons at the Philadelphia and New York Navy yards that had influenced design on the *North Carolina* and the *Washington.* Although the designed resistance, as in the *North Carolina,* was 700 pounds of TNT, the effects of similar damage were less severe than in the earlier ships, as shown in the comparison of calculated equivalent damage effects (Table 3-7).

TABLE 3-7

Torpedo Hit Calculations

	North Carolina	South Dakota
Uncorrected list, one hit	7°	3.7°
Armor freeboard after hit	0.10'(.030m)	5.1'(1.554m)
Water needed to right ship	644 (654 m.t.)	440 (447 m.t.)
Metacentric height reduction	1.57'-1.881' (.479-.552m)	1.04'-1.15' (.317-.350m)
Draft increase by counter-flooding	10.6"(.269m)	7.5"(.191m)

Fundamentally, this revised system featured four bulkheads parallel to the side shell. The third bulkhead inboard was the lower side belt, with armor tapering from 12.2 inches to 1 inch. The two outboard compartments were normally liquid loaded at all times, while the two inboard compartments in the protective layer were normally void.* The effect of the relocation inboard of the void compartments is apparent in the improved performance of the side protective system after a single torpedo hit. The multiple-bulkhead side protective system was characteristic of almost all modern capital ships, with variations in liquid loading, scantlings, and bulkhead spacing being of the greatest importance.

Liquid loading. The side protective layer relied upon the great strength of heavy armor plates and the energy-absorbing capabilities of lighter plates when elastically and plastically deformed. Simultaneously, liquid loading permitted the deformation of the outboard bulkheads, with consequent energy absorption, before the loading of the lower side belt and the holding bulkhead beyond it. The effectiveness of a side protective system is highly dependent on the maintenance of the designed scheme of liquid loading. With the possible exception of the French *Richelieu*, no foreign battleships contemporary to this U. S. class had side protective systems of comparable efficiency and effectiveness.

In addition to its function in resisting armor-piercing projectiles, the internal lower side belt structure was believed to result in a considerable improvement in the effectiveness of the side protective system. The internal sloping armor was expected to reduce the deflection of the holding bulkhead. On this basis, the number of bulkheads within the side protective system was reduced from five to four and the breadth of the system slightly reduced. With tanks outboard of the armor belt, the gas jet from an underwater detonation could be somewhat vented upwards, thereby moderating the forces on the inboard bulkheads. Internal armor belts, however, do require the addition of some splinter protection to the shell plating to lessen the likelihood of shell fragments and smaller projectiles holing the side of the ship. The framing and butt straps necessary in the structure of an internal armor belt somewhat increase the structural weight of the overall system, as compared to that of an external belt.

Radar.

The *South Dakota*-class ships, throughout their operational careers, benefitted from the development of radar fire control and used it with notable success in controlling both the main and secondary batteries. The main battery guns were controlled by Mark 3 radar in the early part of the war. During the Guadalcanal campaign this gave U. S. forces a great advantage over the Japanese, who at that time had only optical fire-control equipment. The Mark 8 radar, successor to the Mark 3, was first installed on the *Indiana* in August 1942. Most important of its many improvements was the "B" scope presentation of targets in a plot of range versus bearing. These systems permitted accurate surface fire under complete radar control during night engagements, an inestimable advantage over optical systems.

---

*Information from French sources.

The Mark 4 radar, essentially a modified Mark 3 suitable for antiaircraft fire control, won its reputation on 26 October 1942, when the *South Dakota* shot down 26 enemy aircraft. In that engagement, approaching Japanese aircraft were detected at a range of 55 miles. The Mark 4 was also suited for use against surface targets, perfectly matching the excellent dual-purpose capabilities of the 5-inch guns.

Rapid development in radar made virtually all components obsolete within two years after introduction into service. The combination of long-range search radar with accurate fire-control radar equipment for the direction of gunfire at shorter ranges gave the U. S. Navy a great technological advantage in the war against Japan. No Axis ships carried such sophisticated electronic equipment.

By February of 1944, the *Alabama* was reporting the following *average* aircraft detection ranges:

SK radar	40,000 to 80,000 yards
SG radar	30,000 to 40,000 yards (on occasional low-flying aircraft)
Mark 4 GFCS radar	20,000 to 30,000 yards

Propulsion Plant.

Early design studies on the possibility of a 30-knot maximum speed indicated that this speed was only attainable with a hull appreciably longer than that of the *North Carolina* class, combined with more than 200,000 shaft horsepower. As a consequence of the desire to adhere to the treaty displacement limitations while improving protection, a speed of 27.5 knots—the same as for the *North Carolina*—was established as a design goal.

Steam conditions. The ship was driven by four sets of geared turbines and eight *Somers*-type boilers, similar to those in the *North Carolina*. The decision to employ steam pressure of 600 pounds per square inch at a temperature of 850°F. came too late to benefit earlier ships, but the turbine nozzles, steam piping, and other equipment in the *South Dakota*-class ships, designed from the beginning for the best possible use of steam conditions, produced the designed maximum speed.

Machinery arrangement. The propulsion plant arrangement was similar to that of the *North Carolina*-class ships; four main machinery spaces with two air-encased boilers, one set of geared turbines, and auxiliary equipment in each compartment, permitted the complete isolation of the main propulsion machinery and consequently improved overall resistance to damage. There were no longitudinal bulkheads subdividing these compartments, as design doctrine prohibited them wherever possible. The boilers in machinery rooms 1 and 3 were to port with the turbines to starboard; 2 and 4 had the opposite arrangement. The boilers were elevated sufficiently above the inner bottom to provide for better shaft clearances than in the first two new battleships. The evaporators were located forward of machinery room 1.

Power output. The high-pressure, high-temperature steam cycle made it possible to increase normal maximum shaft horsepower from 115,000 to 130,000 (overload ratings were 121,000 and 135,000), with improved specific weight of the machinery plant, as indicated in Table 3-8.

The close proximity of the forward tower and the uptakes permitted mutual structural support and protection, a design precedent to be followed in many later designs and modernizations, such as the battleships rebuilt after being damaged at Pearl Harbor.

TABLE 3-8
Machinery Weight Comparison

	North Carolina	South Dakota
Year completed	1941	1942
Shaft horsepower (overload)	121,000 (122,679 mhp)	135,000 (136,872 mhp)
Weight (tons)	3,444 (3,499 m.t.)	3,580 (3,637 m.t.)
Pounds per horsepower	63.8 (28.74 kg/mhp)	59.4 (26.57 kg/mhp)

Hull Characteristics. The shorter hull form of the *South Dakota* led to somewhat improved maneuverability as compared with the *North Carolina*, and her speed and handling characteristics were extremely good.

Model basin tests. Model basin tests of the twin-skeg stern shape adopted on the *North Carolina* were so impressive in comparison with the normal stern form that the latter was never considered for the *South Dakota*. Increased propeller efficiency allowed reduced propeller diameters. The twin skegs improved propulsion efficiency and the vibration problems encountered in the *North Carolina* were eliminated.

Speed and endurance. Cruising speed was retained at 15 knots and gave an endurance of 17,450 nautical miles. Long cruising range, an absolute necessity for these ships, was given high priority in their design. At the relatively high speed of 25 knots, the endurance was 6,400 nautical miles, an impressive figure when compared to foreign battleships.

Summary. The battleships of the *South Dakota* class were the best of those designed to the 35,000-ton standard displacement limitation imposed by the Washington Naval Treaty and its successors. They combined powerful armament with very good protection and speed adequate for the time in which they were built.

With the evolution of the fast carrier task force, their 27-knot maximum speed was only marginally acceptable, and the postwar requirements of jet aircraft carrier operations soon relegated them to a second-rate status. They were never reactivated after being put in reserve, and all were discarded by the end of 1965.

Their improved protection, as compared to the *North Carolina*-class ships, was their most noteworthy feature. With armor protection against 16-inch guns and an improved system of underwater protection, they were by far the best protected of all the 35,000-ton warships.

Their machinery was well separated and isolated, except for the distilling equipment, which was concentrated in one large compartment. If that space had been flooded, only limited steaming would have been possible.

The U. S. Navy design practice of retaining the heavily armored conning tower was vindicated in the Battle of Guadalcanal, although the vulnerability of the largely unprotected superstructure was once again demonstrated. This was a long-standing fundamental design deficiency of all capital ships that became particularly important with the advent of radar systems, which were especially susceptible to damage.

Damage to the *Indiana* when she was rammed by the *Washington* demonstrated the increased possibility of extensive side shell tearing resulting from adopting an internal inclined side armor belt system. Designers accepted this possibility as the cost of improved resistance to shell and underwater explosive attack. The potentially harmful effects on stability were lessened by the normal use of compartments outboard of the belt armor as fuel or water tanks.

The general arrangements specialists of the Navy who reviewed the layout of the *South Dakota* concluded there was a major deficiency in the internal arrangements in that the spaces over the side protective systems were living and working compartments, normally open to other parts of the ship. This arrangement, similar to the *North Carolina*, exposed the crew to casualties from a torpedo detonation and increased the likelihood of progressive flooding through the deck *above* the side protective system.

The ships of the *South Dakota* class were certainly the most successful of the 35,000-ton "treaty battleships," having a combination of armament, speed, and protection equalled by few other capital ships completed during the World War II era. Their extremely efficient design was apparent in the compact, functionally designed superstructure characteristic of the class. The American designers of these remarkable battleships succeeded so well in meeting the challenge of designing displacement-limited capital ships that only the Japanese giants *Yamato* and *Musashi* were clearly capable of defeating a *South Dakota*-class ship in a traditional gunnery engagement.

South Dakota Class

Name & hull number	*South Dakota* (BB-57)	*Indiana* (BB-58)
Builder	New York Shipbuilding Corp., Camden, N.J.	Newport News Shipbuilding & Dry Dock Co., Newport News, Va.
Laid down	5 July 1939	20 November 1939
Launched	7 June 1941	21 November 1941
Commissioned	20 March 1942	30 April 1942
Operational*	August 1942	9 November 1942
Dispositon	Sold 25 October 1962 to Lipsett Div., Luria Brothers. Scrapped. Parts of ship sold to state of S.Dak. for war memorial at Sioux Falls.	Sold on 24 May 1961 to Lipsett Div., Luria Brothers, for $757,000. Scrapped.

Name & hull number	*Massachusetts* (BB-59)	*Alabama* (BB-60)
Builder	Bethlehem Steel Co., Quincy, Mass.	Norfolk Navy Yard, Portsmouth, Va.
Laid down	20 July 1939	1 February 1940
Launched	23 September 1941	16 February 1942
Commissioned	12 May 1942	16 August 1942
Operational*	October 1942	March 1943
Disposition	Dedicated as a war memorial at Fall River, Mass. on 12 June 1965.	Dedicated as a war memorial at Mobile, Ala. in 1964.

*Based on first sortie on an operational mission.

Displacement

South Dakota

(13 Oct. 1942)	34,563 tons (35,118 m.t.)	Light ship
	38,664 tons (39,285 m.t.)	Standard (calculated)
	43,178 tons (43,871 m.t.)	Optimum battle
	44,519 tons (45,233 m.t.)	Full load
	46,218 tons (46,959 m.t.)	Emergency load
(1945)	38,506 tons (39,124 m.t.)	Standard (calculated)
	46,200 tons (46,941 m.t.)	Full load

Indiana

(18 Apr. 1942)	34,044 tons (34,591 m.t.)	Light ship
	43,053 tons (43,744 m.t.)	Optimum battle
	44,374 tons (45,068 m.t.)	Full load
	45,610 tons (46,342 m.t.)	Emergency load
(1942)	35,900 tons (36,476 m.t.)	Standard
	44,600 tons (45,316 m.t.)	Full load

Massachusetts

(10 May 1942)	35,113 tons (35,677 m.t.)	Light ship
	43,884 tons (44,588 m.t.)	Optimum battle
	45,216 tons (45,942 m.t.)	Full load
	47,006 tons (47,760 m.t.)	Emergency load

(1945) 38,988 tons (39,614 m.t.) Standard (calculated)
      43,178 tons (43,871 m.t.) Optimum battle
      46,314 tons (47,057 m.t.) Full load

Alabama
(30 Sep. 1942) 34,791 tons (35,349 m.t.) Light ship
(25 Feb. 1945) 35,223 tons (35,789 m.t.) Light ship

Dimensions

South Dakota
680′ 4.250″ (207.362 m) Length overall
666′ 0.000″ (202.997 m) Waterline length
108′ 1.500″ (32.946 m) Maximum beam
 27′ 9.250″ (8.464 m) Mean draft @ 34,563 tons
 33′ 11.625″ (10.354 m) Mean draft @ 42,900 tons
 34′ 0.250″ (10.370 m) Mean draft @ 43,178 tons
 34′ 11.250″ (10.649 m) Mean draft @ 44,519 tons
 36′ 2.250″ (11.030 m) Mean draft @ 46,218 tons
 36′ 4.000″ (11.074 m) Maximum draft

Indiana
680′ 0.000″ (207.264 m) Length overall
666′ 0.000″ (202.997 m) Waterline length
108′ 2.000″ (32.969 m) Maximum beam
 27′ 9.500″ (8.471 m) Mean draft @ 34,044 tons
 33′ 9.813″ (10.308 m) Mean draft @ 42,545 tons
 34′ 0.500″ (10.376 m) Mean draft @ 43,053 tons
 34′ 11.500″ (10.655 m) Mean draft @ 44,374 tons
 35′ 9.500″ (10.909 m) Mean draft @ 45,610 tons
 36′ 2.000″ (11.024 m) Maximum draft

Massachusetts
680′ 9.813″ (207.513 m) Length overall
666′ 0.000″ (202.997 m) Waterline length
108′ 2.250″ (32.976 m) Maximum beam
 28′ 7.000″ (8.712 m) Mean draft @ 35,113 tons
 33′ 8.500″ (10.274 m) Mean draft @ 42,545 tons
 34′ 7.500″ (10.554 m) Mean draft @ 43,884 tons
 35′ 6.000″ (10.820 m) Mean draft @ 45,216 tons
 36′ 3.250″ (11.055 m) Mean draft @ 46,314 tons
 36′ 9.000″ (11.201 m) Mean draft @ 47,006 tons
 36′ 9.000″ (11.201 m) Maximum draft

Alabama
679′ 5.313″ (207.094 m) Length overall
666′ 0.000″ (202.997 m) Waterline length
108′ 1.500″ (32.946 m) Maximum beam
 28′ 4.000″ (8.636 m) Mean draft @ 34,791 tons
 33′ 9.813″ (10.308 m) Mean draft @ 42,545 tons
 36′ 2.000″ (11.024 m) Maximum draft

Frames

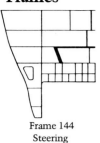

Frame 144
Steering

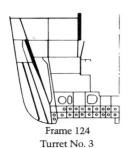

Frame 124
Turret No. 3

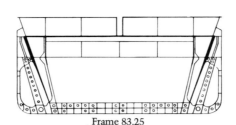

Frame 83.25

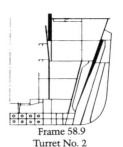

Frame 58.9
Turret No. 2

Frame 42
Turret No. 1

Frame 12.5

Hull Characteristics at D.W.L.

Displacement	42,545 tons (43,228 m.t.)
Mean draft	33' 9.813" (10.308 m) *Indiana*
	33' 8.500" (10.274 m) *Massachusetts*
	33' 9.813" (10.308 m) *Indiana*
Hull depth amidships	52' 0.000" (15.850 m)
Freeboard at bow	28' 7.000" (8.712 m)
Freeboard at stern	20' 7.125" (6.277 m)
Block coefficient	0.615
Prismatic coefficient	0.618
Waterplane coefficient	0.709
Midship section coefficient	0.993
Ton per inch immersion	121.6 (48.645 m.t./cm.)
Moment to trim one inch	4,200 foot-tons (one cm: 508.46 m-m.t.)
(GM) metacentric height	7.18' (2.189 m)
Wetted surface	90,760 sq. ft. (8,431.9 sq. m.)

Armament

Nine 16-inch/45 caliber (Mark 6) (406mm)
Sixteen 5-inch/38 caliber (Mark 12) (127mm) BB-57
Twenty 5-inch/38 caliber (Mark 12) (127mm) Others

Antiaircraft machine guns

	40mm/56	1.1"/75 (28mm)	20mm/70	.50 cal. (12.7mm)
South Dakota				
(Mar. 1942)	none	28	16	8
(Sep. 1942)	16	20	36+	none
(Feb. 1943)	68	none	35	none
(Dec. 1944)	68	none	72	none
(Mar. 1945)	68	none	77	none
Indiana				
(June 1942)	24	none	16	none
(Dec. 1944)	48	none	55	none
(1945)	48	none	52	none
Massachusetts				
(May 1942)	24	none	35	none
(Dec. 1944)	72	none	38	none
(June 1945)	72	none	33	none
(Nov. 1945)	72	none	41	none
Alabama				
(Aug. 1942)	24	none	22	none
(Dec. 1944)	48	none	52	none
(Feb. 1945)	48	none	56	none
(Nov. 1945)	48	none	52	none

Armor Protection (Refer to plans for arrangement details.)

Immunity zone from 17,700 to 30,900 yards (16,185-28,255 m) (citadel)
U. S. 16"/45 (406mm) firing 2,240 lb. (1,016 kg) shell

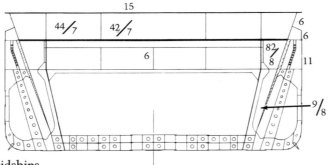

Amidships

Belt armor 12.2" on 0.875" STS, inclined 19° (310mm on 22mm)
Lower belt armor 12.2" tapered to 1.0" on 0.875" STS at lower edge (310mm-25mm on 22mm)

Deck armor	*Centerline*	
main	1.5"	(38mm)
second	5.0" + 0.75"	(127mm + 19mm)
splinter	0.625"	(16mm)
third	0.3"	(8mm)
Total	8.175"	(208mm)
	Outboard	
main	1.5"	(38mm)
second	5.3" + 0.75"	(135mm + 19mm)
splinter	none	none
third	0.3"	(8mm)
Total	7.85"	(199mm)

Barbette armor
  centerline 11.6" (295mm)
  sides 17.3" (438mm)

Turret armor
  face plates 18.0" (457mm)
  sides 9.5" (241mm)
  back plates 12.0" (305mm)
  roof plates 7.25" (184mm)

Secondary gun armor
  gun mounts 2.0" (51mm)
  magazines 2.0" (51mm)

Conning tower armor
  sides 16.0" (406mm)
  roof plates 7.25" (184mm)
  bottom plates 4.0" (102mm)
  comm. tube 16.0" (406mm)

Underwater Protection

Designed resistance 700 pounds TNT (318 kg)
Side protective system depth 17.9' (5.45 m) @ half draft amidships
S.P.S. designed loading (shell) liquid-liquid-void-void
Total bulkhead thickness . . ."
Bottom protective system depth 6' 0" (1.829 m) amidships
upper layer 3' 0" (0.914 m) (void)
lower layer 3' 0" (0.914 m) (liquid loaded)
total plating thickness . . ."

Tank Capacities
(Note: S.D. Book = Ship's Data Book)

Machinery Schematic

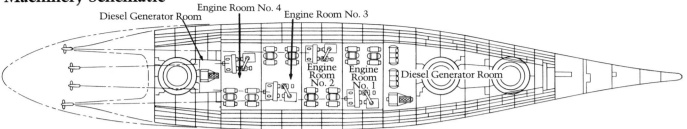

Diesel Generator Room • Engine Room No. 4 • Engine Room No. 3 • Engine Room No. 2 • Engine Room No. 1 • Diesel Generator Room

Boiler
Turbine
Diesel Generator
Evaporator

South Dakota
Fuel oil 7,318.9 tons (7,436.3 m.t.) — 1945
      6,950.9 tons (7,062.4 m.t.) — 1947
      6,607.0 tons (6,713.0 m.t.) — 1949 S.D. Book
Diesel oil 157.1 tons (159.6 m.t.) — 1945-47-49
Gasoline 23.8 tons (24.2 m.t.) — 1945-47-49
Reserve feed water 374.5 tons (380.5 m.t.) — 1947
Potable water 451.3 tons (458.5 m.t.) — 1947

Indiana
Fuel oil 6,434.5 tons (6,537.8 m.t.) — 1945
      7,340.0 tons (7,457.7 m.t.) — 1947
      6,635.0 tons (6,741.5 m.t.) — 1949 S.D. Book
Diesel oil 187.7 tons (190.7 m.t.) — 1945-47-49
Gasoline 21.5 tons (21.8 m.t.) — 1945-47-49
Reserve feed water 341.2 tons (346.7 m.t.) — 1947
Potable water 438.7 tons (445.7 m.t.) — 1947

Massachusetts
Fuel oil 6,875.9 tons (6,986.2 m.t.) — 1945
      6,607.0 tons 6,713.0 m.t.) — 1949 S.D. Book
Diesel oil 157.1 tons (159.6 m.t.) — 1945-49
Gasoline 23.8 tons (24.2 m.t.) — 1945-49

Alabama
Fuel oil 6,974.9 tons (7,086.8 m.t.) — 1945
      6,635.0 tons (6,741.5 m.t.) — 1949 S.D. Book
Diesel oil 185.5 tons (188.5 m.t.) — 1945-49
Gasoline 21.5 tons (21.8 m.t.) — 1945-49
Reserve feed water 341.2 tons (346.7 m.t.)
Potable water 438.7 tons (445.7 m.t.)

Machinery

Boilers	eight three drum express type boilers fitted with two furnaces and double uptakes. Babcock & Wilcox — *South Dakota* and *Massachusetts*; Foster Wheeler — *Indiana* and *Alabama* pressure: 578 psi (40.64 kg/cm²) temperature: 850°F. (454.4°C,)
Turbines	four sets General Electric geared turbines *(South Dakota* and *Massachusetts)* four sets Westinghouse geared turbines *(Indiana* and *Alabama)*
Shaft horsepower	130,000 (131,803 mhp) 32,000 (32,444 mhp) Astern
Maximum speed	27.8 knots @ 185 rpm — 1941 27.0 knots — 1945
Nominal endurance	17,000 nautical miles @ 15 knots — 1945 6,400 nautical miles @ 25 knots — 1945
Generators	seven ship's service turbogenerators (1,000 kw) two emergency diesel generators (200 kw) total ship's service capacity: 7,000 kw, 450 Volts, AC

Propellers	two four-bladed 17' 6" (5.334 m) diameter propellers—inboard
	two four-bladed 17' 8½" (5.398 m) diameter propellers—outboard
Rudders	two rudders with a projected area of the profile of each of 273 sq. ft. (25.4 sq. m.)

Miscellaneous

Complement 1,793 (115 off./1,678 enl.)—design
   (1945) 2,354 (114 off./2,240 enl.)—*South Dakota*
     2,257 (145 off./2,112 enl.)—*Indiana*
     2,354 (114 off./2,240 enl.)—*Massachusetts*
     2,332 (127 off./2,205 enl.)—*Alabama*
   (1947) 2,351 (123 off./2,228 enl.)—*South Dakota*
     1,611 (88 off./1,523 enl.)—*Indiana*
     2,348 (134 off./2,214 enl.)—*Massachusetts*
     2,299 (108 off./2,191 enl.)—*Alabama*

Frame Spacing 4.0' (1.219 m)

Actual GM *South Dakota*—13 October 1942
   7.02' (2.140 m) @ 34,563 tons (35,118 m.t.)
   8.94' (2.725 m) @ 43,178 tons (43,871 m.t.)
   9.51' (2.899 m) @ 44,519 tons (45,233 m.t.)
   9.58' (2.920 m) @ 46,218 tons (46,959 m.t.)

   Indiana—18 April 1942
   6.89' (2.100 m) @ 34,044 tons (34,591 m.t.)
   8.84' (2.694 m) @ 43,053 tons (43,744 m.t.)
   9.36' (2.853 m) @ 44,374 tons (45,086 m.t.)
   9.45' (2.881 m) @ 45,610 tons (46,342 m.t.)

   Massachusetts—10 May 1942
   6.36' (1.939 m) @ 35,113 tons (35,677 m.t.)
   8.38' (2.554 m) @ 43,884 tons (44,588 m.t.)
   8.92' (2.719 m) @ 45,216 tons (45,942 m.t.)
   9.08' (2.768 m) @ 47,006 tons (47,760 m.t.)

   Massachusetts—1945
   9.65' (2.941 m) @ 46,314 tons (47,057 m.t.)

   Alabama—25 February 1945
   6.13' (1.875 m) @ 35,223 tons (35,789 m.t.)

South Dakota (BB-57)
Weight Summary
1942

	Tons	Metric tons	Percent of total
Hull structure (excl. armor)	13,354.946	(13,569.645)	37.99
Armor	13,943.154	(14,167.285)	39.63
Propulsion & electrical	3,441.688	(3,496.957)	9.79
Communication & control	33.365	(33.901)	0.08
Auxiliary systems	730.184	(741.897)	2.07
Outfit & furnishings	1,083.904	(1,101.300)	3.08
Armament	2,607.779	(2,649.604)	7.43
Light Ship Displacement	35,195.020	(35,760.151)	100%
Ammunition	2,283.613	(2,320.255)	
Complement	194.464	(197.586)	
Supplies & stores	936.936	(951.967)	
Aeronautics	53.908	(54.773)	
Standard Displacement	38,663.941	(39,284.495)	
Fuel oil	4,883.440	(4,961.779)	
Reserve feed water	249.840	(253.848)	
Full Load Displacement	43,797.221	(44,500.017)	

Body Plan

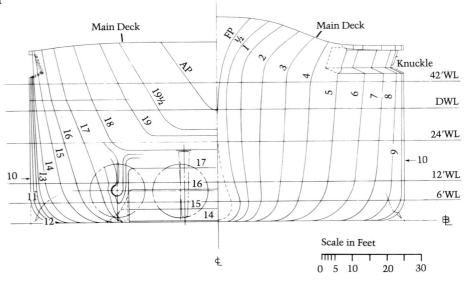

Deck Plans

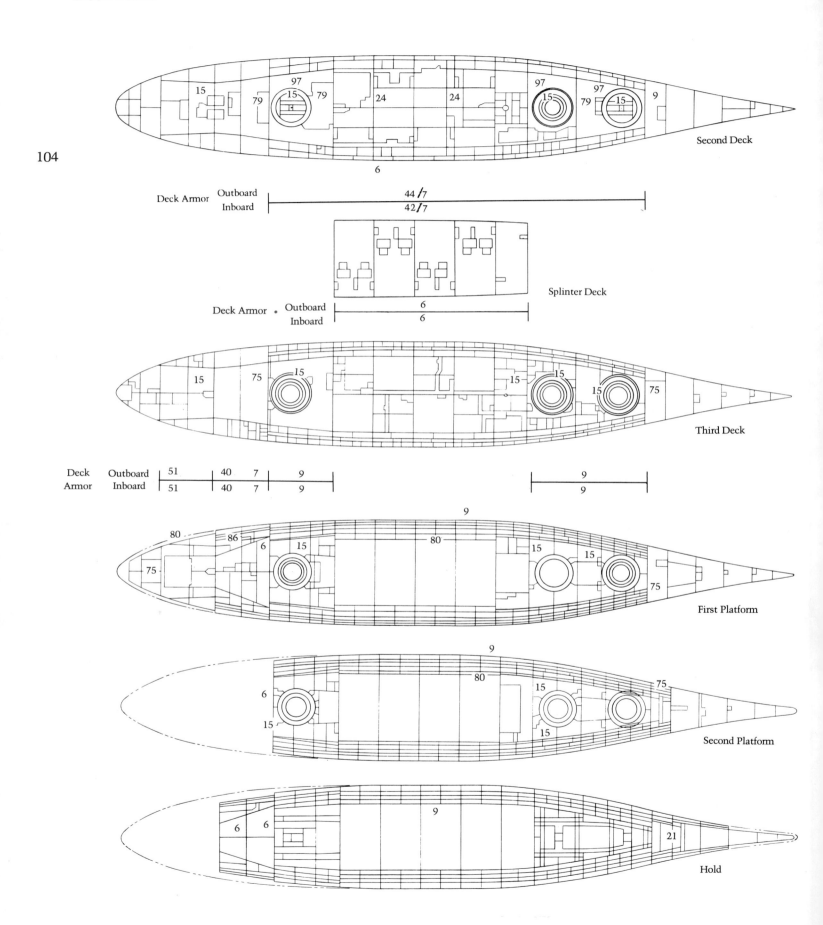

104

Second Deck

15 97 79 15 79 24 24 97 15 79 97 15 9

6

| Deck Armor | Outboard | 44 /7 |
| | Inboard | 42 /7 |

Splinter Deck

| Deck Armor | Outboard | 6 |
| | Inboard | 6 |

Third Deck

15 75 15 15 15 15 75

| Deck | Outboard | 51 | 40 | 7 | 9 | | 9 | |
| Armor | Inboard | 51 | 40 | 7 | 9 | | 9 | |

9

First Platform

80 86 6 15 80 15 15 75 75 75

9

Second Platform

9 80 6 15 15 15 75

Hold

9 6 6 21

Battle Damage

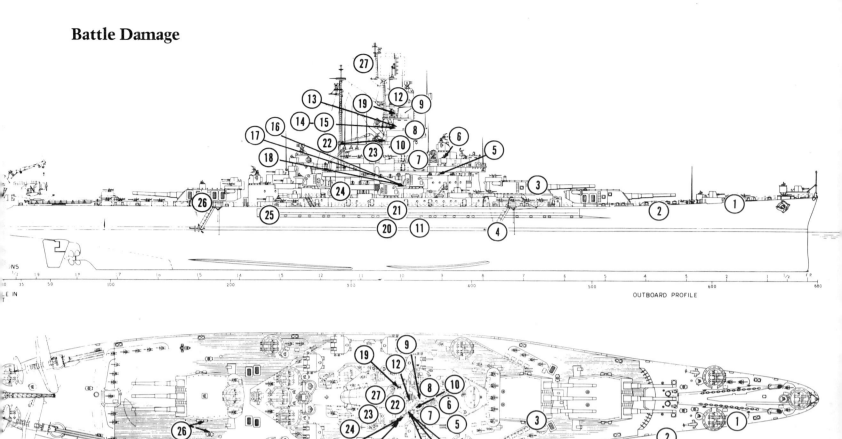

OUTBOARD PROFILE

OVERHEAD VIEW

Armor Thickness

Key No.	Inches	Millimeters	Key No.	Inches	Millimeters	Key No.	Inches	Millimeters	Key No.	Inches	Millimeters
1	.25	6	26	2.80	71	51	6.20	157	76	11.50	292
2	.30	8	27	2.870	73	52	6.30	160	77	11.60	295
3	.375	10	28	2.925	74	53	6.60	168	78	11.70	297
4	.45	11	29	3.00	76	54	6.80	173	79	11.80	300
5	.50	13	30	3.20	81	55	7.00	178	80	12.00	305
6	.625	16	31	3.25	83	56	7.125	181	81	12.10	307
7	.750	19	32	3.30	84	57	7.20	183	82	12.20	310
8	.875	22	33	3.60	91	58	7.25	184	83	12.75	324
9	1.00	25	34	3.75	95	59	7.40	188	84	12.80	325
10	1.125	29	35	3.82	97	60	7.75	197	85	13.00	330
11	1.25	32	36	3.90	99	61	7.80	198	86	13.50	343
12	1.40	35	37	4.00	102	62	7.85	199	87	13.70	348
13	1.425	36	38	4.10	104	63	8.17	208	88	14.00	356
14	1.47	37	39	4.50	114	64	8.50	216	89	14.70	373
15	1.50	38	40	4.75	121	65	9.00	229	90	14.90	378
16	1.625	41	41	4.80	122	66	9.15	232	91	15.00	381
17	1.71	43	42	5.00	127	67	9.30	236	92	15.25	387
18	1.90	48	43	5.26	133	68	9.50	241	93	16.00	406
19	1.91	49	44	5.30	135	69	9.80	249	94	16.10	409
20	1.95	50	45	5.50	140	70	10.00	254	95	16.70	424
21	2.00	51	46	5.60	142	71	10.20	259	96	17.00	432
22	2.05	52	47	5.625	143	72	10.60	260	97	17.30	439
23	2.20	56	48	5.80	147	73	11.00	279	98	17.50	444
24	2.50	64	49	6.00	152	74	11.10	282	99	18.00	457
25	2.70	67	50	6.10	155	75	11.30	287	100	19.50	495
									101	21.30	541

CHAPTER FOUR

The <u>Iowa</u> class

Without question the *Iowa*-class battleships were the best ever built. They possessed an unmatched combination of great offensive power, good protection, and high speed. Ships of other nations occasionally equalled or surpassed them in specific categories, but no other capital ships ever built had such an impressively balanced combination of military characteristics. The *Iowa*-class ships were the World War II equivalents of the superlative World War I-era battlecruisers of the German Navy and the fast *Queen Elizabeth*-class battleships of the Royal Navy.

Late in 1937, the U.S. Navy began investigating battleship designs with a standard displacement of 45,000 tons. This interest was triggered by the possibility that Japan would fail to ratify the 1936 London Naval Treaty, which would automatically increase the displacement limitation from 35,000 to 45,000 tons.

Initial studies evaluated a more heavily armed version of the *South Dakota* design, with the addition of a fourth 16-inch/45 caliber triple turret and an increase in power to 170,000 shp to retain a speed of 27 knots. The other basic attributes of the BB-57 were to be retained, with the added 10,000 tons being consumed by the added turret, the greater expanse of side and deck armor systems, added hull weight, and the increased machinery plant. The main design characteristics are presented in Table 4-1.

The U.S. Navy had long been attracted by the high-speed battleship concept. During the design synthesis of both the *North Carolina*- and the *South Dakota*-class ships, designs for ships with speeds of about 30 knots had been considered, but abandoned, because such speeds, on a 35,000-ton displacement, could be attained only by sacrificing either armament or protection, neither of which was desirable. The Japanese refusal to ratify the London Naval Treaty of 1936 had the effect of raising battleship displacement limitations to 45,000 tons standard, thereby giving the U.S. Navy its first opportunity to design acceptable ships with high speeds.

Design Characteristics. In January 1938 the Preliminary Design Branch of the Bureau of Construction and Repair prepared a series of designs for high-speed battleships, detailed in Table 4-2. The ships were characterized by extremely high maximum speed, great hull length, and light protection. They featured protection against 8-inch guns only, and in this respect they would have been more accurately rated as battlecruisers rather than as battleships. Not surprisingly, this concept was soon abandoned.

In February of 1938 the first fast battleship designs with protection against 16-inch shellfire were prepared (Table 4-3). The displacement of these designs was greatly in excess of the 45,000-ton limitation set by the 1936 London Naval Conference. These studies were noteworthy in that they included 6-inch/47 caliber guns in dual-purpose mounts. Although the

The Iowa *(BB61), name ship of her class, as she moved down the ways at the Brooklyn Navy Yard on 27 August 1942. The tons of anchor chains suspended from her bow were dropped to slow her momentum as she entered the water.*

TABLE 4-1

Four-Turret Version of South Dakota

Date	*Fall 1937*

Displacement
  standard   45,000 tons (45,722 m.t.)
  design waterline   51,500 tons (52,327 m.t.)
  full load   54,200 tons (55,070 m.t.)

Dimensions
  waterline length   770'0" (234.696 m)
  maximum beam   108'3" (32.995 m)
  maximum draft   35'0" (10.668 m)

Armament
  12-16"/45 tripled (406mm)
  20-5"/38 paired (127mm)
  12-1.1"/75 quadrupled (28mm)
  12-0.5" single (12.7mm)

Propulsion
  shaft horsepower   170,000 (172,358 mhp)
  maximum speed   27 knots
  endurance   15,000 nautical miles @ 15 knots

Protection
  Same as for *South Dakota*

TABLE 4-2

High-Speed Battleship Designs, January 1938

Design Scheme	A		B		C		D		E		F	
Displacement												
standard	49,354	(50,146)	49,679	(50,476)	50,004	(50,806)	50,340	(51,147)	50,762	(51,576)	50,949	(51,766)
full load	59,218	(60,159)	59,711	(60,669)	60,223	(61,190)	60,760	(61,735)	61,436	(62,422)	61,700	(62,690)
Dimensions												
waterline length	980'	(298.704)	980'	(298.704)	980'	(298.704)	980'	(298.704)	980'	(298.704)	980'	(298.704)
maximum beam	108'	(32.918)	108'	(32.918)	108'	(32.918)	108'	(32.918)	108'	(32.918)	108'	(32.918)

Armament (all ships)
  12-16"/50 (406mm) tripled
  20-5"/38 (127mm) paired
  12-1.1"/75 (28mm) quadrupled
  12-0.50 cal. (12.7mm) single

Propulsion						
shaft horsepower	221,500 (224,572)	232,600 (235,826)	243,600 (246,979)	256,000 (259,550)	273,500 (277,290)	285,000 (288,95
maximum speed	35.5	35.5	35.5	35.5	35.5	35.5
endurance @ 15	20,000	20,000	20,000	20,000	20,000	20,000

Armor (all ships)
  belt   8.1" tapered to 1.75" (206-44) (inclined 19°)
  16" (406mm) turrets 9.0" faces (229)
            8.0" rear (203)
            6.0" sides (152)
            5.0" roof (127)
  barbettes   10.5" (267)
  conning tower   10.5" sides (267)
            5.0" roof (127)
  bomb deck   1.75" (44)
  armor deck   2.3" + .75" (58 + 19)

Complement (all ships) 2,400 officers and men

High-Speed Battleship Designs, January 1938

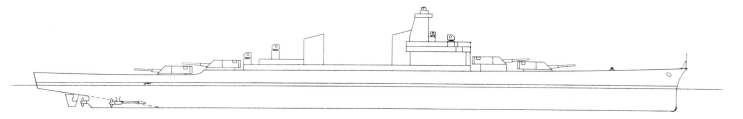

TABLE 4-3

High-Speed Battleship Designs, February 1938

Design Scheme	A	B	C
Displacement			
standard	59,060 (60,008)	52,707 (53,552)	55,771 (56,666)
full load	70,750 (71,865)	63,500 (64,519)	67,280 (68,360)
Dimensions			
waterline length	960' (292.608)	920' (280.416)	960' (292.608)
beam	108¼' (32.994)	108¼' (32.994)	108¼' (32.994)
maximum draft	37½' (11.430)	37½' (11.430)	37½' (11.430)
Armament			
16"/50 (406mm)	12—tripled	9—tripled	9—tripled
6"/47 (152mm)	12—paired	12—paired	12—paired
1.1"/75 (28mm)	12—quadrupled	12—quadrupled	12—quadrupled
0.50 cal. (12.7mm)	12—single	12—single	12—single
Propulsion			
shaft horsepower	277,000 (280,842)	225,000 (228,121)	300,000 (304,161)
maximum speed	32.5	32.5	35.5

Armor (all ships)		
belt	12.6"	(320) (inclined 19°)
16" (406mm) turrets	18.0" faces	(457)
	10.0" sides	(254)
	8.0" roof	(203)
barbettes	16.0"	(406)
conning tower	16.0" sides	(406)
splinter protection	2.5"	(63)
armor deck	5.0"	(127)

improved armor protection, more powerful 16-inch/50 caliber gun armament, and excellent speed were all considered desirable, the need to reduce displacement to conform to treaty requirements necessitated a careful review of all these attributes.

The relatively modest maximum speed of 27 knots given the earlier *North Carolina* and *South Dakota* designs was considered a highly undesirable limit on fleet speed. In March of 1938, as a matter of fact, the controversy regarding the maximum speed of these earlier ships became so intense that several radical changes in capital ship design and construction policy were seriously considered, and then discarded:

- Cease work on BB-55 and BB-56, already under construction, invoke the escalator clause, and redesign the ships with a displacement sufficient to produce 30 knots speed and to permit some improvement in the protection. Build BB-57 through BB-60 to this modified design.

- Complete BB-55 and BB-56 as designed. Accept tactical heterogeneity and invoke the escalator clause for BB-57 and BB-58 and redesign the ships on a displacement sufficient for 30 knots with the same protection and armament. Follow this modified design for BB-59 and BB-60. This would result in two 27-knot and four 30-knot ships.

- Complete BB-55 through BB-58 as designed, with a speed of 27 knots. Invoke the escalator clause for subsequent ships, and revive the old battlecruiser-battleship speed relation in BB-59 and BB-60. This could be accomplished by giving these last two ships approximately the same offensive-defensive power as BB-57, with an increased speed of 32-33 knots. This would result in four 27-knot ships and two ships capable of 32 or 33 knots. [Ultimately, of course, this basic design concept led to the *Iowa*, BB-61.]

- Repeat the BB-55 design when building BB-57 and BB-58, and follow with a new design for BB-59 and BB-60. This would have resulted in four ships built to the *North Carolina* design.

Subsequent to that time, the design evolution of the *Iowa* followed two parallel courses:

- The "slow battleship" version, with the added available displacement used to improve armament and protection while retaining a speed of some 27 knots.

- The "fast battleship" version, with essentially similar armament and protection as that of the earlier *South Dakota* design. Ships designed to this concept utilized the added available displacement to obtain higher speeds.

Slow battleship designs. Table 4-4 details the characteristics of several "slow battleship" design studies completed in April and June of 1938. The April design study is particularly of interest because it projected a main battery armament of nine 18-inch guns. The U. S. Navy completed an 18-inch/48 caliber gun Mark 1 about 1920. Little is known of this gun other than the fact that it fired a 2,900-pound armor-piercing shell at a muzzle velocity of 2,700 feet per second. One 18-inch gun was still preserved at the Naval Proving Grounds, Dahlgren, Virginia, as recently as 1966. A triple turret for 18-inch guns was estimated to weigh some 3,000 tons, almost half again as much as a triple turret for the 16-inch/45 caliber gun. The April 1938

Speed, power, protection, and utility, four essential elements of ship design that made the Iowa-class battleships the best of their type, are apparent in the waterline model prepared during the preliminary design process.

TABLE 4-4

Slow Battleship Design Studies

Date	April 1938	June 1938	June 1938
Displacement			
standard	45,495 (46,225)	45,292 (46,019)	45,099 (45,823)
optimum battle	54,495 (55,370)	54,077 (54,945)	53,984 (54,850)
full load	56,595 (57,504)	55,397 (56,286)	55,338 (56,226)
Dimensions			
waterline length	800'0" (243.840)	785'0" (239.268)	800'0" (243.840)
maximum beam	108'3" (32.994)	108'3" (32.994)	108'3" (32.994)
maximum draft	35'11½" (10.96)	35'11½" (10.96)	35'11½" (10.96)
Armament			
18"/48 (457mm)	9—tripled	none	none
16"/50 (406mm)	none	12—tripled	12—tripled
5"/38 (127mm)	20—paired	20—paired	20—paired
1.1"/75 (28mm)	12—quadrupled	12—quadrupled	12—quadrupled
0.50 cal. (12.7mm)	12—single	12—single	12—single
Propulsion			
shaft horsepower	130,000 (131,803)	130,000 (131,803)	115,000 (116,595)
maximum speed	27.5	27	27
endurance @ 15 knots	15,000	15,000	15,000

Protection	(For April 1938 design only)
belt	14.75" on 0.75" (375 + 19) (inclined 19°)
18" (457mm) turrets	20.0" faces (508mm)
	10.0" roof (254mm)
barbettes	21.0" (533mm)
conning tower	21.0" sides (533)
	10.0" roof (254)
transverse bulkheads	16.75" (425)
splinter protection	2.5" (63)
bomb deck	1.5" (38)
armor deck	5.1" + .75" (130 + 19)
splinter deck	0.625" (16)

version of the "slow battleship" was given massive armor protection, sufficient to provide immunity against the 18-inch gun from 20,000 to 29,000 yards.

The June versions of the "slow battleship" were much more conventional with regards to the main battery, featuring twelve 16-inch/50 caliber guns in four triple turrets. After evaluating possible lengths varying from 755 to 830 feet, it was decided that the most economical length from a weight viewpoint was about 810 feet, although it was possible to accept a length of 785 feet without a great increase in the standard displacement. Beyond 810 feet, for the basic geometric configuration being considered, the displacement increased rapidly.

The construction of such large ships posed some problems, since the building ways at the New York Navy Yard were inadequate and would require remodeling. Despite this, it was generally concluded that it was practicable to build a 27-knot, 45,000-ton battleship with twelve 16-inch/50 caliber guns in triple turrets. With a maximum acceptable draft of 36 feet, the minimum practicable length was 785 feet. The operational advantages of higher speeds were considered to be of such importance, however, that these "slow battleship" design studies were ultimately abandoned in terms of further development and refinement.

Fast battleship designs. "Fast battleships" of the 45,000-ton class were first designed in April of 1938 (Table 4-5). The emphasis was still on high speed (32-plus knots), good protection, and powerful armament (nine 16-inch guns). The secondary armament was reduced from 6-inch to 5-inch guns in an effort to minimize the displacement. Design Scheme II was a variation with the 16-inch/45 caliber gun given the *South Dakota*, while Schemes I, III, and IV were armed with the more powerful 16-inch/50 caliber gun. The four studies were given protection similar to that of the *South Dakota*. The most important variable was the length of the machinery box and the available shaft horsepower, which resulted in design maximum speeds varying from 32.25 to 32.5 to 33 knots.

The variation in turret weights for the two 16-inch guns was considerable, as can be seen from the following tabulation:

	16"/45 triple turret	*16"/50 triple turret*
Barbette diameter	39.25'	39.33'
Weight*	565 tons	780 tons

*Weight for ordnance and machinery *only, not* including armor and supporting structure.

The design schemes with the 16-inch/50 caliber gun all slightly exceeded the standard displacement limitation. It was concluded that further refinements of Scheme I might reduce the displacement, but at the price of altering some of the desired characteristics. Schemes III and IV demonstrated the effects of accepting somewhat reduced speeds, while Scheme IV also benefitted from slight reductions in armor protection.

As the design continued, several basic decisions were made that fundamentally influenced the ultimate form taken by the *Iowa:*

- The permissible draft was increased to a maximum of 36 feet.
- The main battery would probably be 16-inch/50 caliber guns.
- The armor protection was to be to the same scale as that of the *South Dakota*, despite the improved performance of the 16-inch/50 caliber guns.

In June of 1938, the General Board selected the "fast battleship" design of May 1938 (Table 4-6) for further development leading to the construction of the *Iowa*. The decision to adopt the improved 16-inch/50 caliber gun was eased by the success of the Bureau of Ordnance in redesigning the triple turret so that a weight savings of some 275 tons per turret was

TABLE 4-5

The First 45,000-ton "Fast Battleships"

Scheme	I	II	III	IV
Date	April 1938	April 1938	April 1938	April 1938
Displacement				
standard	46,585 (47,333)	44,540 (45,255)	45,495 (46,225)	45,375 (46,103)
full load	55,685 (56,579)	53,440 (54,298)	54,495 (55,370)	54,375 (55,248)
Dimensions				
waterline length	860' (262.128)	832' (253.594)	840' (256.032)	840' (256.032)
beam	108.25' (32.995)	108.25' (32.995)	108.25' (32.995)	108.25' (32.995)
maximum draft	34.6' (10.546)	34.6' (10.546)	34.6' (10.546)	34.6' (10.546)
Armament				
16"/50 (406mm)	9 — triple	None	9 — triple	9 — triple
16"/45 (406mm)	None	9 — triple	None	None
5"/38 (127mm)	20 — twin	20 — twin	20 — twin	20 — twin
1.1"/75 (28mm)	12 — quad	12 — quad	12 — quad	12 — quad
0.50 cal (12.7mm)	12 — single	12 — single	12 — single	12 — single
Propulsion				
shaft horsepower	230,000 (233,190)	230,000 (233,190)	210,000 (212,913)	218,000 (221,024)
maximum speed	33.0	33.0	32.25	32.5
endurance @ 15 knots	15,000	15,000	15,000	15,000
Armor				
Immunity zones (all ships)				
16"/50 2240 lb. AP shell	21,800-32,100 yards (19,934-29,352 m.)			
16"/45 2240 lb. AP shell	18,000-30,000 yards (16,459-27,432 m.)			
Thicknesses				
belt (@ 19°)	12.2" (310)	12.2" (310)	12.2" (310)	12.2" (310)
turrets — face	18" (457)	18" (457)	18" (457)	17.5" (445)
— roof	7.25" (184)	7.25" (184)	7.25" (184)	7.0" (178)
barbettes	17.3" (439)	17.3" (439)	17.3" (439)	17.3" (439)
splinter protection	2.5" (63)	2.5" (63)	2.5" (63)	2.5" (63)
armor deck	5.1" + 1.75" (130 + 44)	5.1" + 1.75" (130 + 44)	5.1" + 1.75" (130 + 44)	5.1" + 1.75" (130 + 44)

TABLE 4-6

Fast Battleship Design Study, May 1938

Displacement	44,560 tons (45,275) standard
	53,460 (54,317) optimum battle*
	55,710 (56,604) full load
Waterline length	860″ (262.128 m)
Maximum beam	108′3″ (32.994 m)
Maximum draft	35′11.5″ (10.960 m)
Armament	9-16″/50 cal (406mm) tripled
	20-5″/38 cal (127mm) paired
	12-1.1″/75 cal (28mm) quadrupled
	12-0.5 cal (12.7mm) single
Protection	To resist 16″ projectiles
Shaft horsepower	200,000+ (202,774+)
Maximum speed	33 knots
Endurance	15,000 nautical miles at 15 knots.

*The best loading condition to sustain battle damage.

realized. Furthermore, guns of this type had already been completed and were on hand, thereby avoiding a potential source of delay in the construction of the ships.

As might be expected in the design of an American battleship, high speed was considered of secondary importance to adequate offensive and protective capabilities. The improved 16-inch/50 caliber gun appeared to at least equal main battery weapons in foreign capital ships. The armor system was designed to resist the 16-inch/45 caliber guns carried by BB-55 — BB-60, and the side protective system was to be the most effective possible, incorporating the latest technical research and experience. Tests on one-third scale models of sections of the *South Dakota*-class ships provided valuable information for the design of the side protective system.

The structural design was basically that of the earlier *South Dakota*-class ships, with allowances for the modified protective system and hull length. The detailed scantlings were adjusted as necessary to handle larger loads resulting from the increased displacement and greater length.

The *Iowa* and *New Jersey*, lead ships of the class, were formally authorized on 17 May 1938, shortly before the final characteristics were officially confirmed. The *Missouri* and *Wisconsin* were authorized for construction on 6 July 1939. Finally, in the summer of 1940, the last two ships of the class were authorized. The ships were assigned to building yards as follows: *Iowa* (BB-61) and *Missouri* (BB-63) to the New York Navy Yard; *New Jersey* (BB-62), *Wisconsin* (BB-64), and *Illinois* (BB-65) to the Philadelphia Navy Yard; and the *Kentucky* (BB-66) to the Norfolk Navy Yard.

In December of 1941, in response to queries from the Chief of Naval Operations regarding the protection of the *Iowa*-class, two basic points were made:

- "... what improvements would be necessary to BB-61 class to give them as good protection as that possessed by the BB-57 class?"

Reply—Basic protection of the BB-61 is directly patterned after that of BB-57. The only area where the ship suffers by comparison is the greater unprotected length (56 feet) forward. This is offset by the greater subdivision of the larger ship.

- "BB-61 class (45,000 tons)—is there a possibility of increasing protection to equal BB-67 class (60,000 tons)?"

Reply—To increase the armor and underwater protection of BB-61 to the equivalent of that on BB-67 would require the alteration of an immense number of plans and the re-ordering of all side armor to new dimensions. The increase in protective weight would, moreover, be so great that some large compensating weights (such as large units of main machinery) would have to be omitted. In other words, the design of the entire ship would be upset and a makeshift would only result at the expense of as much more time as though a completely new design were laid down.

Iowa—Operational History.

The keel of the *Iowa*, name ship of the class, was laid on 27 June 1940. The ship was launched on 27 August 1942, and was commissioned on 22 February 1943. The first year of service was not auspicious, as the ship gashed her bottom and later narrowly escaped being hit by a friendly torpedo.

Grounding damage. The grounding occurred during the afternoon of 16 July 1943, as the ship was completing passage from New York to Casco Bay, Maine. According to the official "Damage Report—U.S.S. *Iowa*," dated 31 July 1943, the ship cut a long gash in her bottom while entering Casco Bay shortly after low water. The narrow, winding channel required radical maneuvering, including a tight S turn that covered a distance of only seven ship lengths, and all this was complicated by strong currents. In the previous seven months, the ship had entered the bay five times.

Marks on the hull showed that the first contact with the bottom was made at frame 75 on the port side. The damaged area consisted of shell plating from frame 82½ to 139¾ (232 feet) on the *F* strake, and from frame 76¾ to 137¾ (244 feet) on the *G* strake. A total of eighteen plates required replacement, and sixteen fuel tanks were opened to the sea.

As the commanding officer of the *Iowa* had been his naval aide, President Roosevelt personally reviewed reports of the accident, and ordered that no blame was to be placed on him. The damage was repaired at the Boston Navy Yard.

Atlantic operations. On 27 August 1943, the *Iowa* sailed for Argentia, Newfoundland, where she spent several weeks on the chance that the *Tirpitz* might try to enter the Atlantic.

The *Iowa* left Hampton Roads, Virginia, on 13 November 1943, with President Roosevelt on board, en route to Africa for the Cairo and Teheran conferences. The following day the destroyer *William D. Porter* was making practice torpedo runs on the *Iowa*, and the President and his party were topside witnessing antiaircraft fire, when the destroyer accidentally fired a torpedo. She immediately signalled "Torpedo is coming your way," followed by "Torpedo is

It's all in the point of view. The slim prow of the Iowa, and her squat, round stern, appear to belong to two different ships. The overall view, made off Pearl Harbor in 1952, puts the whole ship in proper perspective.

Framed between the barrels of a quad 40mm mount, the national flag of the Republic of Korea marks the visit of President Syngman Rhee aboard the Iowa in Pusan Harbor, 12 May 1952 (top, left.)

A close-up look at the Iowa's superstructure shows an intricate composition of armament, armor, fire control, communications and ship control elements, including the ship's bell.

Floats on the port side indicate she is guarded by a submarine net (top, right).

The Navy's advance base concept enabled ships to remain in forward areas instead of returning to the continental United States for interim repairs. Here the Iowa is in a floating drydock, whose sections were towed individually to an island base, then assembled to handle the largest ships afloat (bottom).

The mothball fleet at the Philadelphia Naval Shipyard in April 1967 contained the Wisconsin, New Jersey, and Iowa as units of the Atlantic Reserve Fleet. (Top)

On her decommissioning after World War II, in 1949, the Iowa went into the reserve fleet at San Francisco, California. On 14 July 1951, she was hauled out for reactivation and service in the Korean conflict. (Bottom, left)

By the time of the Korean action, helicopters had replaced fixed wing aircraft aboard all battleships and cruisers. Removal of catapults opened up the fantail for parking visiting whirleybirds. Off Inchon, Korea, in 1952, the Iowa landed one Marine and two Air Force craft for a high-level conference. (Bottom, right)

118

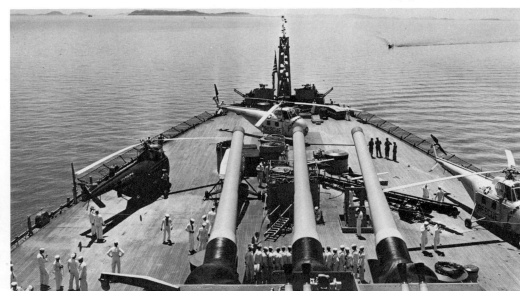

The tapering hull of the Iowa-class ships forward of the citadel is plainly shown in this bow view of the Iowa from the bridge, made in October 1944. The array of 20mm and 40mm mounts, and directors, forward of No. 1 turret, were all added after the ship was first designed. Note Marine detachment on starboard side of forward turret, ready for inspection.

A full broadside by the Iowa's nine 16" guns weighed about twelve tons. Its arrival on target was even more impressive than the departure pictured here at top, right.

A unique photograph, made in 1954, shows all the Iowa-class ships (from the foreground, Iowa, Wisconsin, Missouri, and New Jersey) steaming in formation. This was the only time they all operated together.

mine. I am investigating." The *Iowa* went to full speed—29 knots—and turned toward the *Porter*. The torpedo wake could be seen about 1,000 yards on the starboard quarter; the torpedo destroyed itself with an explosion which felt, aboard the *Iowa*, like a depth charge detonation.

Investigation showed no negligence. Salt spray had apparently bridged an open switch on the torpedo tube and activated the firing mechanism. The President ordered that no one be disciplined for the affair. Full details of the incident are contained in the classified report *"Special Employment of Task Group 27.5 . . . October 24, 1943 to December 16, 1943."*

When the *Iowa* returned on 16 December 1943, she had steamed 16,161 miles at an average of 22.5 knots—a speed so great that relays of destroyers had been required to screen her.

Pacific operations. The ship left the United States on 2 January 1944 for the Pacific, and joined the Fifth Fleet on 22 January. On 18 March, in company with the *New Jersey*, a carrier and several destroyers, she bombarded Mili Atoll in the Marshalls and was hit by two Japanese 152mm shells. One detonated on the port side at frame 134, and tore a jagged hole some 30 x 50 inches in size, with the top of the hole about 12 inches below deck level. The second projectile detonated on impact on the left side of turret 2 about 18 inches above the barbette. Fragments caused minor damage to the turret range finder. Overall, the *Iowa* received negligible material damage, and there were only two minor injuries.

Following support of air strikes in the Carolines and New Guinea area, the ship participated in the invasion of Saipan and Tinian. Early in August she went to Eniwetok for replenishment and rest. In September she resumed carrier support operations in the Central Philippines and the Palau Islands. In the Battle for Leyte Gulf, the *Iowa* was part of the fast-battleship—carrier force decoyed to the north by a Japanese force, thereby opening the San Bernardino Strait to a more powerful Japanese force and the Battle of Samar.

The *Iowa* operated with carriers in Philippine waters until December 1944, then departed for an overhaul at Hunter's Point Navy Yard in San Francisco from 15 January to 19 March 1945. She returned to the war zone in April and for the remainder of the war supported carrier operations off Okinawa and Kyushu, bombarded Hokkaido and Honshu in mid-July, and entered Tokyo Bay on 29 August.

Final Disposition.
After the war ended, the ship performed routine training exercises until she was inactivated at San Francisco in September of 1948. She was placed out of commission in reserve on 24 March 1949. Recommissioned on 25 August 1951, she conducted gunnery and training exercises off the West Coast for several months. On 1 April 1952 she became the Seventh Fleet flagship, based in Japan, for operations in the Korean War. She made periodic strikes on targets in the Wonsan area until October 1952, then returned to the United States for overhaul at Norfolk. The *Iowa* was placed out of commission in reserve at the Philadelphia Navy Yard on 24 February 1953.

Conversion proposals. The excellent speed and endurance of the *Iowa*-class ships, coupled with their great gunpower and heavy protection, were such that the ships were desirable candidates for conversions designed to take advantage of these attributes by upgrading the capabilities of the battleships for modern combat missions.

In June 1958, the Bureau of Ships completed a study on the feasibility of converting the *Iowa*-class ships to guided missile ships by removing all of the main battery and replacing it with two Talos twin missile systems, two Tartar twin missile systems, an ASROC antisubmarine missile launcher, and a Regulus II installation with four missiles.

The conversion would have included adding a bow-mounted SQS-26 sonar, facilities for two ASW helicopters, Talos and Tartar fire control systems, and flagship facilities. Stability requirements called for added low weights to replace the main battery installation; this would have been met by adding approximately 8,600 tons of fuel oil capacity. The resulting net capacity of 16,500 tons would have compared favorably with smaller fleet-type oilers.

The proposed conversion would have produced a powerful guided missile ship with excellent flag communication facilities and the capability of refueling destroyers and cruisers. The cost was estimated at $178 million per ship, plus another $15 million for four Tartar launchers.

This was considered to be prohibitively expensive, so a partial conversion was then evaluated: forward turrets were to be retained, only one Talos, one Tartar and one ASROC were to be added, but two Regulus systems with six missiles were included. One 600-kw, 400-cycle generator was to be installed and 300-kw emergency diesel generators were to be replaced by two 1,000-kw units. Fuel capacity was to total 11,600 tons.

Substantial superstructure changes would have added macks to allow better arrangement of the missile armament and electronics systems, and the conning tower would have been replaced. This conversion was estimated at $84 million, or slightly less if the ASROC and sonar systems were not added.

During 1962, the Navy and Marine Corps seriously investigated the possibility of reactivating the mothballed *Iowa*-class ships as force bombardment and assault ships. Projected alterations would have eliminated the after 16-inch turret and some 5-inch gun mounts to make room for a helicopter platform extending from the after superstructure to the stern. The landing craft would have been carried by Welin-type davits. Plans envisioned berthing for an embarked Marine battalion, with a capacity for 20 helicopters and 16 landing craft. The two forward 16-inch turrets were to be retained for landing force gunnery support. The conversion, estimated to cost between $15 and $20 million per ship, was never authorized.

New Jersey — Operational History.

The keel of the *New Jersey*, second ship of the class, was laid on 16 September 1940. The ship was launched on 7 December 1942 and was commissioned on 23 May 1943.

Pacific operations. The *New Jersey* sortied from Funafuti, in the Ellice Islands, on 23 January 1944 on her first combat operation, primarily antiaircraft defense of a carrier task force. On 17 February, during a sweep around Truk, the *New Jersey* fired on a fleeing Japanese destroyer at ranges of from 34,000 to 39,000 yards. The gunnery was excellent; the ship obtained several

The New Jersey *(BB62), second of the* Iowa *class, as she appeared in October 1943, top, and August 1944. She served in World War II, Korea, and Vietnam, and was the last battleship on active duty in the U. S. Navy.*

This striking overhead view of the New Jersey made in August 1944 clearly shows the arrangement of the secondary and antiaircraft batteries in the superstructure and at the extremities of the ship.

Battleship guns were especially effective in long-range shore bombardment because of their pin-point accuracy. Here the New Jersey, *lying to off Chong Jin, Korea, fires a salvo from No. 3 turret. The circle marks the projectiles en route to the target.*

The New Jersey *and* Wisconsin, *temporarily relieved from the firing line in Korea, at anchor in Yokosuka, Japan, in 1951. (Bottom)*

124

Deck-loaded with launches and barges, left, the New Jersey makes a 32-knot speed run en route to Norfolk, Virginia, from Guantanamo Bay, Cuba, in 1951.

With scaffolding masking her superstructure, the New Jersey was moved into drydock at the Philadelphia Naval Shipyard on 20 September 1967, to reactivate for service with the Seventh Fleet off Vietnam. She remained in Drydock No. 3 until 13 January 1968. (Bottom)

125

The unusual camera angle gives the New Jersey *a fishlike appearance. The view is from the drydock floor, directly under the forefoot of the ship, with her starboard anchor in the foreground and the hawseholes overhead.*

With her World War II clutter of light antiaircraft weapons and aircraft catapults removed, the New Jersey *has a spacious helicopter landing deck on her fantail.* (Top, right)

Docked for reactivation, 1967. Note the four-bladed screws outboard, five-bladed screws inboard, and twin rudders. (Bottom)

126

In order to permit them to clear the locks of the Panama Canal, ships had to be less than 110 feet in beam, for that was the width of the locks. The little room for maneuvering available to the 108-foot-wide New Jersey is evident in this photo made during her transit in 1968. (Left)

Loading ammunition from barges alongside, the New Jersey uses crawler cranes on deck to handle the man-sized powder cans. (Center)

Off Vietnam in September 1968, the New Jersey fires her main battery at a target 12 miles away. Note that the center gun of No. 1 turret is not firing. (Right)

Trim and clean-cut in bright sunlight, the New Jersey here closely resembles the waterline design development model of the class pictured earlier. (Bottom)

straddles (but no hits) at those extreme ranges. She was Third Fleet flagship during the Battle for Leyte Gulf. On 23 December the *New Jersey* received minor damage when a 5-inch shell fired by a destroyer escort during target practice hit her main deck. One man was injured. She took part in all subsequent naval actions against Japan, except for the brief period between April and July 1945, when she was overhauled at Bremerton, Washington. During her wartime service she steamed more than 220,000 miles and shot down 20 enemy aircraft—five in one day. She was placed out of commission in reserve at Bayonne, New Jersey, on 30 June 1948.

Korean operations. Recommissioned on 21 November 1950, the *New Jersey* served in the Korean theater during April-November 1951 and March-November 1953. On 21 May 1951, while anchored in Wonsan Harbor for fire support, she was fired on and straddled by a shore battery. One small shell, about 4-inch caliber, exploded on the roof of number 1 turret, causing negligible damage. There were no casualties. Then an air burst off the port quarter killed one and wounded three members of a machine-gun crew. They were the only combat losses on the *New Jersey* throughout her career.

The ship returned to Norfolk in November 1953 for overhaul and, after the end of the Korean hostilities, carried out routine training exercises. She was again decommissioned and placed in reserve at Bayonne, New Jersey, on 21 August 1957. Later the ship was moved to Philadelphia.

Vietnam operations. As a result of the urgent need for heavy gunfire support of land operations in Vietnam, the *New Jersey* was selected for recommissioning in 1967. The other *Iowa*-class ships were considered less suitable for reactivation for the following reasons:

- *Iowa*—electronics installation was out of date.
- *Missouri*—a speed limitation had been imposed on the ship after her grounding in 1950.
- *Wisconsin*—needed repairs to circuitry in the area of the forward 16-inch turrets, damaged by an electrical fire during the last inactivation overhaul.

The *Iowa* and the *Wisconsin* were cannibalized to expedite the recommissioning of the *New Jersey,* whose forward bridge tower was remodeled to accommodate sophisticated electronics countermeasures and counter-countermeasures equipment. The ship was given improved gunfire-control computers, and other weapons systems were updated. The obsolete 40mm machine gun batteries were removed, and a helicopter landing area was installed on the fantail. Medical facilities were improved, and other improvements in habitability were also made.

The *New Jersey* was recommissioned at the Philadelphia Naval Shipyard on 6 April 1968. She began gunfire support missions off Vietnam on 30 September 1968, and served with notable effectiveness until the end of March 1969.

The Missouri *(BB63) off New York in July 1944, shortly after being commissioned. After shakedown in the Atlantic, most of her career was spent in the Pacific.*

Final Disposition.
The *New Jersey* returned to Long Beach on 5 May 1969. In September she sailed to Bremerton, Washington, where she was decommissioned on 17 December 1969. With the retirement of the last battleship in the U.S. Navy, a long and colorful era of naval history came to a close.

Missouri — Operational History.
The last of the *Iowa*-class ships to be completed, the *Missouri* was laid down on 6 January 1941, launched on 29 January 1944, and commissioned at the New York Navy Yard on 11 June 1944. She was destined to become one of the most famous warships of the U.S. Navy, although not because of any noteworthy combat exploits.

Pacific operations. The *Missouri* reached Ulithi on 6 January 1945 in time for the final assaults against Japan. She shot down her first Japanese plane while operating off Iwo Jima in February of 1945.

On 11 April, off southern Kyushu, a Zeke fighter plane crashed into the starboard side just below the main deck level, about twenty feet aft of number 3 turret. Wreckage littered the starboard side, and a small gasoline fire was quickly extinguished. Damage was superficial.

Five days later, two aircraft attempted to crash the ship. One was destroyed by antiaircraft fire; the second was severely damaged but hit the aircraft crane on the fantail, spun in, and exploded, spraying the ship with debris. Again, damage was superficial.

The *Missouri* spent the rest of the war in operations off Okinawa and Japan proper. The Japanese signed formal surrender documents aboard the ship on 2 September 1945, while she was anchored in Tokyo Bay.

Grounding damage. The *Missouri* remained in commission after World War II. On 17 January 1950, while on a routine training operation, she ran hard aground at the entrance to Chesapeake Bay. At the time she was making only 12 knots and was at deep draft, which advantages were offset by the fact that she grounded at high tide.

A full report of the grounding and salvage was issued on 1 June 1950 as "*NavShips 250-694-3.*" This report has since been declassified, and is the source for the following details. Careful calculations showed that the ship had a ground loading of about 11,700 tons. Her draft before grounding was 35.75 feet forward and 36.75 feet aft; after grounding it was 27.7 feet forward and 31.3 feet aft. Her displacement on getting under way was 57,666 tons. In two weeks of intensive work, 11,758 tons of fuel, ammunition, and supplies were removed to reduce the ground loading to less than 1,000 tons.

The salvage effort involved heavy beaching gear, pontoons, 13 tugs and salvage vessels, and the dredging of a deep channel to simplify moving the ship to the main channel. The first attempt to refloat the ship, on 31 January 1950, failed, largely because a previously undetected

Starboard side view of the Missouri, July 1944. The camouflage scheme was not permanent, but could be changed according to operational requirements. Wartime censorship deleted all evidence of electronics in this photo.

Construction scene while the Missouri was on the ways at the New York Navy Yard, 3 July 1942. Foreground objects are boilers.

A remarkable fast-action camera shot shows the six projectiles fired by the Missouri's two forward turrets. Note the blast effect of the guns reaching out several hundred feet across the sea.

130

On 11 April 1945, a kamikaze plane struck the starboard side of the *Missouri* despite intense gunfire. One wing of the plane and the pilot's body hit gun mounts forward, but caused only superficial damage.

The Japanese surrender was signed aboard the Missouri in Tokyo Bay on 2 September 1945. Immediately afterward, a victory parade of hundreds of aircraft filled the sky over Tokyo. (Top, left)

The Japanese surrender delegation boarding the Missouri, just before the ceremony. The table in the foreground is now at the U. S. Naval Academy Museum. (Top, right)

Some five years after she ceased firing on Japanese targets, the Missouri was back in action, firing on Korean targets. She is shown off-shore from Chong Jin on 21 October 1950, about 40 miles from the Soviet border. (Bottom)

132

The Missouri *aground on Thimble Shoals in Hampton Roads, Virginia. After five days spent offloading fuel and ammunition, the ship pulled clear on 1 February 1950, with aid of a fleet of tugs and a high tide. (Left)*

On keel blocks in dry dock, the Missouri *shows fuel oil tanks ripped open when she ran aground at Thimble Shoals. (Below)*

The Iowa *and* Missouri *at anchor in the Korean theatre, October 1952. Note hull number painted on No. 1 turret, 5" ammunition cases on fantail of* Iowa. *(Bottom)*

wreck impaled her bottom in way of three fuel tanks. On the morning of 1 February, the ship was finally broken free from the shoals where she had sat for two weeks. The salvage effort cost $225,000. The Norfolk Naval Shipyard repaired the bottom damage in five days.

As the only battleship operational when South Korea was invaded, the *Missouri* was the first to join operations there. She served in Korean waters for approximately one year, at three times between mid-September 1950 and 7 April 1953, and was awarded the Korean Presidential Unit Citation for that service.

Final Disposition. Eleven years of active duty ended for the *Missouri* on 26 February 1955, when she was placed out of commission in reserve at the Puget Sound Naval Shipyard, Bremerton, Washington.

Wisconsin — Operational History.
The keel of the *Wisconsin*, the fourth ship of the *Iowa* class, was laid on 25 January 1941. The ship was launched on 7 December 1943 and was the second ship of the class to be launched on an anniversary of the Japanese attack on Pearl Harbor. The *Wisconsin* was commissioned on 16 April 1944, sailed for the western Pacific on 24 September, and joined the Third Fleet on 9 December. She participated in all major Pacific naval operations during the remainder of the war.

Korean operations. The *Wisconsin* was inactivated on 1 July 1948 at the Norfolk Naval Shipyard. She was recommissioned on 3 March 1951 and served in the Korean War from November 1951 through March 1953. On the afternoon of 15 March 1952, she received the only combat damage of her entire career when a coastal battery near Songjin scored one hit with a 152mm shell. The projectile ripped a 24 x 30-inch hole on the 02 level deck between frames 144-145 on the starboard side. Three men were wounded by fragments. The *Wisconsin* immediately engaged the enemy shore battery and scored two hits with 16-inch shells.

On 19 March 1952 the ship left the Korean area to carry out routine duties, including a tour as flagship of the Seventh Fleet, that lasted from September 1953 through June 1954. On 6 May 1956, off Norfolk, she collided with and sank the escort destroyer *Eaton*. The *Wisconsin* was repaired at the Norfolk Naval Shipyard, where an accelerated work schedule made her ready for duty in 16 days. The damaged bow was replaced by a 120-ton, 68-foot bow section from the incomplete *Kentucky*.

Final Disposition. The *Wisconsin* was placed out of commission in reserve at Bayonne, New Jersey, on 8 March 1958. Her retirement was inevitable, convincing evidence

The Wisconsin (BB64) slides down the launching ways at the Philadelphia Navy Yard on 7 December 1943. Note the rails lined with workmen riding her down. (Left)

The Navy's "official photograph" of the Wisconsin. The large hull numbers indicate a peacetime pose—they were much smaller during World War II. (Right)

After a short 9-month wartime career, the Wisconsin was a part of the peacetime Navy from 1945 to 1948, and from 1951 to 1958. Here she is pictured firing main battery guns during a midshipman training cruise in 1947. Note distance of recoil (exaggerated by the perspective) of the firing gun in the forward turret. (Bottom)

The keel of the Illinois *(BB65) was laid at Philadelphia on 25 January 1945. By 7 July work had progressed to this point. Construction was halted a month later, when the ship was cancelled.*

136

The Kentucky (BB66) was laid down on 6 December 1944. Work was suspended in 1947 when she was about seventy-five percent complete. Bow of the Kentucky was removed to replace damaged bow on the Wisconsin, after her collision with the Eaton (DDE-510). Bow sections on deck are undamaged portions of the Wisconsin's bow structure. Gun mounts and other equipment stored on deck, awaiting final disposition.

at the end of the battleship era. These expensive warships had become obsolete for the mission for which they had been designed and built. For the first time since 1895, the United States Navy had no battleship in service.

Illinois — Partial Construction.

The keel of the fifth ship of the class, the *Illinois*, was laid on 6 December 1942. The *Illinois* and *Kentucky* differed from the earlier ships in being designed for all-welded construction. Work went very slowly and the ship was formally cancelled on 11 August 1945, when about 22 per cent complete. The hulk was eventually scrapped; demolition commenced in September 1958.

Kentucky — Partial Construction.

The last ship of this class, the *Kentucky*, was laid down on 6 December 1942. Work continued intermittently, was suspended and resumed again in 1944, halted in August 1946, and resumed on 17 August 1948. The *Kentucky* was floated out of the building dock on 20 January 1950. She was then 73 per cent complete, with propelling machinery already installed.

No further work was done, and the hulk was stricken from the Navy List on 9 June 1958. It was sold in September 1958 and towed away for scrapping in February 1959. The propulsion machinery was saved and eventually installed in the fast replenishment ships *Sacramento* and *Camden*, which were completed in 1964 and 1966, respectively.

Armament.

Gun characteristics for these ships are shown in Table 4-7. Nine 16-inch/50 caliber guns, Mark 7, the most powerful ever mounted on a U. S. warship, were mounted in well-protected triple turrets. These were considerably more powerful versions of the Mark 6 guns installed on earlier battleships. The combination of a longer barrel and a heavier propelling charge increased the muzzle velocity, thus improving maximum range and armor penetration. Captain Edward Snyder of the *New Jersey* was quoted in 1969 as stating that the armor-piercing shell was capable of penetrating 32 feet of reinforced concrete.

Although there has been no release of official data on the actual performance of the Mark 7 gun, an approximate calculation of armor penetration can be derived from the known ballistic properties. A comparison of armor penetration capabilities (Table 4-8) indicates the improved performance, although the increased angle of fall with the shorter 45 caliber gun gave it superior deck penetration at any given range. This gun was also provided with a 1,900-pound, high-capacity projectile carrying a high-explosive charge of 154 pounds. Maximum range was 41,622 yards when fired with the normal propelling charge of 660 pounds, with a muzzle velocity of 2,690 feet per second.

TABLE 4-7

Gun Characteristics

Gun	16"/50	(406mm)	5"/38	(127mm)
Shell weight (lb.)	2,700	(1,225 kg.)	53.85	(24.43 kg.)
Muzzle velocity (FPS)	2,500	(762 m/s)	2,600	(792 m/s)
Maximum range (yd.)	42,345	(38,720 m)	17,575	(16,070 m)
Maximum elevation	45°		85°	

Gun	1.57"/60	(40mm)	0.79"/70	(20mm)
Shell weight (lb.)	1.98	(0.898 kg.)	0.27	(0.122 kg.)
Muzzle velocity (FPS)	2,890	(881 m/s)	2,770	(844 m/s)
Maximum range (yd.)	*11,000	(10,058 m)	4,800	(4,389 m)
Maximum elevation	90°		90°	

*Fuze self-destructive at 5,000 yards (4,572 m).

TABLE 4-8

Armor Penetration Comparison

16"/45 Gun (Mark 6) 2,700 lb. (1,225 kg.) AP shell
2,300 FPS (701 m/s) muzzle velocity

	Belt penetration	Deck penetration
@ Muzzle	29.74" (775mm)	. . .
@ 10,000 yd. (9,144 m)	23.51" (597mm)	1.87" (47mm)
@ 20,000 yd. (18,288 m)	17.62" (447mm)	4.29" (109mm)
@ 30,000 yd. (27,432 m)	12.77" (324mm)	7.62" (194mm)

16"/50 Gun (Mark 7) 2,700 lb. (1,225 kg.) AP shell
2,500 FPS (762 m/s) muzzle velocity

	Belt penetration	Deck penetration
@ Muzzle	32.62" (829mm)	. . .
@ 10,000 yd. (9,144 m)	26.16" (664mm)	1.71" (43mm)
@ 20,000 yd. (18,288 m)	20.04" (509mm)	3.90" (99mm)
@ 30,000 yd. (27,432 m)	14.97" (380mm)	6.65" (169mm)

TABLE 4-9

Ballistics, 16" Reduced Charge

Shell weight (lb.)	2,700 (1,225 kg.)	1,900 (862 kg.)
Muzzle velocity (FPS)	1,800 (549 m/s)	2,075 (632 m/s)
Maximum range (yd.)	24,181 (22,112 m)	27,350 (25,009 m)

For shore bombardment support, a 315-pound reduced charge decreased bore wear and resulted in the performance shown in Table 4-9.

When the *New Jersey* was reactivated in 1968, a new, cooler-burning powder was adopted in order to prolong bore life. With the new powder, the armor-piercing shell was fired at a muzzle velocity of 2,425 feet per second to a maximum range of 40,185 yards.

The rotating weight of the turrets, less projectiles, varied from 1,701 to 1,708 tons. The maximum training rate was 4 degrees per second; the elevating rate was 12 degrees per second. The outside diameter of the roller path was 34 feet 5 inches. The maximum length of recoil was 4 feet. All turrets had training arcs of 300 degrees. A minimum crew of 77 men was required for each turret. The rate of fire was 2 rounds per minute per gun.

Secondary battery. The secondary armament was typical of the U. S. Navy design practice, with twenty 5-inch/38 caliber dual-purpose guns, Mark 12, in ten twin mounts. Design development work on a twin dual-purpose turret for the much more powerful 6-inch/47 caliber gun had been initiated in September of 1937. Design calculations indicated that six twin dual-purpose turrets for 6-inch guns would weigh 1,667 tons, while ten twin 5-inch dual-purpose mounts would weigh only some 1,267 tons. As a result of the weight penalties associated with the adoption of the heavier gun for dual-purpose armament, coupled with the developmental status of the 6-inch turret, the concept of a 6-inch dual-purpose armament was abandoned. For various reasons, the 6-inch turrets were not introduced into service until 1948.

Antiaircraft battery. The *Iowa*-class ships benefitted by early combat lessons of World War II, especially in the antiaircraft machine-gun batteries. As initially designed, each ship was to have carried twelve 1.1-inch and twelve .50-caliber machine guns. As built, a maximum of eighty 40mm Bofors and fifty 20mm Oerlikons were mounted. The increased hull length of the ships permitted much improved arcs of fire which, with excellent fire-control systems, gave them the greatest antiaircraft capability of any ships in World War II. Although the *Yamato* had more guns, they were less effective, owing to inferior fire control.

Japanese use of suicide planes proved the 40mm and 20mm machine guns to be too light and too short-ranged to disable such planes before they crashed into ships, and many U. S. ships were so damaged. Postwar firing tests against Nakajima-type planes showed that one 3-inch/50 caliber gun was as effective as two 40mm quadruple mounts. The advantage was even more pronounced against the Baka bomb; one 3-inch gun was worth five quadruple 40mm mounts. These improved results were accomplished beyond the effective range of the 40mm guns, a convincing argument in favor of the larger gun. Accordingly, 3-inch guns in single or twin mounts were to be substituted for the 40mm guns. The larger gun fired a 13-pound shell to a maximum range of 14,600 yards and had a ceiling of about 29,800 feet. Plans to rearm the *Iowa*-class ships with some fifteen twin 3-inch mounts in place of 20mm and 40mm batteries were never carried out.

Despite repeated proposals to modify the antiaircraft batteries, only the machine guns were changed; the 20mm guns were removed after World War II. When the *New Jersey* was reactivated in 1968, her 40mm guns were removed, but the gun tubs were retained.

Aircraft. Each ship originally had two fantail catapults and carried four aircraft for spotting long-range fire. There were no hangar facilities below decks. In 1950 planes and catapults were removed and replaced by helicopters for operations off Korea.

Protection.
The protective systems of the *Iowa*-class ships were patterned after those of the successful *South Dakota* designs; the considerable increase in displacement was largely attributable to the weight and volume requirements of the greater length (for high speed) and the more powerful machinery plant.

The armor protection of the *Iowa* provided an immunity zone of from 17,600 to 31,200 yards against the old 16-inch/45 caliber gun firing 2,240-pound AP shells; against the more modern 16-inch/45 caliber gun firing 2,700-pound AP shells, this zone extended only from 20,400 to 26,700 yards.

The 12.1-inch main side belt armor of the *Iowa* was superimposed on 0.875-inch STS backing plates. The armor system was inclined outboard some 19 degrees from the vertical, giving protection equal to that of 17.3-inch vertical plates. The lower side belt plating, with the same inclination as the heavy main belt, tapered from 12.1 inches at the top to 1.625 inches at the bottom.

Deck armor. One of the most noteworthy developments in the evolution of battleship design was the increased importance of adequate horizontal protection. This trend was clearly evident in the design of American capital ships, and the *Iowa*-class ships had particularly heavy deck armor protection, as shown in Table 4-10.

TABLE 4-10
Deck Armor Thickness

	Over machinery		Over magazines	
Main deck	1.50″	(38mm)	1.50″	(38mm)
Second deck	4.75″ + 1.25″	(121mm + 32mm)	4.75″ + 1.25″	(121mm + 32mm)
Splinter deck	0.625″	(16mm)	none	
Third deck	0.5″ or 0.625″	(13mm or 16mm)	1.00″	(25mm)
Total (maximum)	8.75″	(222mm)	8.50″	(216mm)

The most difficult problem in the design of the armor deck system involved its use as a strength member in the hull structure. Class B armor, such as that used on armor decks, could also be used for structural purposes if fixed rigidly to the underlying structure. Deck armor to be used solely for protection could be left relatively free to work independently as the hull structure worked in a seaway. After exhaustive full-scale welding tests at the Philadelphia Navy Yard, the decision was made to have the armor plates butt-welded and held down to an undercourse of heavy STS plates by heavy rivets.

High-level bombing before World War II was not sufficiently accurate to pose a serious threat to ships, but its potential menace caused much concern to naval architects responsible for the horizontal protection of ships. At Pearl Harbor the Japanese dropped what were believed to be 14-inch armor-piercing shells modified for use as bombs. The Germans were reported to have used heavy caliber projectiles in the same manner. The nearly vertical impact of such projectiles gave them much greater penetrative power against deck armor as compared with the more oblique impact of shells fired at long ranges. Design and construction of the *Iowa*-class ships were too far advanced to compensate for this new threat, which soon made it practically impossible to provide horizontal protection against armor-piercing bombs.

Conning tower. The conning tower structure was typically heavily armored, with 17.5-inch side plating, 7.25-inch roof plates, and 4-inch deck armor. The communications tube armor was 16 inches thick.

The forward armored bulkhead tapered in thickness from 11.3 inches at the second deck to 8.5 inches at the inner bottom. Aft, the transverse bulkhead was 11.3 inches thick between the second and third decks. Between the third deck and the second platform, splinter protection only was provided by 0.625-inch plates. Between the second and third platform, 2-inch armor was installed. The unique gradations aft were a function of the shielding effect of heavy deck armor (5.6 inches on 0.75 inches) which protected accesses to the steering gear, coupled with heavy side armor plating 13.5 inches thick. Superstructure control positions were given limited splinter protection by 1.5-inch plating.

Side protection. Details of the side protective system are sparse. Published photographs of the ships under construction confirm the similarity of the structural arrangements to those of the earlier *South Dakota* design, although the designed liquid-loaded arrangement cannot be confirmed. Clearly, the system was a conventional multilayered arrangement. It is known that the *South Dakota* had a four-layer system, with the two outboard layers liquid loaded. The later *Montana* design was given a similar arrangement, with variations in detail.

For the first time in the design of an American battleship, equal importance was given to both the side protective system and the traditionally important armor protection against shells and bombs. This was a noteworthy development; the *Montana* carried the trend even farther.

Radar. The completion of these ships late in World War II permitted them to take full advantage of the advances in radar technology. By the end of the war, the *Iowa*, for example, mounted the following radar systems:

Surface-search radar	SC-2
Air-search radar	SK
Main-battery GFCS (2)	Mark 38
	Mark 27 radar (conning tower)
	Mark 13 radar (directors)

The rapid development of radar and communications equipment soon resulted in battleship superstructures being crowded beyond description. In this view of the New Jersey, *the only visible ties with the early history of battleships are a few signal halliards and radio antennae.*

Secondary battery GFCS	Mark 37
(4)	Mark 12/22/32 radars
MG battery GFCS	Mark 56
(40mm)	Mark 35 radar

Superstructures soon became overcrowded because of the need to locate all electronic equipment as close as possible to the antennas. The eventual result, as the CIC evolved into a primary battle control station, was progressive crowding of living accommodations as parts of the available hull and superstructure volume were taken up by electronic installations. The use of communications equipment also increased rapidly; by the end of the war the *Missouri* carried 21 radio transmitters, with the strongest rated at 5,000 watts, and 65 receivers, thus offering a full range of voice and CW transmission.

Propulsion Plant. Design specifications called for a 33-knot maximum speed (*Jane's* later reported 35 knots in service operation) and a large cruising radius, coupled with a power plant arrangement that permitted flexible operations despite heavy battle damage. Maintenance and repair of machinery and the ship's structure demanded the maximum possible accessibility. The machinery arrangement had to be carefully planned in order to attain the required power in as compact an installation as possible.

Machinery arrangement. The power plant was the most powerful installation in any battleship, with a normal maximum of 212,000 shaft horsepower. The machinery arrangement was superb, featuring outstanding compartmentation and excellent provision for cross-connection of boilers and turbines. The eight boilers were arranged in four fire rooms, with each turbine set located in a separate engine room. From forward aft, the arrangement was fire room, engine room, repeated four times. The eight main machinery spaces, without longitudinal bulkheads, permitted an admirable isolation of all key propulsive components.

Boilers. The boilers were the usual two-drum, double-furnace, single-uptake type. The superheater was installed between the two furnaces, and the hot gas from the superheater furnace passed over the superheater into the saturated furnace and thence through the boiler bank and economizer, exiting through a single uptake connection.

Efforts to develop a compact, light power plant for the *Iowa*-class ships were successful, as comparison with the *South Dakota*-class ships (Table 4-11) shows. Endurance was remarkably good: 5,300 nautical miles at 29.6 knots; 15,900 nautical miles at 17 knots; 18,000 nautical miles at 12 knots.

The electrical installations were extremely complex, including over 900 electric motors on each ship, and demanded considerable generating capacity. Eight ship's service turbo-generators, each rated at 1,250 kw, provided an electrical capacity of 10,000 kw. Two 250-kw diesel generators could provide emergency power within seven seconds after a casualty.

TABLE 4-11

Propulsion Plant, Weight-Horsepower

	Iowa	South Dakota
Normal maximum shp	212,000	130,000
Machinery weight (tons)	4,992	3,580
Pounds per shp	52.7	61.69

The power plants proved reliable in service; the *Missouri* once steamed continuously for 58 days. With a reliable, powerful, and efficient power plant, and an efficient hull form for high-speed operations, the ships satisfied the basic design specifications in every respect.

Hull Characteristics.

Although the *Iowa*-class ships had a relatively fine hull form, as might be expected for a fast ship, they still had ample stability, with a metacentric height of 9.26 feet at the design displacement of 54,889 tons. The block coefficient at the design displacement was 0.593; the prismatic coefficient was 0.596.

High speeds dictated great hull length with a relatively fine underwater hull form. A very thin and fragile-appearing bow form was coupled with a moderate-sized bulb to improve high-speed resistance characteristics. The stern form featured the twin skegs characteristic of earlier ships. Despite the fragile appearance of the fine bow structure, it developed no structural problems. Admittedly, the ships were never damaged in that apparently vulnerable section.

During the design period, studies of the sheer and bending forces that might be encountered in a seaway indicated that the armor should be fitted in sections. Longitudinal bulkheads in the side protective system, one on each side, were extended beyond the forward transverse armor bulkheads to reinforce the bow structure. Aft, they terminated in the twin skegs, which were in effect twin keels, and greatly increased the longitudinal girder strength of the after hull structure.

Summary.

The *Iowa*-class battleships were the best ever built. While not outstanding in every specific characteristic, all of their major attributes were at least very good, and most were outstanding. That they were completed too late to serve the traditional battleship role is irrelevant, as is their undistinguished combat record. They did their assigned jobs—shore bombardment and antiaircraft defense—superlatively well. Their retention for service, many years after the end of World War II, was a tribute to their capabilities, power, high speed, and excellent endurance.

As of 1975, the *Iowa, New Jersey, Missouri* and *Wisconsin* remain in the reserve fleet, but their reactivation is most unlikely, owing to their age, inevitable deterioration, and the obsolescence of all components and systems.

Iowa Class

Name & hull number	*Iowa* (BB-61)	*New Jersey* (BB-62)
Builder	New York Navy	Philadelphia Navy Yard
Laid down	27 June 1940	16 September 1940
Launched	27 August 1942	7 December 1942
Commissioned	22 February 1943	23 May 1943
Operational*	27 August 1943	December 1943
Disposition	Out of commission in reserve, Philadelphia, Pa.	Out of commission in reserve, Bremerton, Wash.

Name & hull number	*Missouri* (BB-63)	*Wisconsin* (BB-64)
Builder	New York Navy Yard	Philadelphia Navy Yard
Laid down	6 January 1941	25 January 1941
Launched	29 January 1944	7 December 1943
Commissioned	11 June 1944	16 April 1944
Operational*	December 1944	24 September 1944
Disposition	Out of commission in reserve, Bremerton, Wash.	Out of commission in reserve, Philadelphia, Pa.

Name & hull number	*Illinois* (BB-65)	*Kentucky* (BB-66)
Builder	Philadelphia Navy Yard	Norfolk Navy Yard, Portsmouth, Va.
Laid down	6 December 1944	6 December 1942
Launched		20 January 1950
Commissioned		
Disposition	Construction cancelled 11 August 1945. Ship scrapped 1958.	Sold on 31 October 1958 to Boston Metals Co. for $1,176,666.16. Scrapped

*Based on first sortie on an operational mission.

Displacement

Iowa
(28 Mar. 1943) 43,875 tons (44,579 m.t.) Light ship
48,425 tons (49,202 m.t.) Standard (calculated)
55,424 tons (56,314 m.t.) Optimum battle
57,540 tons (58,464 m.t.) Full load
59,331 tons (60,283 m.t.) Emergency load

New Jersey
(13 June 1943) 43,944 tons (44,649 m.t.) Light ship
45,649 tons (56,542 m.t.) Optimum battle
57,216 tons (58,134 m.t.) Full load
59,300 tons (60,252 m.t.) Emergency load

Missouri
(1945) 57,540 tons (58,464 m.t.) Full load

Frames

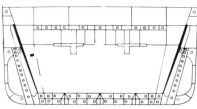

Frame 188

Frame 160½
Turret No. 3

Frame 101 Midships

Frame 74
Turret No. 2

Frame 56
Turret No. 1

Frame 13

Wisconsin
(1945) 57,216 tons (58,134 m.t.) Full load

Illinois and *Kentucky*
(Design) 45,000 tons (45,722 m.t.) Standard
55,250 tons (56,137 m.t.) Full load

Dimensions

Iowa
887' 2.750" (270.427 m) Length overall
859' 5.750" (262.689 m) Design waterline length
108' 2.063" (32.971 m) Maximum beam
28' 8.250" (8.744 m) Mean draft @ 43,875 tons
35' 0.750" (10.687 m) Mean draft @ 55,424 tons
36' 2.250" (11.030 m) Mean draft @ 57,540 tons
37' 2.000" (11.328 m) Mean draft @ 59,331 tons
37' 9.000" (11.506 m) Maximum draft

New Jersey
887' 6.625" (270.526 m) Length overall
859' 10.250" (262.084 m) Design waterline length
108' 1.375" (32.953 m) Maximum beam
28' 8.500" (8.750 m) Mean draft @ 43,944 tons
35' 2.000" (10.719 m) Mean draft @ 55,649 tons
36' 0.250" (10.973 m) Mean draft @ 57,216 tons
37' 1.750" (11.278 m) Mean draft @ 59,300 tons
38' 0.000" (11.582 m) Maximum draft

Missouri
887' 3.000" (270.434 m) Length overall
860' 0.000" (262.128 m) Waterline length
108' 2.000" (32.969 m) Maximum beam
37' 9.000" (11.506 m) Maximum draft

Wisconsin
887' 3.000" (270.434 m) Length overall
860' 0.000" (262.128 m) Waterline length
108' 2.000" (32.969 m) Maximum beam
37' 9.000" (11.506 m) Maximum draft

Illinois and *Kentucky*
(Design) 887' 3.000" (270.434 m) Length overall
860' 0.000" (262.128 m) Waterline length
108' 2.000" (32.969 m) Maximum beam
35' 10.000" (10.922 m) Maximum draft

Hull Characteristics at D.W.L.

Displacement	54,889 tons (55,770 m.t.)
Mean draft	34' 9.250" (10.597 m) *Iowa* and *New Jersey*
Hull depth amidships	52' 11.875" (16.151 m)
Block coefficient	0.593
Prismatic coefficient	0.596

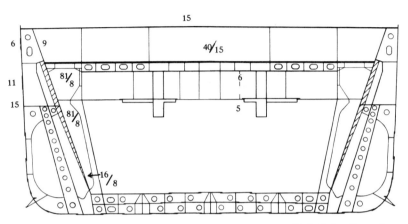

Midship Section

Waterplane coefficient 0.694
Midship section coefficient 0.996
Tons per inch immersion 153.88 (61.552 m.t./cm.)
Moment to trim one inch 6,670 foot-tons (one cm: 817.434 m-m.t.)
(GM) metacentric height 9.26' (2.822 m)
Wetted surface 113,600 sq. ft. (10,553.5 sq. m)

Actual GM *Iowa*—28 March 1943

   4.88' (1.487 m) @ 43,875 tons (44,579 m.t.)
   7.68' (2.341 m) @ 55,424 tons (56,314 m.t.)
   8.40' (2.560 m) @ 57,540 tons (58,464 m.t.)
   8.68' (2.646 m) @ 59,331 tons (60,283 m.t.)

   New Jersey—13 June 1943
   5.15' (1.570 m) @ 43,944 tons (44,649 m.t.)
   7.95' (2.423 m) @ 55,649 tons (56,542 m.t.)
   8.57' (2.612 m) @ 57,216 tons (58,134 m.t.)
   8.80' (2.682 m) @ 59,300 tons (60,252 m.t.)

Armament

Nine 16-inch/50 caliber guns (Mark 7) (406mm)
Twenty 5-inch/38 caliber guns (Mark 12) (127mm)

Antiaircraft machine guns

	40mm/56	20mm/70
Iowa		
(Feb. 1943)	60	60
(Dec. 1944)	76	52
(1957)	80	none
New Jersey		
(May 1943)	80	49
(Dec. 1944)	80	49
(Aug. 1945)	80	57
(1968)	none	none
Missouri		
(June 1944)	80	49
(Dec. 1944)	80	49
(Nov. 1945)	80	43
Wisconsin		
(Apr. 1944)	80	49
(Dec. 1944)	80	51
Illinois and *Kentucky*		
(Design)	80	?

Armor Protection (Refer to plans for arrangement details.)

Immunity zone from 20,400 to 26,700 yards (Citadel) (18,647 to 24,406 meters)
   U. S. 16"/45 (406mm) firing 2,700 lb. (1,225 kg) shell
   from 17,600 to 31,200 yards (Citadel) (16,088 to 28,519 meters)
   U. S. 16"/45 (406mm) firing 2,240 lb. (1,016 kg) shell

Main side belt 12.1″ on 0.875″ (inclined 19°) (307mm on 22mm)
Lower side belt 12.1″ tapered to 1.625″ (inclined 19°) (307mm to 41mm)

Deck armor

main	1.50″	(38mm)
second	4.75″ + 1.25″	(121mm + 32mm)
splinter	0.625″	(16mm)
third	0.5″ or 0.625″	(13mm or 16mm)

Barbette armor
17.3″-11.6″ (439-295 m) to 2nd deck
3″ (76 m) 2nd-3rd deck
1.5″ (38 m) below 3rd deck

Turret armor
face plates 17.0″ + 2.7″ (432mm + 63mm)
sides 9.5″ (241mm)
back plates 12.0″ (305mm)
roof plates 7.25″ (184mm)

Secondary gun armor
mounts 2.5″ (63mm)
handling rooms 2.5″ (63mm)

Conning tower armor
sides 17.5″ (444mm)
roof 7.25″ (184mm)
deck 4.0″ (102mm)
communications tube 16.0″ (406mm)

Underwater Protection

(Refer to the text for discussion of underwater protection based on unofficial sources.)

Tank Capacities
(Note: S.D. Book = Ship's Data Book)

Iowa
Fuel oil 8,624.3 tons (8,765.0 m.t.)—1945
            8,841.0 tons (8,983.0 m.t.)—1949 S.D. Book
Diesel oil 187.2 tons (190.2 m.t.)—1945
Gasoline 22.4 tons (22.8 m.t.)—1945
Reserve feed water 491.2 tons (499.1 m.t.)
Potable water 777.2 tons (789.7 m.t.)

New Jersey
Fuel oil 8,084.1 tons (8,213.5 m.t.)—1943
            8,341.0 tons (8,983.0 m.t.)—1949 S.D. Book
Diesel oil 187.2 tons (190.2 m.t.)—1945
              192.0 tons (195.1 m.t.)—1947
Gasoline 22.4 tons (22.8 m.t.)—1945
              25.2 tons (25.6 m.t.)—1947

Machinery Schematic

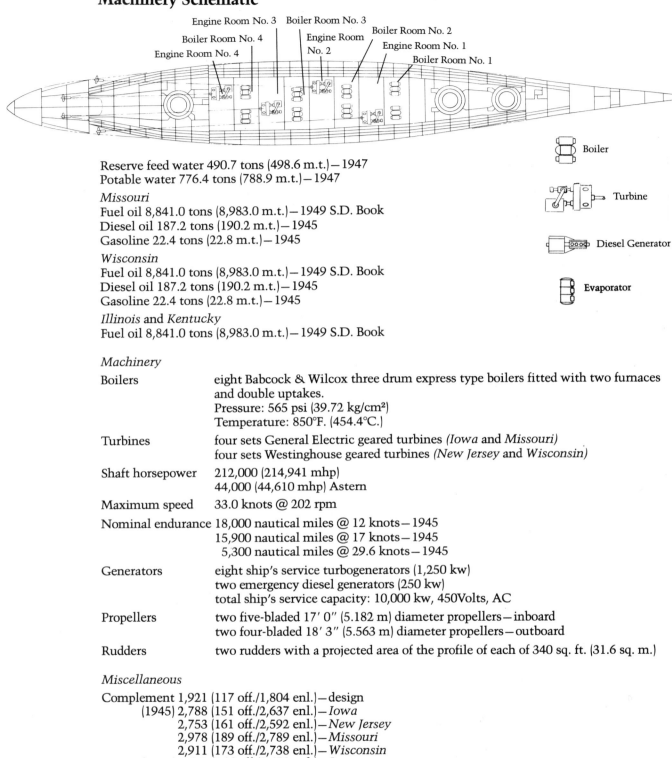

Engine Room No. 4
Boiler Room No. 4
Engine Room No. 3
Boiler Room No. 3
Engine Room No. 2
Boiler Room No. 2
Engine Room No. 1
Boiler Room No. 1

Boiler

Turbine

Diesel Generator

Evaporator

Reserve feed water 490.7 tons (498.6 m.t.) — 1947
Potable water 776.4 tons (788.9 m.t.) — 1947

Missouri
Fuel oil 8,841.0 tons (8,983.0 m.t.) — 1949 S.D. Book
Diesel oil 187.2 tons (190.2 m.t.) — 1945
Gasoline 22.4 tons (22.8 m.t.) — 1945

Wisconsin
Fuel oil 8,841.0 tons (8,983.0 m.t.) — 1949 S.D. Book
Diesel oil 187.2 tons (190.2 m.t.) — 1945
Gasoline 22.4 tons (22.8 m.t.) — 1945

Illinois and *Kentucky*
Fuel oil 8,841.0 tons (8,983.0 m.t.) — 1949 S.D. Book

Machinery

Boilers	eight Babcock & Wilcox three drum express type boilers fitted with two furnaces and double uptakes. Pressure: 565 psi (39.72 kg/cm²) Temperature: 850°F. (454.4°C.)
Turbines	four sets General Electric geared turbines *(Iowa* and *Missouri)* four sets Westinghouse geared turbines *(New Jersey* and *Wisconsin)*
Shaft horsepower	212,000 (214,941 mhp) 44,000 (44,610 mhp) Astern
Maximum speed	33.0 knots @ 202 rpm
Nominal endurance	18,000 nautical miles @ 12 knots — 1945 15,900 nautical miles @ 17 knots — 1945 5,300 nautical miles @ 29.6 knots — 1945
Generators	eight ship's service turbogenerators (1,250 kw) two emergency diesel generators (250 kw) total ship's service capacity: 10,000 kw, 450Volts, AC
Propellers	two five-bladed 17' 0" (5.182 m) diameter propellers — inboard two four-bladed 18' 3" (5.563 m) diameter propellers — outboard
Rudders	two rudders with a projected area of the profile of each of 340 sq. ft. (31.6 sq. m.)

Miscellaneous

Complement 1,921 (117 off./1,804 enl.) — design
(1945) 2,788 (151 off./2,637 enl.) — *Iowa*
2,753 (161 off./2,592 enl.) — *New Jersey*
2,978 (189 off./2,789 enl.) — *Missouri*
2,911 (173 off./2,738 enl.) — *Wisconsin*
(1949) 2,617 (166 off./2,451 enl.) — *Iowa*
2,688 (234 off./2,454 enl.) — *New Jersey*
2,406 (151 off./2,255 enl.) — *Missouri*
2,672 (169 off./2,503 enl.) — *Wisconsin*
(1968) 1,626 (70 off./1,556 enl.) — *New Jersey*

Frame spacing 4.0' (1.219 m)

New Jersey (BB-62)
Weight Summary
1943

	Tons	Metric tons	Percent of total
Hull structure (excl. armor)	15,491.224	(15,740.104)	34.31
Armor	19,311.570	(19,621.565)	42.77
Propulsion & electrical	4,797.159	(4,874.119)	10.62
Communication & control	27.733	(28.178)	0.06
Auxiliary systems	1,182.635	(1,201.661)	2.62
Outfit & furnishings	795.937	(808.712)	1.76
Armament	3,549.109	(3,606.097)	7.86
Light Ship Displacement	45,155.367	(45,879.863	100%
Ammunition	2,592.340	(2,633.922)	
Complement	283.757	(288.307)	
Supplies & stores	1,473.960	(1,497.646)	
Aeronautics	51,696	(52.525)	
Standard Displacement	49,657.120	(50,453.664)	
Fuel oil	8,084.140	(8,213.890)	
Reserve feed water	490.650	(498.520)	
Full Load Displacement	58,131.910	(59,065.031)	

Body Plan

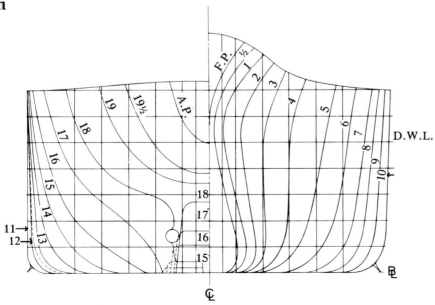

Deck Plans

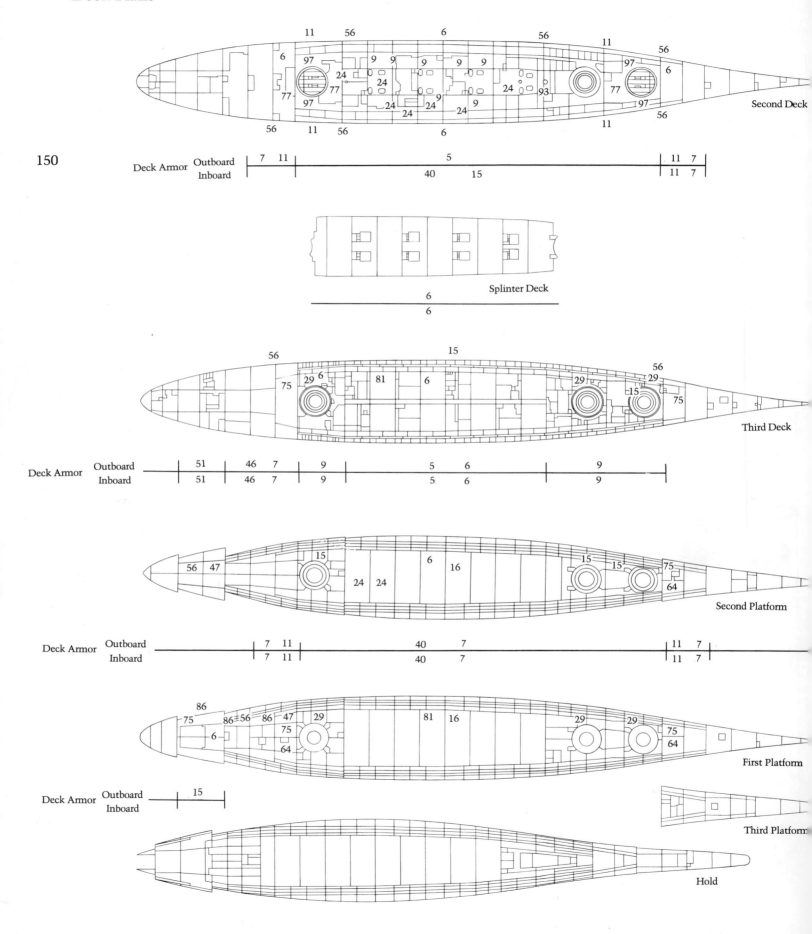

150

Second Deck

Deck Armor	Outboard	7	11		5				11	7
	Inboard				40	15			11	7

Splinter Deck

		6		
		6		

Third Deck

Deck Armor	Outboard	51	46	7	9	5	6	9
	Inboard	51	46	7	9	5	6	9

Second Platform

Deck Armor	Outboard	7	11	40	7	11	7
	Inboard	7	11	40	7	11	7

First Platform

Deck Armor	Outboard	15	
	Inboard		

Third Platform

Hold

Armor Thickness

Key No.	Inches	Millimeters	Key No.	Inches	Millimeters
1	.25	6	51	6.20	157
2	.30	8	52	6.30	160
3	.375	10	53	6.60	168
4	.45	11	54	6.80	173
5	.50	13	55	7.00	178
6	.625	16	56	7.125	181
7	.750	19	57	7.20	183
8	.875	22	58	7.25	184
9	1.00	25	59	7.40	188
10	1.125	29	60	7.75	197
11	1.25	32	61	7.80	198
12	1.40	35	62	7.85	199
13	1.425	36	63	8.17	208
14	1.47	37	64	8.50	216
15	1.50	38	65	9.00	229
16	1.625	41	66	9.15	232
17	1.71	43	67	9.30	236
18	1.90	48	68	9.50	241
19	1.91	49	69	9.80	249
20	1.95	50	70	10.00	254
21	2.00	51	71	10.20	259
22	2.05	52	72	10.60	260
23	2.20	56	73	11.00	279
24	2.50	64	74	11.10	282
25	2.70	67	75	11.30	287
26	2.80	71	76	11.50	292
27	2.870	73	77	11.60	295
28	2.925	74	78	11.70	297
29	3.00	76	79	11.80	300
30	3.20	81	80	12.00	305
31	3.25	83	81	12.10	307
32	3.30	84	82	12.20	310
33	3.60	91	83	12.75	324
34	3.75	95	84	12.80	325
35	3.82	97	85	13.00	330
36	3.90	99	86	13.50	343
37	4.00	102	87	13.70	348
38	4.10	104	88	14.00	356
39	4.50	114	89	14.70	373
40	4.75	121	90	14.90	378
41	4.80	122	91	15.00	381
42	5.00	127	92	15.25	387
43	5.26	133	93	16.00	406
44	5.30	135	94	16.10	409
45	5.50	140	95	16.70	424
46	5.60	142	96	17.00	432
47	5.625	143	97	17.30	439
48	5.80	147	98	17.50	444
49	6.00	152	99	18.00	457
50	6.10	155	100	19.50	495
			101	21.30	541

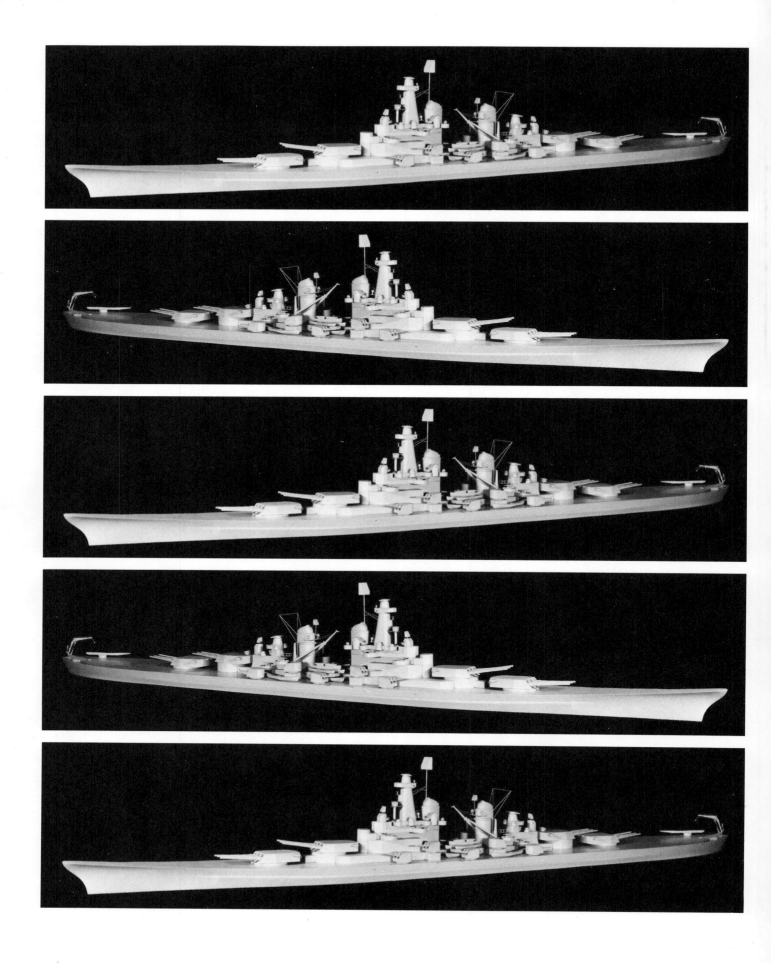

CHAPTER FIVE

The *Montana* class

The *Montana*-class battleships were the most powerful and best-protected ships ever projected for the United States Navy. The design of this class was initiated early in 1940 after the *Iowa*-class design was completed. The ships were fated never to be laid down.

Although the basic decision had been made in the summer of 1938 that the *Iowa*-class ships should be given high speeds, the Navy's interest in somewhat slower, more heavily protected, and more heavily armed ships persisted. As a result, before the basic decision to accept significant increases in displacement, the Navy prepared an exhaustive series of some twenty preliminary designs of 27-knot battleships of the 45,000-ton class.

Slow Battleship Designs. These follow-on "slow battleship" design studies had standard displacements ranging from 41,627 tons to 46,668 tons. All but one of the studies would have mounted 16-inch/50 caliber guns in either twin, triple, *or* quadruple turrets, the one exception being a design with 14-inch/50 caliber guns in equadruple turrets. At a minimum, the protection was equal to that of the *Iowa*, and in many cases the sacrifice in speed was accompanied by improvements in protection.

Representative examples of these follow-on design studies to the *Iowa* are presented in Table 5-1.

Dual-purpose guns. At this stage of development, the most common projected dual-purpose armament featured the 5-inch/38 caliber gun, although a few studies were given a 6-inch/47 caliber dual-purpose gun armament. Improved versions of the standard fleet antiaircraft gun were being contemplated. In the summer of 1939, a series of candidates to replace the 5-inch/38 caliber gun were on the drawing boards:

5.4-inch/47 caliber	75 lb. projectile
5-inch/58 caliber	75 lb. projectile
5-inch/50 caliber	75 lb. projectile
5-inch/32 caliber	56.25 lb. projectile

Ultimately, the Navy selected a 5-inch/54 caliber dual-purpose gun design for further development. This gun, firing a 70-pound projectile, was selected for incorporation in the dual-purpose batteries given the *Montana* design. None of the "slow battleship" designs of the 45,000-ton class were given this gun. The 5-inch/54 caliber gun first entered service with the *Midway*-class aircraft carriers, completed in 1945-47.

Five Montana*-class ships were to be built, but despite extensive design studies, none of them were ever laid down. The general arrangement of the ships was indicated in waterline models, but these were subject to change. Undoubtedly, had the ships been built, helicopters would have replaced floatplanes and the fantail catapults would have been eliminated.*

TABLE 5-1

45,000-ton Slow Battleships

Summer 1939 Design Studies

Design Scheme*		BB 65-A	BB 65-D	BB 65-J
Displacement				
light ship		45,435 (46,164)	44,020 (44,727)	
standard		46,668 (47,417)	45,308 (46,035)	44,380 (45,092)
Dimensions				
waterline length		800' (243.84)	800' (243.84)	800' (243.84)
beam		108' (32.918)	108' (32.918)	108' (32.918)
maximum draft		36' (10.973)	36' (10.973)	36' (10.973)
Armament				
16"/50	(406mm)	12	12	. .
14"/50	(356mm)	. .	. .	12
arrangement		3-3-A-3-3	4-4-A-4	3-3-A-3-3
6"/47	(152mm)	. .	12—twin	. .
5"/38	(127mm)	20—twin	. .	20—twin
1.1"/75	(28mm)	12—quad	12—quad	16—quad
0.50 cal.	(12.7mm)	12—single	12—single	12—single
Propulsion				
shaft horsepower		130,000 (131,803)	130,000 (131,803)	130,000 (131,803)
maximum speed, knots		26	26	26
endurance @ 15 knots		15,000	15,000	15,000
Armor				
immunity zone				
16"/45	2700 lb.	20,500-26,500 (18,745-24,232)	20,500-26,500 (18,745-24,232)	16,700-27,900 (15,270-25,512)
16"/45	2240 lb.	18,000-30,000 (16,459-27,432)	18,000-30,000 (16,459-27,432)	14,700-31,900 (13,442-29,169)
Thicknesses				
belt		12.1" (307)	12.1" (307)	14.3" (363)
turrets—face		17" + 2.5" (432 + 63)	17" + 2.5" (432 + 63)	20" (508)
—roof		7.25" (184)	7.25" (184)	7.75" (197)
barbettes		17.3" (439)	17.3" (439)	19.9" (505)
conning tower—sides		17.3" (439)	17.3" (439)	19.9" (505)
splinter protection		2.5" (63)	2.5" (63)	2.5" (63)
armor deck		4.75" + 1.25" (121 + 32)	4.75" + 1.25" (121 + 32)	5.5" + 1.25" (140 + 32)

*At this date, BB-65 and BB-66 had not been authorized as units of the *Iowa* class.

Early in 1940, it appeared significant to the General Board that all major navies were continuing their building programs, with substantial emphasis on battleship construction, as indicated in Table 5-2.

TABLE 5-2

Battleship New Construction, 1940, Worldwide

	Completed by 1940	Building or Projected
Germany	2	6
Italy	2	2
France	2	2
Japan	0	4
United Kingdom	1	4
Soviet Union	0	2
United States	0	10

TABLE 5-3

Preliminary Design Characteristics

Designation Date	BB 65-8D* 23 Feb. 1940	BB 65-5 March 1940	BB 65-5A March 1940
Displacement			
standard	66,500 (67,567)	57,500 (58,423)	58,500 (59,439)
full load	79,700 (80,979)	68,000 (69,091)	69,700 (70,818)
Dimensions			
waterline length	1,050' (320.040)	930' (283.464)	880' (268.224)
maximum beam	120' (36.576)	118' (35.966)	122' (37.186)
maximum draft	35' (10.668)	35' (10.668)	35' (10.668)

Armament (all ships)	12 — 16"/50	(406mm)	tripled
	20 — 5"/54	(127mm)	paired
	16 — 1.1"/75	(28mm)	quadrupled
	12 — 0.50 cal.	(12.7mm)	single

Protection — all ships — to withstand 16"/50 (406mm) 2,700 lb. (1,225 kg) shell fired at normal battle range.

Propulsion			
shaft horsepower	293,000 (297,064)	150,000 (152,080)	150,000 (152,080)
maximum speed, knots	33	28	28
endurance @ 15 knots	15,000	15,000	15,000

*Fast battleship version of *Montana* class.

Although the Montana-class ships were never built, much of their design detail would have followed that established by earlier ships of the type. With slight modifications, they would have resembled the Iowa, pictured here, in much of her superstructure arrangement.

Preliminary designs called for thiry-two 40mm guns, such as these in action aboard the Wisconsin, below. This number would probably have been increased if the ship had gone into service.

156

The Montana-class ships were designed to carry twenty 5" dual purpose guns, clustered amidships in much the same arrangement featured on Iowa-class ships.

Ammunition requirements for the Montana-class ships were essentially the same as for previous battleships. The proposed secondary battery of twenty 5" guns required thousands of projectiles, such as pictured at bottom.

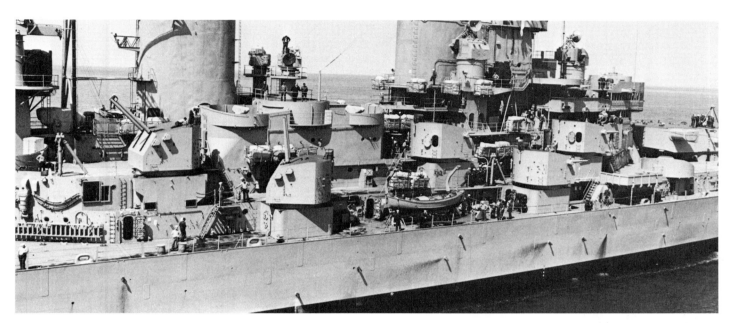

Battleships, heavily armed, well protected, and designed to withstand plunging fire of the heaviest armor-piercing projectiles, seemed to be least affected by the rapid development of aircraft. Even admitting the practicability of accurate bombing in the face of determined resistance, heavy bombs were considered to be certainly less destructive than armor-piercing shells.

After evaluating the 45,000-ton "slow battleship" studies prepared in 1939, the General Board decided to accept major increases in displacement in order to obtain more desirable characteristics, primarily improved protection. Fifteen preliminary designs were submitted to the General Board between March and July of 1940. Representative examples are given in Table 5-3. In marked contrast to the *Iowa* design, in which speed was a paramount concern, the *Montana*-class ships were to be well protected, with heavy armament and only modest maximum speed.

Design Characteristics. After evaluating the studies, the General Board on 21 August 1940 made several basic decisions regarding the new ships:

- The construction of a group of high-speed capital ships (the *Iowa* class) must be given first priority, and the ships should be completed as soon as possible.
- Treaty limitations on the displacement of all future capital ships are no longer in effect.
- All limitations on the beam of warships are suspended in view of the plans either to enlarge the Panama Canal or to build a wider canal in Nicaragua. [No such plans were carried out.]
- The hitting power of sixteen-inch shells has improved so that the defensive characteristics must also be improved.
- These new battleships must be stronger defensively and offensively by twenty-five per cent than any other ships completed or under construction.
- These important characteristics are desired in the new battleships:
  a. Improved engineering plant and arrangement.
  b. Greater efficiency in gunnery.
  c. Lessons learned from wartime experiences in the European theater should be incorporated in the design.
  d. High speed.

At that time, the General Board approved the basic characteristics for the final design of the *Montana*-class ships (Table 5-4).

Length was limited because some ships were to be built at the New York Navy Yard, where the launching ways could not handle a ship of 58,000 tons. Dry dock number 4 there was enlarged so ships could be built in it and floated out, rather than launched conventionally. The length and displacement limitations complicated problems confronting the Preliminary Design Branch.

TABLE 5-4

Preliminary Design Requirements, 1940

Displacement	58,000 tons standard (58,931 m.t.)
Waterline length	Not to exceed 890' (271.272 m)
Beam	Compatible with other characteristics, to give superior stability.
Draft	Not to exceed 36.5' (11.125 m)
Armament	12 – 16"/50 tripled (406mm)
	20 – 5"/54 paired (127mm)
	24-32 – 1.1"/75 quadrupled (28mm)
	. . – 0.5" machine guns (12.7mm)
Protection	Armor – To provide immunity zone of from 18,000 to 32,000 yards (16,459-29,261 m) against 2,700 lb. (1,225 kg) 16" shell. Main side belt to extend 8' (2.438 m) above *and* below battle condition waterline.
	Side: best obtainable protection against underwater damage.
	Subdivision: complete protection and localization of damage, as practical by compartmentation with intact bulkheads.
Propulsion	Speed of 28 knots, provided by 212,000 shp.
Endurance	15,000 nautical miles at 15 knots.

Design variations. Several design variations were produced late in 1940 (Table 5-5). Design Study BB67-1, based on preliminary design study BB65-5A, was used as the basis for the development of more detailed designs. Study BB67-2 satisfied all the requirements outlined by the General Board, but the standard displacement of 61,400 tons far exceeded the desired 58,000 tons. It resulted from errors inherent in the approximate methods used to estimate the displacement of the earlier study, increased requirements, and reports of modifications and weight increases in the *Iowa*-class ships. Weight estimates, based on data for the *Iowa*, had to be modified as better information on actual weights became available.

The possibility of using a smaller power plant while retaining adequate maximum speed was first studied in November of 1940. This proved worthwhile because such a power plant was eventually selected. Table 5-6 shows the effects of the number of boilers and the required maximum shaft horsepower on the machinery weight.

Drastic design modifications were necessary to approach the specified displacement while retaining the required speed, armament, and protection. Design study BB67-3 (Table 5-5) resulted from these alterations. It had an improved hull form similar to that of the *Iowa*, although length, beam, and draft remained the same as in BB67-2. The primary change was in the propulsion plant, where a reduction to 180,000 shaft horsepower permitted improvements in the machinery arrangement and better protection against underbottom explosions. This reduced the length of the machinery spaces and contributed to reduction in the overall length of the armor box by twelve feet.

Further weight savings accrued from the modification of the after armor belt. The originally rather generous distribution of armor was sharply curtailed, and armored tubes were

TABLE 5-5

Detailed Design Variations

Designation	BB 67-1	BB 67-2	BB 67-3
Date	Sept. 1940	Oct. 1940	Nov. 1940
Displacement			
standard	61,000 (61,979)	61,400 (62,385)	59,700 (60,658)
full load	73,000 (74,171)	72,400 (73,561)	70,600 (71,733)
Dimensions			
waterline length	890' (271.272)	890' (271.272)	890' (271.272)
maximum beam	118' (32.918)	118' (32.918)	118' (32.918)
maximum draft	36' (10.973)	36' (10.973)	36' (10.973)
Armament			
16"/50 (406mm) tripled	12	12	12
5"/54 (127mm) paired	20	20	20
40mm/60 quadrupled	none	none	24
1.1"/75 (28mm) quadrupled	16	24	none
0.50 cal. (12.7mm) single	12	12	12

Protection (all ships) to resist 16"/50 (406mm) 2,700 lb. (1,225kg) AP shell fired at normal battle range.

Propulsion			
shaft horsepower	212,000 (214,941)	212,000 (214,941)	180,000 (182,497)
maximum speed, knots	29	29	28

adopted to protect the steering-gear leads. This sharply reduced the armor weight, but left little protection to the reserve buoyancy in the after part of the ship.

The reductions in armor and power resulted in net weight savings of 1,700 tons, and the improved hull form reduced the initial costs of the hull structure and power plant, as well as permitting marked reductions in operational costs.

The General Board ordered the Bureau of Ships to prepare a detailed design study conforming to the characteristics of BB67-3 and urged further modifications to attain the specified 58,000-ton displacement. The Board discussed the reduction of the after waterline belt and the deck armor. Complete deck protection was desired, because improved AP shells and bombs made armor protection mandatory above the propeller shafts. Deck armor would also provide better protection for the steering-gear leads.

By January of 1941 there was a general acceptance of a larger displacement than 58,000 tons, a slightly greater length, reduced power for a better machinery arrangement, and improved internal subdivision. A proposal to save weight by using 5-inch/38 caliber guns instead of the 5-inch/54 caliber was rejected. The substitution of 40mm Bofors machine guns for the 1.1-inch quadruple machine gun mounts was approved. As a result, major alterations to the proposed basic design characteristics were authorized (Table 5-7).

Final design characteristics. A new design study, BB67-4, accepted a shaft horsepower of 172,000 good for a maximum speed of 28 knots. Proposals to increase hull length to compen-

TABLE 5-6

Comparison—Boiler-Turbine Weight vs. Shaft Horsepower

Maximum shp	No. Boilers	Machinery Weight (m.t.)	Machinery Length
212,000	8	5,315 tons (5,400)	308' (93.878 m)
(214,491 mhp)	12	5,390 tons (5,476)	272' (82.906 m)
180,000	8	4,740 tons (4,816)	
(182,497 mhp)	12	4,770 tons (4,847)	

TABLE 5-7

Alterations to 1940 Design

Displacement	60,000 tons standard (60,963 m.t.)
Waterline length	Not to exceed 910' (277,368 m)
Armament	Possible substitution of 40mm Bofors for 1.1"/75 (28mm)

TABLE 5-8

Approved Design Characteristics, March 1941

Displacement	60,500 tons standard (61,471 m.t.)
	70,500 tons full load (71,631 m.t.)
Waterline length	890' 0" (271.272 m)
Beam	120' 8" maximum over armor (36.779 m)
	118' 0" underwater (35.966 m)
Draft	36' 0" full load (10.973 m)
Armament	12—16"/50 tripled (406mm)
	20—5"/54 paired (127mm)
	32—40mm/60 quadrupled
	8—20mm/70 single
Shaft horsepower	172,000 (174,386 mhp)
Maximum speed	28 knots

TABLE 5-9

Design Characteristics, June 1942

Displacement	63,221 tons standard (64,236 m.t.)
	70,965 tons full load (72,103 m.t.)
Waterline length	890' 0" (271.272 m)
Beam	120' 8" maximum over armor (36.779 m)
	121' 2" underwater (36.932 m)
Draft	36' 0" full load (10.973 m)
Armament	12—16"/50 tripled (406mm)
	20—5"/54 paired (127mm)
	32—40mm/60 quadrupled
	20—20mm/70 single
Shaft horsepower	172,000 (174,386 mhp)
Maximum speed	28 knots

sate for reduced power were rejected because a complete time-consuming design would have been necessary, and it was desired to have construction commence as soon as possible. This study, issued by the Bureau of Ships on 21 March 1941 and approved by the General Board as that to which the *Montana*-class ships would be built, had the characteristics shown in Table 5-8.

The eight boilers were located in individual fire rooms. This added compartmentation reduced possible flooding from underbottom damage. The undesirability of asymmetrical flooding was recognized, but the designers had sufficient confidence in the side protective system and overall stability to revert to longitudinal subdivision of primary engineering spaces amidships.

Armor freeboard was increased from eight to nine feet, providing a better chance of side armor protection after underwater damage. Even with increased displacement, the residual freeboard would remain greater than in the original design.

The .50 caliber machine guns were replaced by 20mm Oerlikons, which the Bureau of Ordnance estimated to be at least ten times more effective. A proposal to substitute two quadruple 40mm Bofors machine gun mounts for these light machine guns, which would have increased the displacement, was set aside for further study. As late as April 1942 the General Board decided that work on the ships would be continued, but after the modified design was issued on 4 June, all work stopped. The ships were formally cancelled on 21 July 1943. Final basic characteristics were as shown in Table 5-9. The increased underwater beam was the consequence of improved underwater protection.

Construction.
Five ships of the class were projected, all to be built in U. S. navy yards: the *Montana* (BB-67) and *Ohio* (BB-68) at Philadelphia, the *Maine* (BB-69) and *New Hampshire* (BB-70) at New York, and the *Louisiana* (BB-71) at Norfolk. Construction was authorized by Congress on 19 July 1940, although on 19 May the Navy had already placed orders for their construction to the BB67-4 design scheme. Scheduled completion dates varied from 1 July to 1 November 1945. Actual construction would probably have been delayed by design changes and alterations.

Large Battleship Designs.
Early in July 1944, rough sketch outlines were prepared for a very large, new type battleship. The object was to determine whether repositioning main-battery turrets would provide sufficient hull volume for adequate side protection against torpedo hits in way of the magazines. The estimated characteristics of this study were as follows:

Displacement:		
full load (est.)*	106,500 tons	(108,204 m.t.)
Dimensions:		
length waterline	1,160 feet	(353.443 m)
length overall	1,200 feet	(365.631 m)
maximum beam	136 feet	(41.438 m)
maximum draft (est)*	38 feet	(11.578 m)
Armament:		
main battery (est.)*	12-16″/50	(406mm)

*Authors' estimates.

The dimensional analysis employed was specifically shown as a proportioning of similar dimensions for the *Montana*. This was used for estimating the draft and displacement.

This study was never the basis for serious consideration for design development, was never developed even to the level of detail of a preliminary design, and merely stands as an interesting footnote to the history of the battleship in the United States Navy.

Main battery guns for the Montana-*class ships would have fired this type of projectile, to a maximum range of 42,345 yards.*

Armament. Gun characteristics were as shown in Table 5-10.

TABLE 5-10
Gun Characteristics

Gun	16"/50 (406mm)	5"/54 (127mm)
Shell weight (lb.)	2,700 (1,225 kg)	70 (31.75 kg)
Muzzle velocity (FPS)	2,500 (762 m/s)	2,650 (808 m/s)
Maximum range (yd.)	42,345 (38,720 m)	25,900 (23,683 m)
Maximum elevation	45°	85°
Gun	1.57"/60 (40mm)	0.79"/70 (20mm)
Shell weight (lb.)	1.98 (0.898 kg)	0.27 (0.122 kg)
Muzzle velocity (FPS)	2,890 (881 m/s)	2,770 (844 m/s)
Maximum range (yd.)	11,000 (10,058 m)*	4,800 (4,389 m)
Maximum elevation	90°	90°

*Fuze self-destructive at 5,000 yards (4,572 m).

Main battery. The most noteworthy feature was the addition of a triple 16-inch turret aft. The main battery of twelve 16-inch/50 caliber guns, Mark 7, in four turrets was the most powerful ever projected for an American battleship. The equal distribution of firepower fore and aft was an improvement over that of earlier ships. The weight of the main-battery salvo, 32,400 pounds, was by far the heaviest ever given an American battleship.

Secondary battery. The secondary battery of twenty 5-inch/54 caliber guns, Mark 16, in twin mounts was the most versatile and powerful dual-purpose gun ever selected for use by the U. S. Navy. It fired a heavier shell at greater range and with a rate of fire similar to that of the less effective 5-inch/38 caliber gun. In the mid-1970s improved, fully automatic models of the 5-inch/54 caliber gun were still being mounted on new destroyer-type ships.

Antiaircraft battery. Although the final machine-gun armament had not been established, the thirty-two 40mm Bofors machine guns and twenty 20mm Oerlikon machine guns projected in June of 1942 were indicative of a powerful defense. In view of the ship's greater length and beam, the machine-gun armament probably would have exceeded that of the *Iowa* class.

Aircraft. Three floatplanes and two fantail catapults were planned. One plane was to be carried on each catapult and one was to be stowed on deck. As battleships normally operated with carriers during World War II, it is probable that by the time the ships were completed no aircraft would have been carried.

Protection. Armor protection in these ships was by far the most effective ever projected for an American capital ship. It was calculated to provide an immunity zone for the armored citadel of from 18,000 to 31,000 yards on the basis of the performance of the 16-inch/45 caliber gun firing a 2,700-pound AP shell. Against the older 16-inch/45 caliber gun firing a 2,240 pound AP shell, the immunity zone was calculated to be 16,500 to 34,500 yards.

Citadel. The sides of the armored citadel were protected by a very heavy inclined armor belt system. The main side belt was comprised of 16.1-inch plates (tapered to 10.2 inches at the lower edge) on 1-inch STS backing plates, inclined 19 degrees from the vertical with the lower edge inboard. This increased the effective resistance to about that of 21-inch vertical plates. Inner belt armor supplemented the main side belt, with its top edge approximately at the level of the lower edge of the main side belt.

This internal armor varied from 1.5 to 8.5 inches in thickness over the magazines and from 1.0 to 7.2 inches over the machinery and served a dual purpose of providing ballistic protection while increasing the resistance of the side protective system.

Deck armor. The increasing threat of plunging shell and bomb attack lead to the provision of remarkably heavy deck armor, as shown in Table 5-11. The third deck served as the splinter deck over the citadel. The steering gear accesses were given only limited protection, with the 2.25-inch main deck supplemented by 1.25-inch armor on the second deck. Forward, the deck construction served primarily structural purposes.

TABLE 5-11
Deck Armor Thickness

	Amidships — centerline	
Main deck	0.75″ + 1.5″	(19mm + 38mm)
Second deck	5.8″ + 1.25″	(147mm + 32mm)
Third deck	0.62″	(16mm)
total	9.92″	(252mm)
	Amidships — outboard	
Main deck	0.75″ + 1.5″	(19mm + 38mm)
Second deck	6.1″ + 1.25″	(155mm + 32mm)
Third deck	0.75″	(19mm)
total	10.35″	(263mm)

Very late in the design development the main transverse armor bulkheads were reduced in thickness to permit scaling up horizontal protection on the main-battery turret roofs. As finally planned, the forward transverse bulkhead would have been 16 inches thick, while the upper part of the after bulkhead would have been 14 inches thick, with the lower segment 12.75 inches thick.

The steering-gear room would have been even more heavily protected than was normal, with sides 16.7 inches thick inclined 10 degrees from the vertical to increase the effective thickness to about that of 19-inch vertical plates. The after bulkhead was 15.25 inches thick; the forward bulkhead was 18 inches thick. Wiring leads were protected by armored tubes of 6-inch plates. Weight problems precluded adequate shielding of the accesses to the steering gear, hence the partial solution to the problem by the use of armored tubes.

Turrets and mounts. The main-battery turrets were to have extremely heavy armor. The face plates were 22.5 inches thick overall, with 18-inch plates superposed on 4.5-inch backing plates. The sides were 10 inches thick, the back plates were 12 inches thick, and the roof was 9.15 inches thick, ample protection against 16-inch fire at normal battle ranges. The barbettes were likewise well protected, with thicknesses ranging from 18 to 19.5 to 21.3 inches. The secondary mounts and magazines were protected in accordance with standard practice; STS plating 2.5 inches thick provided ample protection against fragmentation and strafing damage.

Conning tower. This was a double-level structure; the upper level served as a gunfire control station. Sides were 18 inches thick, the roof was 7.75 inches thick, and the floor was 4 inches thick. The communications tube was of 16-inch plates.

Side protection. The design of the entire protective system was strongly influenced by developments in aerial warfare. The use of heavier, more powerful bombs forced the provision of very heavy horizontal protection, while high-speed torpedo bombers increased the chances of extensive torpedo damage and forced emphasis on underwater protection and subdivision.

Underwater protection. The designed loading of the side protective system was calculated to minimize the lists resulting from underwater damage. The four-compartment system featured two outboard liquid-loaded compartments and two void inboard compartments. The inner belt armor comprised the bulkhead between the void compartments. The armor system was designed to bend elastically—a critical design assumption. It was never tested in combat. The transverse depth of the system amidships at half draft was 20.5 feet.

The *Montana*-class ships were the first American ships designed with such heavy emphasis on underwater protection.

Prominent features of the design were the blisters and the considerable beam. With restrictions on the beam relaxed, it was possible to provide greatly improved underwater protection and subdivision. The blisters were designed to serve as cushions against torpedoes, to help support heavy side armor, and to reinforce underwater subdivision. Although considerably modified for use on fast battleships, they were clumsy and reduced speed. The need to counter torpedoes armed with powerful explosive charges forced such a system on the designers.

Technical information on explosions under the bottoms of ships called for a triple bottom the full length of the citadel. Although triple bottoms are difficult to design and install, they were considered necessary to give these ships at least that limited protection. The great strength of the triple bottom was designed to confine flooding resulting from an underbottom detonation, as was the extensive subdivision of the major engineering spaces. It was acknowledged that the effects of an underbottom explosion could not be contained within the confines of the protective system.

Underwater protection cannot be uniform along the length of the armored citadel, for the hull form and internal arrangements tend to force reduced effectiveness of the side protective system nearer the ends of the citadel. In the design of the *Iowa* and *Montana* classes, this problem was overcome to a great extent as indicated in the summary (Table 5-12) of the designed performance of the side protective system of the *Montana*-class ships.

TABLE 5-12

Torpedo Hit Effect, Calculations

	Torpedo Hit Amidships	Torpedo Hit Forward
Initial armor freeboard	8.5′ (2.591 m)	8.5′ (2.59 m)
Minimum damaged condition freeboard	4.5′ (1.372 m)	6.8′ (2.073 m)
Angle of heel	3° 34′	1° 54′
Residual metacentric height	7.83′ (2.387 m)	8.16′ (2.487 m)

The side protection was an impressive improvement over the *North Carolina*-class ships, which had an anticipated armor freeboard, after damage, of one foot with maximum heel angle of about 7 degrees, assuming torpedo damage amidships. The *Montana*-class ships at a displacement of 70,965 tons had a designed metacentric height of 9.31 feet.

These battleships were unquestionably the best-protected warships ever designed for the United States Navy. Their armor protection was outstanding, and their side protective system and extreme subdivision gave them a hitherto unmatched resistance to underwater damage.

Propulsion Plant.
The improved subdivision of the main machinery spaces improved resistance to damage, but at the cost of greater machinery weight and a reduction in power, as shown by comparison with the *Iowa*-class design (Table 5-13).

Turbines. Four sets of geared turbines, rated at 565 pounds per square inch pressure at 850°F delivered a normal maximum of 172,000 shaft horsepower, good for a maximum of 28 knots at 160 rpm with a displacement of 70,500 tons.

Each geared turbine set consisted of high-pressure and low-pressure turbines, and an astern turbine in the low-pressure turbine casing. Helical, locked-train, double-reduction gears permitted higher turbine speeds and desirably low shaft speeds. The two-group setup, which somewhat limited the complete flexibility of the plant, was a disadvantage that should have been avoided.

TABLE 5-13

Horsepower-Weight Comparison

Ship	Iowa	Montana
Year completed	1943	1945 (schedule)
Shaft horsepower	212,000 (214,941)	172,000 (174,386)
Weight (tons)	4,992 (5,072)	5,030 (5,111)
Pounds/shp	52.70 (23.58)	65.50 (29.30)

Boilers. The boilers were of the two-drum, double-furnace single-uptake air-encased type, with the superheater installed between the furnaces. Hot gases from the superheater furnace passed over the superheater tubes into the saturated furnace, through the boiler tube bank and economizer and out through a single-uptake connection. The boilers were divided into groups of four, each group supplying steam for two engine rooms.

Steam conditions. Although higher steam pressures and temperatures would have been more efficient, the designers retained the same conditions used in earlier ships. Assured reliability was considered more important than a possible small economy in fuel consumption. Very-high-pressure cycles are better suited for very-high-speed operation, and increased power would not have offset reduced reliability.

Because of the amount and complexity of planned electrical equipment, there were to be ten AC ship's service turbogenerators, rated at 1,250 kw, 450 volts, and two 500 kw emergency diesel generators.

Hull Characteristics. The twin skeg stern form was retained although model

basin tests, conducted for the first time since the design of the *North Carolina*, indicated that the conventional stern form was superior to the twin skeg version, a complete reversal of the *North Carolina* tests. The new tests indicated a superiority of about 7 per cent through the entire speed range and 9.5 per cent at the design speed of 28 knots. The retention of the twin skegs, despite these tests results, was a consequence of their undeniable structural and protective advantages over the conventional stern form.

A major design concern was the problem of armor production. Specifications called for armor thickness never before produced in the United States that would have taxed existing equipment to its limit. The design project necessitated experiments to produce forged armor of the thickness specified.

Improved welding techniques for Class B armor were also devised, and experiments with high-carbon steel promised an improvement in the quality of plates delivered to the shipyards. The consistent increase in the proportion of structural welding would unquestionably have been continued in these ships.

Summary. The *Montana*-class design provided for the most powerful armament ever given an American capital ship (other than the few conceptual studies with 18-inch guns) combined with unprecedentedly extensive and effective protection against all forms of attack.

The machinery arrangement, dictated by the desire for extensive subdivision and isolation of components, suffered from a fundamental design deficiency; it was arranged in two groups, and boilers in one group could not supply steam to turbines in the other. Although the extreme subdivision diminished the possibility of losing all boilers in any one group, this deficiency remained a weakness in what was otherwise a very damage-resistant and flexible arrangement.

These ships were admirably suited to the classic battleship mission, but their 28-knot speed was marginal for fast carrier task force operations, and soon would have relegated them to the reserve fleet in peacetime, as it did all U. S. battleships other than the *Iowa*-class. The powerful armament was admirably suited for shore bombardment, where speed was not essential.

The *Montana*-class battleships were the most formidable capital ships projected by any nation during World War II. The Japanese ships, the *Yamato* and *Musashi*, with 18.1-inch guns, were more powerful, but the *Montana*, with more numerous main-battery guns of comparable power, would have essentially matched the power of the Japanese ships, and superior U. S. fire-control systems would have increased the effectiveness of her guns. In every regard except speed, the *Montana*-class ships would have been at least the equal of any other capital ship projected for construction during World War II.

Armor Thickness

Key No.	Inches	Millimeters	Key No.	Inches	Millimeters	Key No.	Inches	Millimeters	Key No.	Inches	Millimeters
1	.25	6	26	2.80	71	51	6.20	157	76	11.50	292
2	.30	8	27	2.870	73	52	6.30	160	77	11.60	295
3	.375	10	28	2.925	74	53	6.60	168	78	11.70	297
4	.45	11	29	3.00	76	54	6.80	173	79	11.80	300
5	.50	13	30	3.20	81	55	7.00	178	80	12.00	305
6	.625	16	31	3.25	83	56	7.125	181	81	12.10	307
7	.750	19	32	3.30	84	57	7.20	183	82	12.20	310
8	.875	22	33	3.60	91	58	7.25	184	83	12.75	324
9	1.00	25	34	3.75	95	59	7.40	188	84	12.80	325
10	1.125	29	35	3.82	97	60	7.75	197	85	13.00	330
11	1.25	32	36	3.90	99	61	7.80	198	86	13.50	343
12	1.40	35	37	4.00	102	62	7.85	199	87	13.70	348
13	1.425	36	38	4.10	104	63	8.17	208	88	14.00	356
14	1.47	37	39	4.50	114	64	8.50	216	89	14.70	373
15	1.50	38	40	4.75	121	65	9.00	229	90	14.90	378
16	1.625	41	41	4.80	122	66	9.15	232	91	15.00	381
17	1.71	43	42	5.00	127	67	9.30	236	92	15.25	387
18	1.90	48	43	5.26	133	68	9.50	241	93	16.00	406
19	1.91	49	44	5.30	135	69	9.80	249	94	16.10	409
20	1.95	50	45	5.50	140	70	10.00	254	95	16.70	424
21	2.00	51	46	5.60	142	71	10.20	259	96	17.00	432
22	2.05	52	47	5.625	143	72	10.60	260	97	17.30	439
23	2.20	56	48	5.80	147	73	11.00	279	98	17.50	444
24	2.50	64	49	6.00	152	74	11.10	282	99	18.00	457
25	2.70	67	50	6.10	155	75	11.30	287	100	19.50	495
									101	21.30	541

Montana Class

Name & hull number	*Montana* (BB-67)	*Ohio* (BB-68)	
Builder	Philadelphia Navy Yard	Philadelphia Navy Yard	
Authorized	19 July 1940	19 July 1940	
Cancelled	21 July 1943	21 July 1943	
Name & hull number	*Maine* (BB-69)	*New Hampshire* (BB-70)	
Builder	New York Navy Yard	New York Navy Yard	
Authorized	19 July 1940	19 July 1940	
Cancelled	21 July 1943	21 July 1943	
Name & hull number	*Louisiana* (BB-71)		
Builder	Norfolk Navy Yard		
Authorized	19 July 1940		
Cancelled	21 July 1943		

Displacement

Montana and *Ohio* (nominal design values)
60,500 tons (61,471 m.t.) Standard
70,500 tons (71,631 m.t.) Full load

Maine, New Hampshire, and *Louisiana* (from detail weight summary)
57,772 tons (58,699 m.t.) Light ship
63,221 tons (64,236 m.t.) Standard
70,965 tons (72,104 m.t.) Full load
71,922 tons (73,076 m.t.) Emergency load

Dimensions (All ships)

925' 0.000" (281.940 m) Length overall
890' 0.000" (271.272 m) Waterline length
121' 2.000" (36.932 m) Maximum beam
 29' 11.188" (9.123 m) Mean draft @ 57,534 tons
 35' 1.375" (10.703 m) Mean draft @ 68,317 tons
 36' 10.188" (11.232 m) Mean draft @ 71,922 tons
 33' 2.188" (10.114 m) Maximum draft @ 57,534 tons
 36' 1.937" (11.032 m) Maximum draft @ 68,317 tons
 36' 10.563" (11.244 m) Maximum draft @ 71,922 tons

Hull Characteristics at D.W.L.

Displacement	68,317 tons (69,413 m.t.)
Mean draft	35' 1.375" (10.703 m)
Hull depth amidships	
Freeboard at bow	
Freeboard at stern	
Block coefficient	0.673

Midship Section

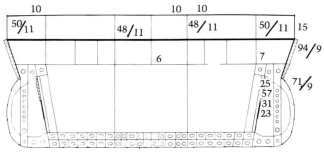

Prismatic coefficient	0.660
Midship section coefficient	1.020
Moment to trim one inch	8,652 foot-tons (one cm: 1,059.39 m-m.t.)
(GM) metacentric heights	8.14' (2.481 m)

Armament (June 1942 design)

Twelve 16-inch/50 caliber guns (Mark 7) (406mm)
Twenty 5-inch/54 caliber guns (Mark 16) (127mm)
Thirty-two 40mm/56 caliber machine guns
Twenty 20mm/70 caliber machine guns

Armor Protection (Refer to plans for arrangement details)

Immunity zone from 18,000 to 31,000 (16,459 to 28,346 m) (Citadel)
U. S. 16"/45 (406mm) firing 2,700 lb. (1,225 kg.) shell
from 16,500 to 34,500 yards (15,087 to 31,546 m) 16/45 2,240 lb. (1,016 kg) shell

Amidships

Belt armor 16.1" tapered to 10.2" on 1" (409mm to 259mm on 25mm) STS, inclined 9°
Inner belt armor 7.2" tapered to 1" (183mm to 25mm), inclined 10°

Deck armor	Centerline	
main	0.75" + 1.5"	(19mm + 38mm)
second	5.8" + 1.25"	(147mm + 32mm)
third	0.62"	(16mm)
Total	9.92"	(252mm)
	Outboard	
main	0.75" + 1.5"	(19mm + 38mm)
second	6.1" + 1.25"	(155mm + 32mm)
third	0.75"	(19mm)
Total	10.35"	(263mm)

Barbette armor
  18"-19.5"-21.3" (457mm-495mm-541mm)

Turret armor
  face plates 18" + 4.5" (457mm + 114mm)
  sides 10.0" (254mm)
  back plates 12.0" (305mm)
  roof plates 9.15" (232mm)

Secondary gun armor
  gun mounts 2.5" (64mm)
  magazines 2.5" (64mm)

Conning tower armor
  sides 18.0" (457mm)
  roof plates 7.75" (197mm)
  bottom plates 4.0" (102mm)
  comm. tube 16.0" (406mm)

Machinery Schematic

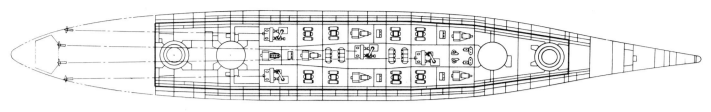

Underwater Protection

Designed resistance . . . pounds TNT
Side protective system depth 20.5′ (6.248 m) @ half draft amidships
S.P.S. designed loading (shell) liquid-liquid-void-void
Total bulkhead thickness . . .″
Bottom protective system depth—amidships
Upper layer—(void)
Lower layer—(liquid loaded)
Total plating thickness . . .″

Tank Capacities

Maine
Fuel oil 7,300 tons (7,417 m.t.) Full load
　　　7,876 tons (7,802 m.t.) Emergency load
Diesel oil 200 tons (203 m.t.) Full load
　　　　203 tons (206 m.t.) Emergency load
Gasoline 35 tons (36 m.t.) Full load
　　　　48 tons (49 m.t.) Emergency load
Reserve feed water 444 tons (451 m.t.)
Potable water 571 tons (580 m.t.) Full load
　　　　639 tons (649 m.t.) Emergency load

Machinery

Boilers	eight two drum boilers fitted with two furnaces and double uptakes.
	pressure: 565 psi (39.724 kg/cm²)
	temperature: 850°F. (454.4°C.)
Turbines	four sets geared turbines
Shaft horsepower	172,000 (174,386 mhp)
	43,000 (43,596 mhp)
Maximum speed	28 knots @ 160 rpm @ 70,500 tons (71,631 m.t.)
Nominal endurance	15,000 nautical miles @ 15 knots
Generators	ten ship's service turbogenerators (1,250 kw)
	two emergency diesel generators (500 kw)
	total ship's service capacity: 12,500 kw, 450 Volts, AC
Propellers	four
Rudders	two

Miscellaneous

Complement 2,247 (113 off./2,134 enl.)—Force Flagship
　　　　2,238 (104 off./2,134 enl.)—Type Flagship
　　　　2,149 (95 off./2,054 enl.)—Division Flagship

Frame spacing 4.0′ (1.219 m)

 Boiler

 Turbine

 Diesel Generator

Evaporator

Frames

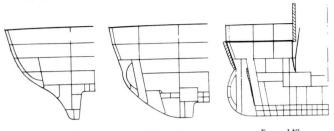  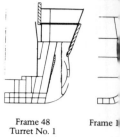

Frame 192	Frame 178	Frame 149 Turret No. 3	Frame 94	Frame 78	Frame 48 Turret No. 1	Frame 1

172

Weight Summary
Maine (BB-69)
May 1942 Design

	Tons	Metric tons	Percent of total
Hull structure (incl. armor)	47,584	(48,347)	82.36
Machinery	5,030	(5,111)	8.70
Outfit & equipment	740	(752)	1.28
Armament	4,018	(4,083)	6.96
Design margin	400	(406)	.70
Light Ship Displacement	57,772	(58,699)	100%
Ammunition	3,423	(3,478)	
Complement	266	(270)	
Supplies & stores	1,706	(1,733)	
Aeronautics	54	(55)	
Standard Displacement	63,221	(64,236)	
Fuel oil	7,300	(7,417)	
Reserve feed water	444	(451)	
Full Load Displacement	70,965	(72,104)	

Body Plan

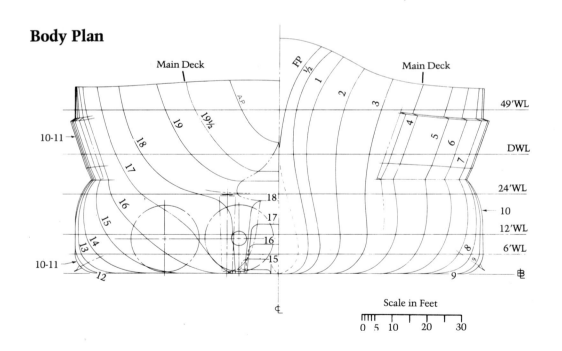

Scale in Feet

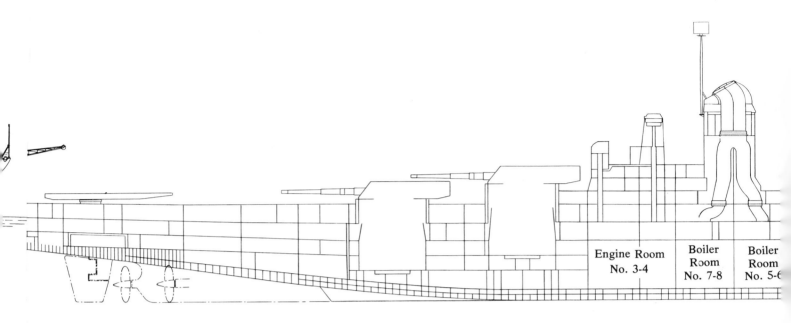

Engine Room
No. 3-4

Boiler
Room
No. 7-8

Boiler
Room
No. 5-6

oard Profile

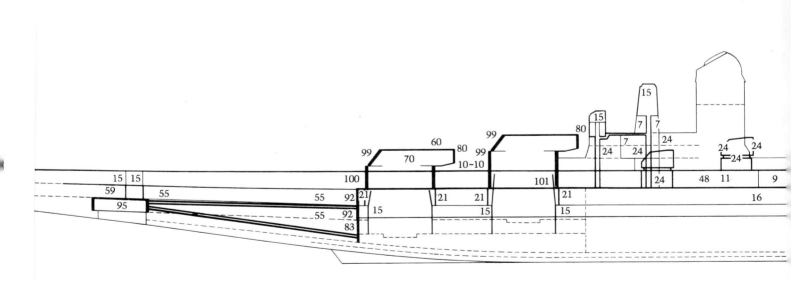

or Profile

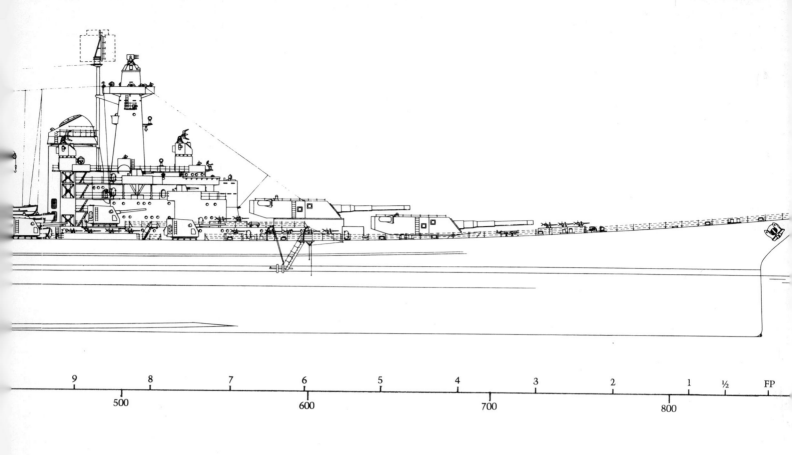

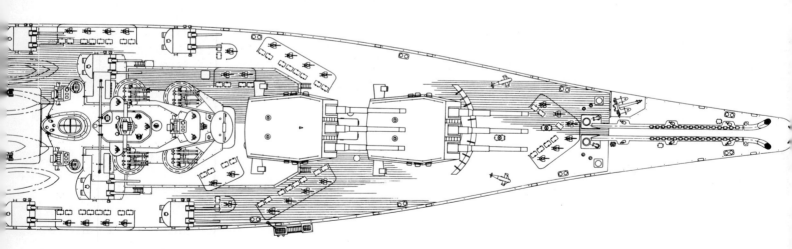

Montana

Outboard Profile

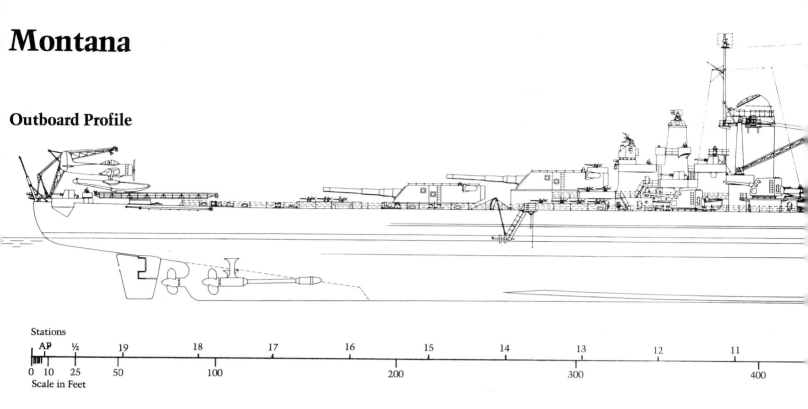

Stations

AP ½ 19 18 17 16 15 14 13 12 11

0 10 25 50 100 200 300 400

Scale in Feet

Overhead View

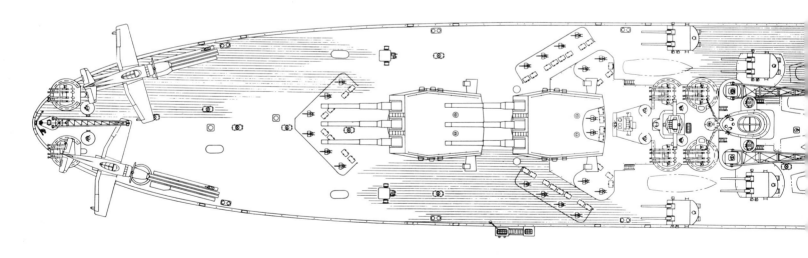

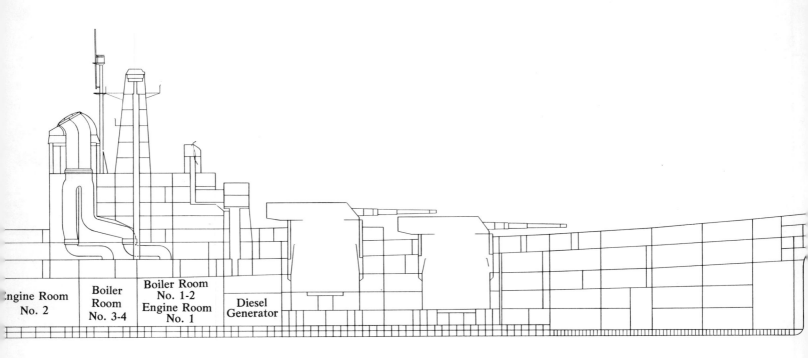

Engine Room No. 2 | Boiler Room No. 3-4 | Boiler Room No. 1-2 Engine Room No. 1 | Diesel Generator

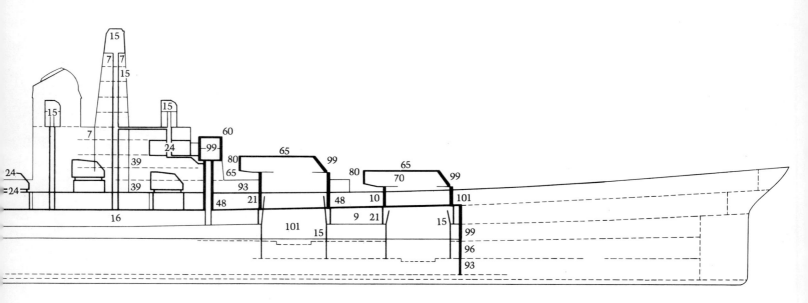

Deck Plans

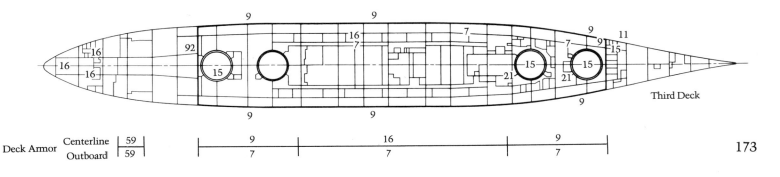

Third Deck

Deck Armor Centerline | 59
Outboard | 59

9 | 16 | 9
7 | 7 | 7

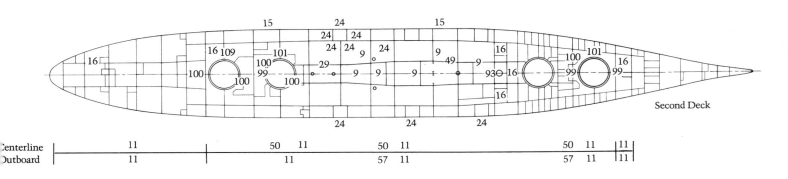

Second Deck

Centerline | 11 | 50 | 11 | 50 | 11 | 50 | 11 | 11
Outboard | 11 | 11 | 57 | 11 | 57 | 11 | 11

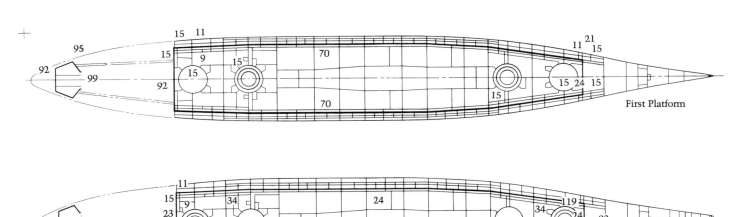

First Platform

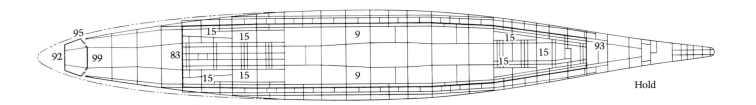

Second Platform

Hold

CHAPTER SIX

The Alaska class

The battlecruisers of the *Alaska* class, too big and expensive to be employed as cruisers yet too weak and vulnerable to operate with battleships, were the least useful of all the capital ships built for the United States Navy during the World War II era. The design and construction of these "white elephants" was largely the result of President Roosevelt's interest, as they had few other enthusiastic backers in the Navy. Although the ships were officially designated "large cruisers," the traditional term, battlecruisers, will be used here, as their design was typical of that type of ship.

Shortly after the outbreak of World War II, the General Board instituted a comprehensive study of all types of naval vessels for consideration for a new and expanded building program. Cruiser studies radically varied in displacement, from the 6,000-ton *Atlanta*-class antiaircraft light cruisers to a 38,000-ton ship armed with twelve 12-inch and sixteen 5-inch guns.

Design Characteristics. As a result of these studies, the Navy decided to further investigate the design of a new class of warships to carry 12-inch guns of a new and powerful type. The characteristics of the alternative design schemes initially evaluated in the development of the design are listed in Table 6-1. Primary concerns in all schemes were the main battery, speed, and protection.

After the initial design studies had been prepared and evaluated, the General Board requested the preparation of an additional series of studies (Table 6-2). The final studies were then evaluated to establish the basic characteristics desired.

Design studies CA-2E and CA-2F differed only in that one had six 12-inch guns, the other had seven. This variation accounted for the 700-ton difference in displacements. Both versions had a triple bottom in way of the magazines, and a double bottom under the machinery. Although bottom structures were carried up to the main armor deck in an effort to provide minimum underwater protection, both schemes were inadequate.

Displacement. The displacement of design scheme CA-2G was 2,700 tons greater than that of CA-2F. The armament of eight 12-inch guns accounted for only 700 tons of this increase; the remaining 2,000 tons resulted from these design modifications intended to improve protection:

- Triple bottom structure extending the length of the machinery spaces.
- Inner bottom (1-inch) in way of machinery spaces.
- Transverse bulkheads (1-inch) in machinery spaces.
- Inner bottom (2-inch) in way of magazines.
- Main side belt increased 2 feet in width over entire length of armor box.

The Alaska-*class battlecruisers paid poor dividends in service for a vast expenditure in building cost. The* Alaska *(CB1) pictured , was in commission for only 32 months after 17 June 1944. The* Guam *(CB2) served only 29 months on active duty. The* Hawaii *(CB3) was never completed. All three ships were scrapped.*

Design Study CA-2F

19 June 1940

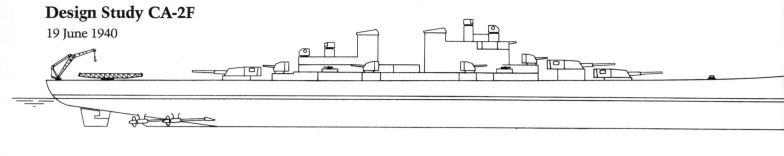

TABLE 6-1

Initial Design Characteristics

Design Scheme			CA-2A	CA-2B	CA-2C
Date	Fall 1939	Fall 1939	17 Jan. 1940	1940	1940
Displacement					
standard	17,300 (17,568)	19,500 (19,797)	25,608 (26,019)	32,550 (33,073)	34,100 (34,648)
design			29,999 (30,480)		
Dimensions					
waterline length			800′ (243.84)		
waterline beam			90′ (27.43)		
draft			26.8′ (8.17)		
Armament					
12″/50 (305mm)	6[1]	8[2]	9[3]	9[3]	9[3]
5″/38 (127mm)					
1.1″/75 (28 mm)					
Armor					
belt—magazines			6.6″ (168) @ 15°		
—machinery			6.6″ (168) @ 15°		
turret faces—triple			7.5″ (191)		
—twin			none		
turret roofs			2.5″ (64)		
turret sides & backs			4.0″ (102)		
barbettes			8.2″ (208)		
conning tower sides			8.2″ (208)		
main deck			1.25″ (32)		1.25″ (32)
second deck			2.5″ (64)		2.5″ (64)
Machinery					
maximum speed	33	33	33	33	33

[1] 2 twin turrets forward, 1 aft
[2] 1 triple, 1 twin turret forward, triple turret aft
[3] 2 triple turrets forward, 1 aft

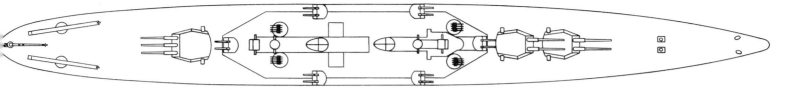

TABLE 6-2

Second Series Design Characteristics, 1940

Design Scheme	CA-2E	CA-2F	CA-2G	CA-2H	CA-2I
Date	7 June	19 June	—June	20 June	—June
Displacement					
standard	24,100 (24,487) [1]	24,800 (25,198)	27,500 (27,941)	27,500 (27,941)	27,100 (27,535)
design	27,600 (28,043)	28,400 (28,855)	31,500 (32,005)	31,500 (32,005)	31,100 (31,599)
Dimensions					
waterline length	740' (225.55)	750' (228.60)	790' (240.79)	790' (240.79)	790' (240.79)
waterline beam	84' (25.60)	84' (25.60)	86' (26.21)	87' (26.52)	86' (26.21)
draft	29' (8.84)	29' (8.84)	30' (9.14)	29' (8.84)	29' (8.84)
Armament					
12"/50 (305mm)	6 [1]	7 [2]	8 [3]	9 [4]	7 [2]
5"/38 (127mm)	12	12	12	12	12
1.1"/75 (28mm)	16	16	16	16	16
Armor		(Note—same for all 3)			
belt—magazines		10.1" (257)		10.1" (257)	10.9" (277)
—machinery		7.7" (196)		7.7" (196)	7.7" (196)
turret faces—triple		12.9" (328)		12.9" (328)	12.9" (328)
—twin		14.2" (361)		None	14.2" (361)
turret roofs		5.0" (127)		5.0" (127)	5.0" (127)
turret sides & backs		6.5" (165)		6.5" (165)	6.5" (165)
barbettes		13.6"-10.6" (345-269)		13.6"-10.6" (345-269)	11.4" (290)
conning tower sides		13.6"-10.6" (345-269)		13.6"-10.6" (345-269)	11.4" (290)
main deck		2.0" (51)		2.0" (51)	2.0" (51)
second deck		3.0" (76)		3.75" (95)	3.75" (95)
Machinery		(Note—same for all 3)			
shaft horsepower		150,000 (152,080)		100,000 (101,387)	120,000 (121,664)
maximum speed		33		30.5	31.5
endurance @ 15 knots		12,000		12,000	12,000

[1] 2 twin turrets forward, 1 aft.
[2] 2 twin turrets forward, 1 triple turret aft.
[3] 1 triple, 1 twin forward, 1 triple turret aft.
[4] 2 triple turrets forward, 1 triple aft.

Protection. Despite the added protection provided in design CA-2G, the underwater protection remained inadequate. The designers decided to investigate the possibility of providing a modest side protective system while retaining the displacement. To attain this added protection, it was necessary to reduce the available shaft horsepower. In the first of these schemes, CA-2H, the provision of only 100,000 shaft horsepower permitted a main battery of nine 12-inch guns and second deck armor thickness of 3.75 inches. Maximum speed was to be 30.5 knots. Design CA-2I, with 120,000 shaft horsepower good for 31.5 knots, had the same protection but a main battery of only seven guns.

These studies made it apparent that the embodiment of all desirable features—speed, offensive power, and armor and underwater protection—would result in a displacement of at least 25,000 tons. As the Board had hoped to obtain a suitable design of less than 25,000 tons, this was a most discouraging conclusion. As a consequence, the General Board reluctantly decided that the new ships would have only the underwater protection provided by a multiple bottom structure.

The preliminary design characteristics promulgated on 30 July 1940 were based on a slightly modified version of scheme CA-2G, with the characteristics shown in Table 6-3. The

TABLE 6-3

Preliminary Design Characteristics, July 1940

Displacement	25,900 tons (26,315 m.t.) light
	27,200 tons (27,636 m.t.) standard
	31,440 tons (31,944 m.t.) design
	32,870 tons (33,398 m.t.) full load
Waterline length	790' (240.79 m)
Waterline beam	86' (26.21 m)
Design draft	29.8' (9.08 m)
Armament	8 - 12"/50 (305mm) (3-2-A-3)
	12 - 5"/38 (127mm) paired
	16 - 1.1"/75 (28mm) quadrupled
Shaft horsepower	150,000 (152,080 mhp)
Maximum speed	33 knots

preliminary design criteria set forth certain fundamental concepts of protection in order to differentiate between these ships and battleships and cruisers. These concepts, followed in the development of all plans, were summarized in a 21 April 1944 memorandum *"Alaska* class— History of Design," submitted to the General Board.

Less than battleship standard

- No armor protection against projectiles falling short that might, by following predicted underwater trajectories, strike below the main side belt.
- Torpedo protection necessarily less.

More than cruiser standard

- Main side belt carried to the second deck between the transverse armor bulkheads, as compared with the third deck amidships and platform deck at the ends in other cruisers.

- Improved side protection (one additional longitudinal bulkhead) provided to minimize damage from misses and to restrict fore-and-aft extent of flooding resulting from torpedo hits.
- Duplication of director leads and splinter-protected crossovers.

In October of 1940 it was decided to maintain constant thickness in the main side belt throughout the length of the armored citadel, a modification necessitated by the installation of 5-inch magazines above the machinery spaces. It was clear that further design compromises would probably be necessary to permit the efficient use of radar equipment then under development.

Revised characteristics issued on 2 June 1941 effected important structural changes. The concept of an equal thickness of belt armor the length of the citadel was formally accepted. Weight previously allocated to the triple bottom in way of the machinery was applied to increasing the scantlings of the double bottom structure, resulting in approximately equivalent underbottom protection. This considerably simplified construction and lowered the center of gravity for the machinery installation. The triple bottom structure was retained in way of the main battery magazines.

TABLE 6-4

Final Design — Basic Characteristics

Displacement
light ship	25,971 tons (26,388 m.t.)
standard	27,000 tons (27,433 m.t.)
full load	34,253 tons (34,803 m.t.)

Dimensions
length overall	808'6" (246.431 m)
waterline length	791'6" (241.249 m)
maximum beam	90'9.375" (27.670 m)
maximum draft	31'9.25" (9.684 m)

Armament
main battery	9 - 12"/50 (305mm)
secondary	12 - 5"/38 (127mm)
antiaircraft	56 - 40mm/56
	34 - 20mm/70

Armor
main side belt	9.0" tapered to 5.0", inclined 10° (229mm − 127mm)
main deck	1.40" (36mm)
second deck — centerline	2.80" + 1.0" (71mm + 25mm)
third deck	0.625" (16mm)

Machinery
shaft horsepower	150,000 (152,080)
maximum speed	33 knots
endurance @ 15 knots	12,000 nautical miles

Detailed weight calculations completed on 31 May had indicated that it was possible to increase the deck armor protection, especially over the magazines, improve the protection over the conning tower communications tube, and increase the main battery to nine guns, at no net increase in displacement. These changes were authorized on 22 July.

The addition of another main battery gun increased the offensive power and resulted in several significant advantages in construction and operation. It simplified the design and reduced the cost of turrets, as only one type was required instead of two. The detail design of the triple turret had progressed to the point that it was demonstrably superior relative to the twin turret in terms of available space and machinery arrangement. The use of one type of turret simplified the spare parts support and maintenance. Designers accepted the fact that the total magazine capacity would probably have to remain at about 1,500 rounds. The final design, as approved, had the basic characteristics shown in Table 6-4.

As the detail design progressed and the construction of the ships started, battle experiences of U. S. and foreign ships led to several important changes, including a much more numerous machine gun battery of 40mm and 20mm weapons. Improved overhead vision from ship control stations was considered so important by June of 1942 that the pilothouse, the "primary ship control station," was relocated from its original position on top of the conning tower to the seventh superstructure level of the forward main battery director tower.

Alaska — Operational History.

The *Alaska*, first battlecruiser built for the U. S. Navy, was laid down at the Camden yard of the New York Shipbuilding Corporation on 17 December 1941. The ship was launched on 15 August 1943 and commissioned on 17 June 1944.

Pacific operations. After training exercises and brief shipyard availabilities, she sailed from Pearl Harbor on 28 January 1945 for combat operations in the western Pacific. She first screened carriers launching raids against Japan and destroyed two Japanese aircraft on 18 March. The next day she helped escort the damaged carrier *Franklin* out of the combat area. On 27 March she bombarded Minami Daito Jima, midway between Iwo Jima and Okinawa, and in late July, with the *Guam*, took part in two sweeps of the East China Sea.

The *Alaska* was operating in the Okinawa area at the time of the Japanese surrender, and on 30 August sailed as part of the Seventh Fleet occupation forces. After supporting minesweeping operations along the Chinese coast up to Chinwangtao, she anchored at Inchon, Korea, on 8 September to support the landing of Army occupation forces. After two weeks, she sailed for Tsingtao to hold that port by a show of force until occupation troops could be landed. On 11 October 1945, Marines landed there unopposed, and two days later the ship was ordered back to the United States.

The *Alaska* was built in the Camden yard of
the New York Shipbuilding Company, and
launched on 15 August 1943. The underway
photographs, made when she was fresh from the
yard, show one marked departure from capital
ship design. There were extensive AA gun
mounts on the fantail, and the aircraft catapults
had been located amidships.

CBG Conversion Design Studies.

In June of 1958, the Bureau of Ships prepared a feasibility study of a guided missile conversion (CBG) of the *Alaska*-class ships. It involved the removal of all guns, and installation of the following missile armament:

- Two Talos twin AA missile systems
- Two Tartar twin AA missile systems
- One ASROC antisubmarine missile launcher
- One Regulus II installation

A modern SQS-26 low frequency long-range sonar system was projected to provide fire control data for the ASROC system and to locate submarine targets for ASW helicopters. Flagship facilities and sophisticated missile fire control systems required by the Talos and Tartar systems were to be provided.

In order to compensate for the removal of the heavy gunnery installations, it was planned to increase the fuel capacity to a total of some 9,700 tons.

The conversion was estimated to cost about $160 million. This prohibitive cost led to evaluation of less extensive changes to the *Alaska* class, completed in October of 1958. The forward batteries were retained, while a reduced guided missile armament was provided aft, as follows:

- Six 12"/50 in two triple turrets forward
- Six 5"/38 in three twin mounts forward
- One Talos twin AA missile system
- One ASROC antisubmarine missile launcher
- Two Regulus II installations with a total of four missiles

The SQS-26 sonar was contemplated, with facilities for two ASW helicopters. The electric generating capacity of the *Alaska* was sufficient for the proposed conversion without any added capability.

This version of the CBG was estimated to cost $82 million. If the ASROC and sonar systems were to be deleted, the conversion cost was estimated at $79,300,000.

Final Disposition.

The *Alaska* was stricken from the Navy List on 1 June 1960. On 30 June 1961 the Lipsett Division of Luria Brothers, New York City, purchased the ship for scrapping.

Guam — Operational History.

The *Guam* was laid down at the Camden yard of New York Shipbuilding Corporation on 2 February 1942. The ship was launched on 12 November 1943 and commissioned on 17 September 1944. She sailed from Pearl Harbor on 3

The Guam, *in starboard bow and starboard quarter views, shows the isolated elements of her superstructure and distinctive mast arrangement. Note numerous small machine gun mounts along the main deck.*

March 1945 and operated in company with the *Alaska* during carrier raids on Japan and sweeps of the East China Sea. While screening carriers off Kyushu on 18 March, the ship destroyed one enemy aircraft.

Subsequent to the Japanese surrender, the *Guam*, as flagship of the North China Force, visited the Asiatic ports of Tsingtao, Port Arthur, and Darien. She arrived at Inchon, Korea, on 8 September and departed on 14 November 1945 for the United States. Her most noteworthy achievement was 61 days of continuous steaming during the Okinawa campaign.

Final Disposition.
The *Guam* was placed out of commission in reserve at Bayonne, New Jersey, on 17 February 1947. Her name was stricken from the Navy List on 1 June 1960, and on 10 July 1961 she was sold to the Boston Metals Company, of Baltimore, Maryland, for scrap.

Hawaii—Partial Construction.
The third ship of this class, the *Hawaii*, was laid down by the New York Shipbuilding Corporation on 20 December 1943, and launched on 11 March 1945. The ship was never completed; 4,241 tons of steel plates and shapes reserved for her were diverted to other construction as early as 1 July 1942.

In September of 1946, there was consideration of converting the ship for use in test and development of guided missiles. This scheme, provisionally designated CB(SW) but never authorized, would have featured eight twin 3-inch/70 caliber gun mounts, with a missile-launching deck forward and two missile-launching pits aft. No armor was required, and installed plating was to be removed as necessary.

With the battlecruiser 85 per cent complete, construction was halted on 16 April 1947. The ship was mothballed with the main-battery turrets in place and the superstructure essentially complete.

Proposed conversion. A conversion of the *Hawaii* to a large tactical command ship (CBC-1) was proposed in August 1951. As 3-inch guns were considered ineffective as the main armament, 5-inch/54 caliber guns would have comprised the main battery. This scheme featured an extensive installation of radar and communication equipment suitable for a flagship. Conversion was actually authorized in 1952, but no contracts were awarded and no work was done.

The *Hawaii* was reclassified CB-3 on 9 September 1954, as all conversion plans had been abandoned. The ship was stricken from the Navy list on 9 June 1958 and scrapped.

Ship Cancellations.
Three more battlecruisers were authorized in 1940, to be built by the New York Shipbuilding Corporation at Camden, New Jersey: the *Philippines*

(CB-4), *Puerto Rico* (CB-5), *and Samoa* (CB-6). None of them were laid down, and construction was formally cancelled on 24 June 1943. Materials allocated for these ships were diverted to aircraft carrier construction.

Armament. Armament characteristics are shown in Table 6-5. The new 12-inch gun, Mark 8, was by far the most powerful weapon of its caliber ever placed in service. It was greatly superior to the earlier Mark 7 (which had been mounted on the *Arkansas*-class battleships completed in 1912), as indicated by the ranges at which given thicknesses of armor could be penetrated (Table 6-6).

TABLE 6-5

Gun Characteristics

Gun	12″/50 (305mm)	5″/38 (127mm)
Shell weight (lb.)	1,140 (517 kg)	53.85 (24.4 kg)
Muzzle velocity (FPS)	2,500 (762 m/s)	2,600 (792 m/s)
Maximum range (yd.)	38,573 (35,271 m)	17,575 (16,070 m)
Maximum elevation	45°	85°
Gun	40mm/56 (1.57″)	20mm/70 (0.79″)
Shell weight (lb.)	1.98 (0.90 kg)	0.27 (0.12 kg)
Muzzle velocity (FPS)	2,890 (881 m/s)	2,740 (835 m/s)
Maximum range (yd.)	11,000* (10,058 m)	4,800 (4,389 m)
Maximum elevation	90°	90°

*Fuze self-destructive at 5,000 yards (4,572 m.)

TABLE 6-6

Armor Penetration — 12″/50 cal. guns

12″/50	(Mark 8)	(Mark 7)
AP shell	1,140 lb. (517 kg)	870 lb. (395 kg)
Muzzle velocity	2,500 FPS (762 m/s)	2,950 FPS (899 m/s)
	vertical (side) armor plates	
13.0″ (330mm)	19,200 yd. (17,556 m)	14,000 yd. (12,802 m)
12.0″ (305mm)	21,400 yd. (19,568 m)	15,700 yd. (14,356 m)
11.0″ (279mm)	23,800 yd. (21,763 m)	17,500 yd. (16,002 m)
10.0″ (254mm)	26,400 yd. (24,140 m)	19,400 yd. (17,739 m)
6.0″ (152mm)	All ranges	34,000 yd. (31,090 m)
	horizontal (deck) armor plates	
3.9″ (99mm)	24,000 yd. (21,946 m)	28,000 yd. (25,603 m)
4.75″ (121mm)	27,400 yd. (25,055 m)	30,700 yd. (28,072 m)

The triple turrets weighed from 922 to 934 tons each. The arc of train was 300 degrees; the maximum training rate was 5 degrees per second. The maximum elevation was 45 degrees; the maximum elevating rate was 11.97 degrees per second. Maximum recoil was 3 feet.

Each gun was located in an individual gun chamber, with separate projectile and powder hoists. The powder hoists had two stages, one extending from the powder-handling level up to the machinery deck level, and the other from the machinery deck level up to the under side of the turret roof plate. The hoist trunks were flametight throughout, with interlocks on the doors to insure flametightness and safety. The rack and pawl type hydraulic projectile hoists, with a maximum capacity of five projectiles each, were located at the rear of each gun chamber with the center hoist nearly vertical and the wing hoists curved to provide suitable locations on the shell-handling platforms.

Secondary battery. The secondary battery consisted of twelve 5-inch/38 caliber dual-purpose guns, Mark 12, in six twin mounts. No changes were formally contemplated in this antiaircraft battery, although the opinion was widespread that such large ships—approaching capital ship size—should have had a more numerous secondary battery. Heavy cruisers of half the displacement were given identical secondary protection.

Machine gun battery. The projected 40mm Bofors machine gun armament incorporated six quadruple mounts, located to minimize gun-crew exposure to blast. As completed, each ship carried fifty-six 40mm guns in fourteen quadruple mounts.

A battery of thirty-two 20mm Oerlikon machine guns was authorized on 4 July 1942. An increase to forty guns was authorized on 24 February 1943, but completed ships carried only thirty-four 20mm in single mounts to make room for more 40mm guns.

As combat experience near the end of World War II showed, the 40mm and 20mm machine guns had inadequate ranges for defense against high-speed aircraft, so a modification to the armament of the *Alaska* and *Guam* was considered. A design study prepared on 12 April 1946 determined that twenty-two 3-inch/50 caliber guns in twin mounts could replace the 40mm batteries. By way of weight compensation, the study projected reducing conning tower armor thickness to 2 inches instead of 5 on the roof, and to 2.5 inches instead of 10.6 on the sides. The net effects of these changes would have been minimal—for the price of a 70-ton increase in the full load displacement and a reduction in conning tower protection, there could have been an enormous increase in effectiveness of the antiaircraft armament.

Aircraft. Originally, the *Alaska*-class ships were to carry six aircraft, four on fantail catapults and two partly dismantled, in small hangars just forward of number 2 turret. The necessity to keep main-battery turrets as low as possible forced designers to relocate hangar and catapults amidships, an unsatisfactory location. The aircraft complement was reduced to four before the ships were completed.

Protection. The designers did not solve the problem of providing adequate protection within the limitations of the desired displacement and other characteristics. The armor provided modest protection against 12-inch guns. The side protection was sufficient only to resist fragmentation from near-miss bombs and mines. The ships had, in effect, no side protective system.

Citadel. The armored citadel provided a limited immunity zone, against a 12-inch gun firing a 1,140-pound shell, of from 23,500 to 25,000 yards. Increased local protection over the magazines moved the outer range limit to 26,600 yards. The ship had inadequate protection against guns of 14-inch or greater caliber.

Side belt. The main side belt, superposed on the shell plating, was 9 inches thick with a taper to 5 inches at its lower edge. The belt armor was inclined some 10 degrees from the vertical, thereby approximating the resistance of 11-inch vertical plates. There was no lower side belt armor. Details of the deck armor protection are shown in Table 6-7.

TABLE 6-7

Deck Armor Thickness

	Amidships	
Main deck	1.40"	(36mm)
Second deck	2.8"-3" + 1.0"	(71mm-76mm + 25mm)
Third deck	0.625"	(16mm)
total (maximum)	6.025"	(152mm)

	Over Magazines	
Main deck	1.40"	(36mm)
Second deck	3.25" + 1.0"	(83mm + 25mm)
Third deck	0.625"-0.75"-1"	(16mm-19mm-25mm)
total (maximum)	6.65"	(169mm)

Turrets and mounts. The main-battery turrets were given the best possible armor protection. The inclined turret front plates, 12.8 inches thick, were proof against 12-inch shellfire at a range of 15,000 yards. The turret roof plates, 5 inches thick, could be penetrated at a range of 28,500 yards. The turret front side plates, 6 inches thick, and the rear side plates, 5.25 inches thick, could be penetrated by 12-inch shellfire at all ranges. The barbettes were similarly protected, with thicknesses of 11, 12, and 13 inches, depending on the location. Below the armor deck, this was reduced to 1.5 inches and eventually to 1 inch.

The dual-purpose gun mounts were protected only against strafing and fragmentation damage, with 1-inch front and roof plates, 0.75-inch side and back plates, and 0.5-inch bottom plates. The 5-inch magazines were shielded by 0.75-inch armor.

Conning tower. The conning tower structure was given an immunity zone of from 24,800 to 28,500 yards. The sides were 10.6 inches thick, the roof was protected by 5-inch armor, and the deck had 2-inch plating. The communications tube was shielded by 9-inch armor down to the main armor deck, and had 0.625-inch splinter protection below that deck.

The forward and after main transverse armored bulkheads, which extended from the armor deck level down to the second platform, were fabricated from 10.6-inch plates, which were immune against 12-inch fire at ranges in excess of 24,800 yards.

The steering gear room was relatively well protected, with 10.6-inch plates on the sides and ends and 1.5-inch plating on the deck. The third deck, directly above, was 4 inches thick. Weight considerations precluded more than 1.5-inch protection for the wiring trunks connecting the steering gear room with the citadel.

Important control positions in the superstructure were given limited protection by plating varying from 0.625 inches to 1.5 inches in thickness. Director positions had 1-inch armor plates.

Side protection. As there was insufficient hull volume to permit an adequate side protective system, the designers compromised by providing limited resistance to underwater damage by a triple hull structure at the sides, with the outboard compartment designed to be kept liquid loaded, while the inboard space was kept void. Over the forward 12-inch turret, the outboard compartment merged with the side shell plating. Amidships, the transverse extent of this system was about 10 feet; it was reduced to about 8 feet over the magazines. Underbottom protection amidships was provided by a double bottom structure with very heavy scantlings. There was a triple bottom structure in way of the magazines.

Underwater protection. Primary underwater protection was provided by the system of subdivision. Between the armored transverse bulkheads, the main divisional bulkheads were watertight to 5 feet above the second deck. At the extremities, where there was relatively little protection, the watertight bulkheads were carried up to the main deck. There was a grave weakness in the system of subdivision in the vicinity of the after main-battery turret. Approximate damaged stability calculations demonstrated that a torpedo hit in this area would jeopardize the transverse stability of the ship, causing it to capsize well before the volume of flooding water would be sufficient to sink it.

Radar. Although radar was not included in the original design, the ships as completed mounted an extensive array of radar systems:

Surface-search radar (2)	SG-1
Air-search radar	SK
Main-battery GFCS (2)	Mark 38
	Mark 8 radar

Secondary battery GFCS (2)   Mark 37
                              Mark 12 radar
MG battery GFCS (40mm)   Mark 57
                              Mark 29/34/39 radars

Note: *Hawaii* (CB-3) was to receive the Mark 13 radar for the Mark 38 GFCS.

The resulting crowding and congestion was criticized by the prospective commanding officer, Captain P. K. Fischler, on 31 March 1944, when he gave the General Board his answer to a request for comments on the new ship type:

> In the *Alaska* and *Guam*, at least, adequate space has not been allocated the CIC. . . . By conference and study we hope we have obtained the best arrangement for the space available, but I must confess that I will have to see the completed installation with the thirty-odd people necessary in the CIC room, before I will be able to believe that it will work efficiently. . . .

Propulsion Plant.

The hull form was more that of a cruiser than a capital ship. High speed was of such paramount consideration that an adequate side protective system was not provided in order to retain the desired speed capability. The design specification stipulated a 33-knot maximum speed with 150,000 shaft horsepower.

Propulsion was by four sets of General Electric cross-compound type geared turbines. The high-pressure turbine was of the 12-stage impulse type, with a double-row first stage and 11 single-row stages. The low-pressure turbine had six single-row, double-flow impulse stages for ahead operation. For astern operation, one double-row impulse stage was fitted at each end of the LP turbine. For full-power ahead operation, the HP turbine turned at 5,327 rpm, the LP turbine at 4,478 rpm, and the propeller shaft at 270 rpm. In full-power astern operation, the turbine turned at 2,614 rpm; the shaft was geared down to 158 rpm.

Steam conditions. Steam, at a maximum pressure of 634 pounds per square inch, was provided by eight Babcock & Wilcox Express boilers, fitted with an integral separately fired superheater of the same basic type installed in new U. S. battleships.

Machinery arrangement. The machinery subdivision was typical of American cruiser design; eight boilers in four fire rooms and two sets of geared turbines in each of two engine rooms. From forward, the arrangement was: fire room, fire room, engine room, fire room, fire room, engine room.

The electrical generating installation was unusual. Each engine room had two General Electric turbogenerators, rated at 1,000 kw, 450 volts AC. Forward and aft of the propulsion plant were diesel generator rooms, with two GE 1,062 kw, 450 volt AC generators driven by Fairbanks-Morse diesel engines in each space. This arrangement was very desirable, for it provided four widely separated sources of power, each capable of providing about one-fourth of the ship's total capacity.

The four-bladed, variable pitch, cast manganese bronze propellers, manufactured by the New York Shipbuilding Corporation, were 14 feet, 10 inches in diameter. The inboard propellers had slightly less pitch than the outboard ones. Shaft diameter at the propellers was 1 foot, 8.125 inches.

Maneuverability. The ships had relatively poor maneuvering characteristics, with a tactical diameter of 870 yards, more than for the *Iowa*-class battleships, which had greater length and displacement. A single-skeg structure and single rudder contributed to this deficiency. The skeg added to the structural strength of the ships, but it is difficult to justify the single rudder.

Summary. Evaluation of the *Alaska*-class battlecruisers shows that they had basic liabilities of the battlecruiser—deficient protection and armament—without the speed advantage previously characteristic of such warships. They were designed in an era when it was possible to give battleships high-speed capabilities.

The greatest deficiency of the design was its vulnerability to underwater attack. There was no conventional side protective system; minimal side protection could have saved the ship from only limited fragmentation damage and flooding. This serious weakness was aggravated by vulnerability to flooding in the vicinity of the after main-battery turret. These ships approached the cost and size of battleships without the protection and offensive power to be expected of such large warships.

Another serious defect was the antiaircraft armament—only equal to that of contemporary heavy cruisers with but half the displacement. A proposal to remove the aircraft and add two twin 5-inch/38 caliber gun mounts was never carried out. Such conversion would have increased displacement by about 50 tons. Cruiser aircraft served little real purpose in 1944-45, and the weight allocated to them could have been better utilized by antiaircraft batteries.

The overall damage-control capabilities of these ships were markedly superior to those of previous cruiser types, although tremendously inferior to those of battleships. In particular, despite the local vulnerability near the after main-battery turret, compartmentation was distinctly superior to that of cruisers, and the detail design of damage-control closures and fittings was excellent.

The designed maximum speed was no greater than that of the *Iowa*-class battleships. This was recognized by Captain Fischler in his letter of 31 March 1944, previously quoted:

> . . . While it is realized that 180,000 horsepower* and 35 knots may be obtained, it would promote a greater feeling of assurance if either this were guaranteed or if, perhaps, 200,000

---

*only in overload condition, and only for a short time.

horsepower were built into the ship. Such horsepower would have resulted in a greater speed differential over the new battleship and aircraft carrier types and greater possibility of useful employment.

The single uptake design, although it improved the arcs of fire of the antiaircraft batteries and provided more deck space, was typical of the difficult design compromises forced on warship designers and led the *Alaska*'s first commanding officer to question

> . . . the soundness of the long horizontal runs for uptakes necessary to obtain the one stack design. These horizontal runs are virtually unprotected, and any damage to them might easily fill a considerable portion of the ship with flue gases. . . .

In his reply to the comments by Captain Fischler, the Chairman of the General Board, Rear Admiral G. J. Rowcliff, concluded:

> Don't overload your ship, for by so doing you make her harder to fight, reduce her armored freeboard and power of survival. Avoid brackets, stanchions, stilts, platforms, hanging gardens, flimsy and inflammable work. [Good advice for any warship skipper!]

> You have a fine ship—the first cruiser to be built absolutely free of old treaty influence. As Captain of a prototype, you have important functions.

Although the *Alaska* carried the formal designation of "large cruiser," the size and displacement approached the battleship scale, and modern naval history has been replete with instances, such as the loss of the *Hood*, demonstrating the dangers inherent in using battlecruisers in company with battleships. The decline of the battleship as a major factor in naval power had long relegated the ships to a somewhat secondary role in naval warfare by the time of the commissioning of these ships. As a result, these "large cruisers" were perhaps not susceptible to the disastrous consequences of their unsuitability for naval combat in terms of their size. However, with only the antiaircraft armament of a heavy cruiser, and main-battery guns vastly inferior to those of the fast battleships of the *Iowa* class, the *Alaska*-class ships were of marginal utility at the time of their completion.

The U. S. Navy would have gained combat strength if it had abandoned construction of the three *Alaska*-class battlecruisers, completing one or two more ships of the *Iowa* class instead. These would certainly have been of greater value to the fleet.

Alaska Class

Name & hull number	Alaska (CB-1)	Guam (CB-2)
Builder	New York Shipbuilding Corp., Camden, N.J.	New York Shipbuilding Corp., Camden, N.J.
Laid down	17 December 1941	2 February 1942
Launched	15 August 1943	12 November 1943
Commissioned	17 June 1944	17 September 1944
Operational	January 1945	February 1945
Disposition	Sold on 30 June 1961 to Lipsett Div., Luria Brothers, New York City. Scrapped.	Sold on 10 July 1961 to Boston Metals Co., Baltimore, Md. Scrapped.

Name & hull number	Hawaii (CB-3)	Philippines (CB-4)
Builder	New York Shipbuilding Corp., Camden, N.J.	New York Shipbuilding Corp., Camden, N.J.
Laid down	20 December 1943	
Launched	11 March 1945	
Disposition	Stricken 9 June 1958. Scrapped.	Construction cancelled 24 June 1943.

Name & hull number	Puerto Rico (CB-5)	Samoa (CB-6)
Builder	New York Shipbuilding Corp., Camden, N.J.	New York Shipbuilding Corp., Camden, N.J.
Disposition	Construction cancelled 24 June 1943.	Construction cancelled 24 June 1943.

Displacement

Alaska and *Guam* (1946)

25,971 tons (26,388 m.t.) light ship
27,000 tons (27,433 m.t.) standard
32,774 tons (33,300 m.t.) normal
34,253 tons (34,803 m.t.) full load

Dimensions

Alaska and *Guam*

808′ 6.000″ (246.431 m) length overall
791′ 6.000″ (241.249 m) waterline length
 90′ 9.375″ (27.670 m) maximum beam
 30′ 9.250″ (9.379 m) maximum draft @ 32,774 tons
 31′ 9.250″ (9.684 m) maximum draft @ 34,253 tons

Hull Characteristics at D.W.L.

Displacement	31,940 tons (32,452 m.t.)
Draft	30′ 2.438″ (9.206 m)
Hull depth amidships	46′ 9.000″ (14.249 m)

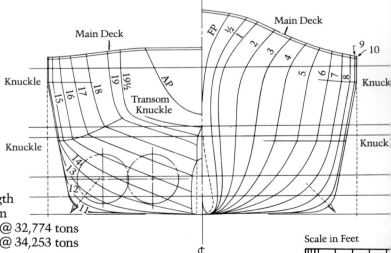

Body Plan

Frames

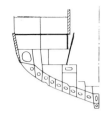

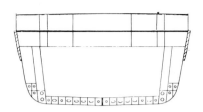

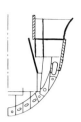

ne 184
eering

Frame 148
Turret No. 3

Frame 98.75
Midships

Frame 62
Turret No. 2

Frame 49
Turret No. 1

Frame 16

193

Freeboard at bow	31′ 2.438″ (9.511 m)
Freeboard at stern	17′ 3.438″ (5.269 m)
Block coefficient	0.5266
Prismatic coefficient	0.5889
Waterplane coefficient	0.7168
Midship section coefficient	0.8943
Tons per inch immersion	120.6 (48.256 m.t./cm.)
Moment to trim one inch	5,140 foot-tons (one cm: 622.36 m-m.t.)
Wetted surface	84,000 sq. ft. (7,804 sq. m.)
Actual GM	8.00′ (2.438 m) @ 32,774 tons (33,300 m.t.)
	8.73′ (2.661 m) @ 34,253 tons (34,803 m.t.)

Armament

Nine 12-inch/50 caliber guns (Mark 8) (305mm)
Twelve 5-inch/38 caliber guns (Mark 12) (127mm)
Fifty-six 40mm/56 caliber guns
Thirty-four 20mm/70 caliber guns
Three floatplanes
Two catapults

Armor Protection (Refer to plans for arrangement details.)

Immunity zone: from 23,500 to 25,000 yards (21,488 to 22,860 m) (citadel)
U. S. 12″/50 (305mm) firing 1,140 lb. (517 kg) shell

Amidships

Belt armor 9.0″ tapered to 5.0″, inclined 10° (229mm to 127mm)

Deck armor

main	1.40″	(36mm)
second	2.80″-3.0″ + 1″	(71mm-76mm + 25mm)
third	0.625″	(16mm)
total	5.825-6.025″	(148-153mm)

Barbettes 11.0″-12.0″13.0″ (279mm-305mm-330mm)

Turret armor
   face plates 12.8″ (325mm)
   front sides 6.0″ (152mm)
   back sides 5.25″ (133mm)
   back plates 5.25″ (133mm)
   roof plates 5.0″ (127mm)

Secondary gun armor
   front plates 1.0″ (25mm)
   side plates 0.75″ (19mm)
   back plates 0.75″ (19mm)
   roof plates 1.0″ (25mm)
   magazines 0.75″ (19mm)

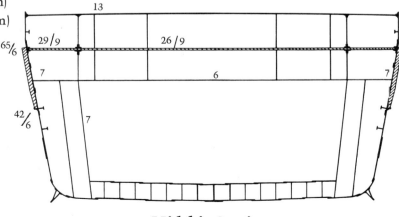

Midship Section

Machinery Schematic

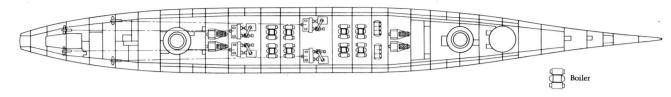

Boiler

Turbine

Diesel Generator

Evaporator

Conning tower armor
    sides 10.6" (269mm)
    roof plates 5.0" (127mm)
    bottom plates 2.0" (51mm)
    comm. tube 9.0" (229mm)

Underwater Protection

Designed resistance . . . pounds TNT
Side protective system depth 10.0' (3.048 m) @ half draft amidships
S.P.S. designed loading (Shell) Liquid-void
total bulkhead thickness — "
Bottom protective system depth 4' 0" (1.219 m) amidships
(double bottom structure, to be kept liquid loaded.)
total plating thickness . . ."

Tank Capacities

Alaska and *Guam*

Fuel oil 3,618.6 tons (3,676.7 m.t.)
Diesel oil 342.4 tons (347.9 m.t.)
Gasoline 31.1 tons (31.6 m.t.)
Reserve feed water 379.6 tons (385.6 m.t.)
Potable water 451.8 tons (459.1 m.t.)

Machinery

Boilers	eight Babcock & Wilcox express type boilers fitted with two furnaces and a single uptake. pressure: 565 psi (39.72 kg/cm²) temperature: 850° F. (454.4°C.)
Turbines	four sets General Electric geared turbines high pressure impulse turbines (12 stages, 5,327 rpm maximum) low pressure impulse turbines (6 stages, 4,478 rpm maximum) astern impulse turbines (2 stages, 2,614 rpm maximum)
Shaft horsepower	180,000 (182,497) overload 150,000 (152,080 mhp) normal maximum
Maximum speed	33 knots @ 270 rpm @ 150,000 shp
Nominal endurance	12,000 nautical miles @ 15 knots
Generators	four ship's service turbogenerators (1000 kw each) four ship's service diesel generators (1062 kw each) . . . emergency diesel generators total ship's service capacity: 8,248 kw, 450 Volts, AC
Propellers	four four-bladed 14' 10" (4.521 m) diameter propellers. Inboard propellers had less pitch than outboard units.
Rudder	one balanced streamline type rudder with a projected area of the profile of about 497.5 sq. ft. (46.22 sq. m.)

Miscellaneous

Complement: 1,517 (73 officers, 1,444 enlisted)
Frame spacing: 4.0' (1.219 m)

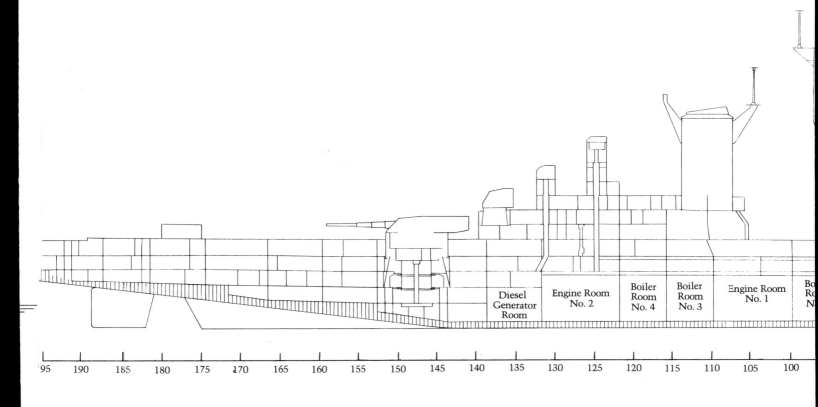

Diesel Generator Room	Engine Room No. 2	Boiler Room No. 4	Boiler Room No. 3	Engine Room No. 1	Bo Ro N

195 190 185 180 175 170 165 160 155 150 145 140 135 130 125 120 115 110 105 100

ard Profile

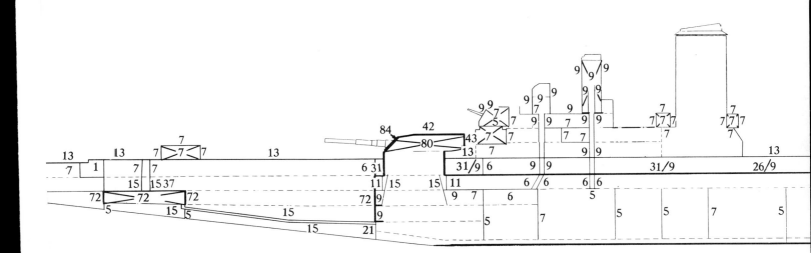

or Profile

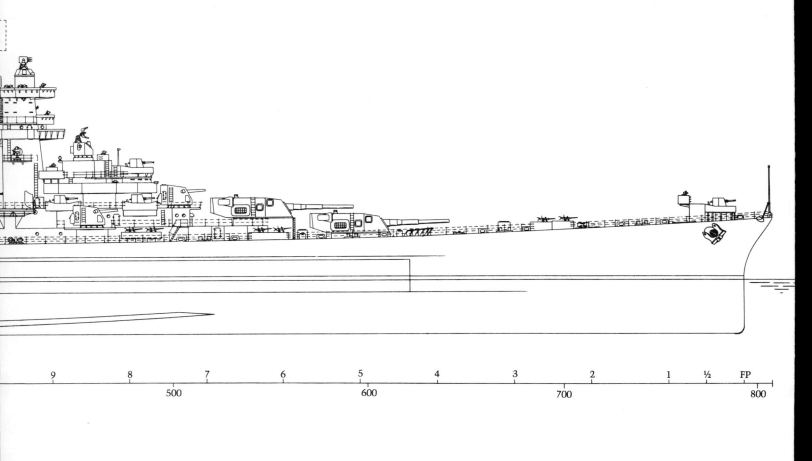

9	8	7	6	5	4	3	2	1	½	FP

500 600 700 800

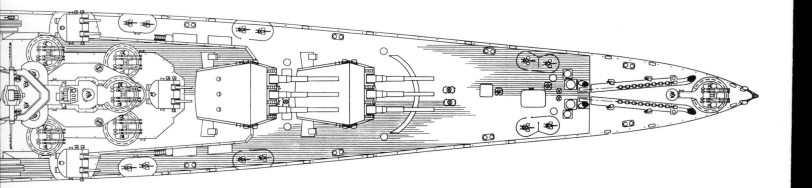

Alaska Class

Outboard Profile

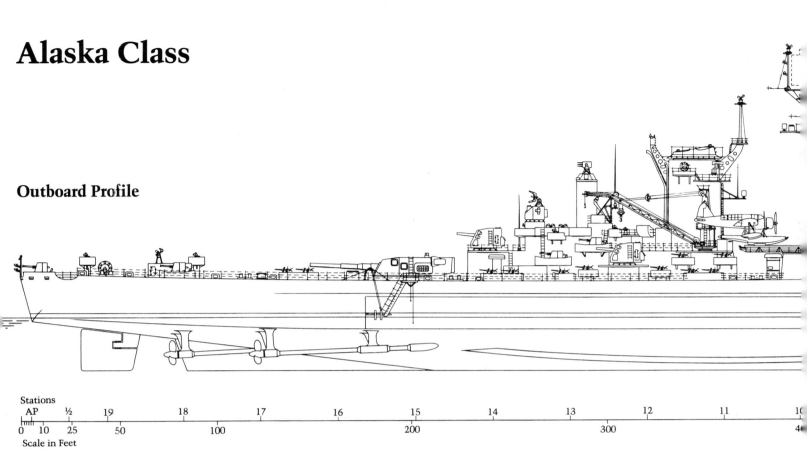

Overhead View

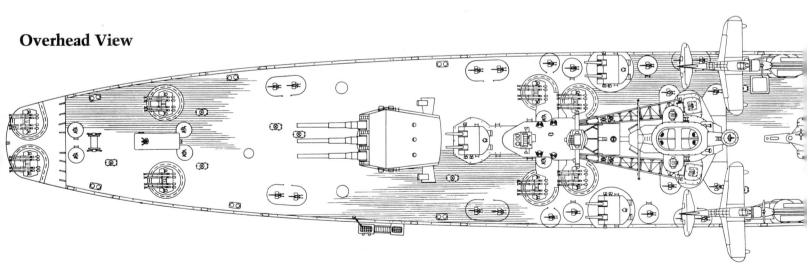

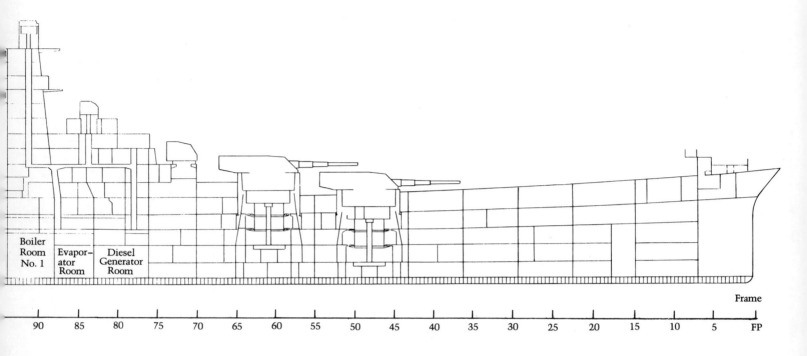

Boiler Room No. 1

Evaporator Room

Diesel Generator Room

Frame

90   85   80   75   70   65   60   55   50   45   40   35   30   25   20   15   10   5   FP

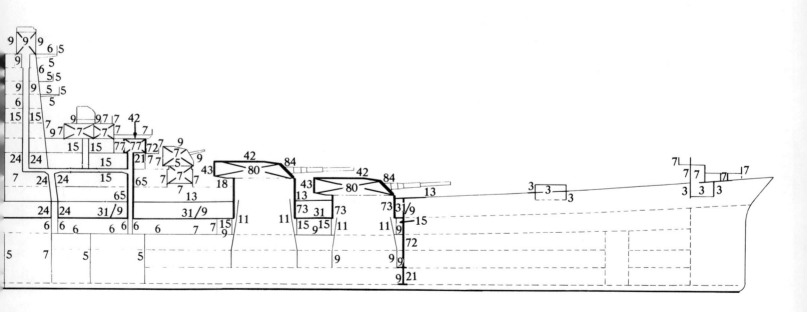

Deck Plans

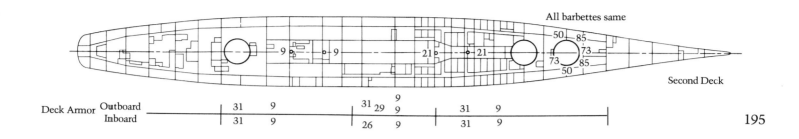

All barbettes same

Second Deck

Deck Armor	Outboard							
	Inboard							

Outboard: 31 9 | 31 29 9/9 | 31 9
Inboard: 31 9 | 26 9 | 31 9

195

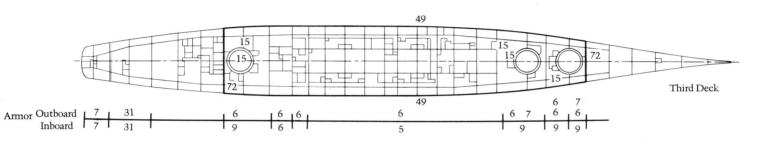

Third Deck

Armor Outboard: 7 31 | 6 | 6 6 | 6 | 6 7 6 6
Armor Inboard: 7 31 | 9 | 6 6 | 5 | 9 9 9

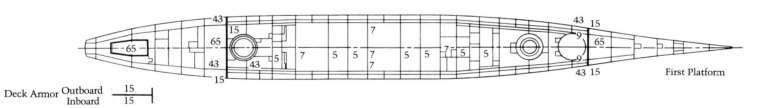

First Platform

Deck Armor	Outboard	15
	Inboard	15

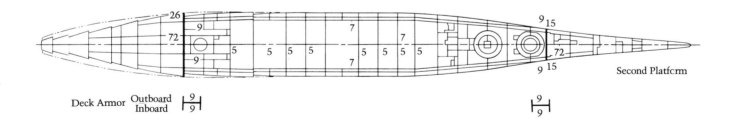

Second Platform

Deck Armor	Outboard	9
	Inboard	9

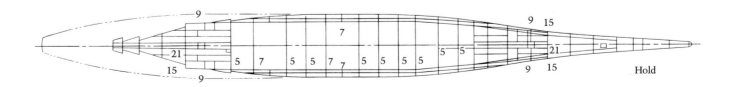

Hold

CHAPTER SEVEN

Conclusion

Capital ships represent an enormous investment of money, material, and personnel. Hence, their construction is almost always the subject of intense public controversy. This was particularly true during the years preceding World War II, when advocates of air power claimed the battleship was obsolete. Their claims were premature, but rapid progress in aircraft design and ordnance technology was destined soon to relegate the battleship to a secondary role in naval warfare.

Limitations on Battleship Design. The Washington and London Naval Treaties and various geographical limitations artificially constrained the designers of most battleships and battlecruisers and complicated the enormously involved design process by forcing difficult compromises affecting the armament, protection, and performance. Most important, of course, was the limit on displacement set by both treaties, which resulted in a partial reversal of the consistent trend towards larger and more powerful warships. Also, dockyard limits (United Kingdom), Panama Canal restrictions on beam (United States and United Kingdom), and draft limitations (Japan, Germany, United States, and United Kingdom) further hampered the design process.

Displacement classifications. In view of the unnatural displacement limitations, one must evaluate the efforts of the naval architects and marine engineers within the limits of the ships concerned, thereby creating several classes of battleships:

- Standard displacements approximating 35,000 tons ("treaty battleships").
- Standard displacements of 40,000-55,000 tons.
- Standard displacements in excess of 60,000 tons.

The United States Navy was the most active of all the navies in the construction of capital ships during the World War II era, both in terms of the number of ships projected, the number of ships completed, and the diversity of ship types. This intense activity produced classic battleships in terms of their general excellence, as well as one superb example of a "white elephant"—the unpopular, politically motivated *Alaska*-class "large cruisers" (battlecruisers) which were of extremely limited value to the Navy.

The capital-ship design philosophy of the United States Navy had traditionally emphasized staying power—the provision of excellent protection and heavy armament—even at the sacrifice of other valuable attributes, such as high speed. Accordingly, American battle-

Battleships fought only a few engagements against enemy ships of their type during World War II. They did conduct numerous shore bombardment operations, but for the most part they had as their primary mission the task of providing air defense for carriers. In many engagements, the battleships never fired their big guns but their extensive secondary and antiaircraft batteries played a critical role in driving off air attack, as shown here.

ships were well armed and well protected, albeit relatively slow, and the new designs continued this emphasis on staying power.

Design philosophy. Despite this emphasis, the U. S. Navy was much attracted by the operational and tactical advantages of high-speed battleships. Fast battleship versions of both the *North Carolina* and the *South Dakota* were proposed, and discarded. The necessary hull length and size of the propulsion plant were prohibitive. The standard displacement limitation of 35,000 tons precluded speeds of 30 knots or more, if adequate armament and protection were to be retained.

Analysis of Ship Types. Although superficially similar in terms of their basic characteristics — the ships were designed to be able to operate together in homogeneous squadrons — the *North Carolina*-class and *South Dakota*-class ships were in fact quite different in many essential aspects.

North Carolina-class ships. The *North Carolina* and the *Washington* were designed to an inferior standard of protection as compared to later battleships. Having initially been projected with an armament of twelve 14-inch/50 caliber guns, the ships were given armor protection adequate to withstand 14-inch shellfire. The side protective system was designed to withstand the detonation of 700 pounds of TNT. Overall, the *North Carolina*-class ships were given only adequate protection, at best.

These first modern American battleships set the pattern for the armament of succeeding designs, with the main battery of nine 16-inch guns supplemented by a dual-purpose battery of twenty 5-inch guns. As the 16-inch/45 caliber gun was a mediocre weapon for its caliber, these battleships were nonetheless powerfully armed.

In general, the *North Carolina* and *Washington* were good but not outstanding examples of the 35,000-ton treaty battleship.

South Dakota-class ships. On the other hand, the four *South Dakota*-class ships were without question the best of all the battleships in their class. By careful design, the Americans succeeded in markedly improving the characteristics of this class as compared to the earlier *North Carolina* class without materially changing the displacement.

The internal arrangement of the *South Dakota* was very different from that of the *North Carolina.* Designed from the outset to withstand 16-inch/45 caliber shellfire, the ships were given similar thicknesses of armor, but with improved arrangement and distribution. Side armor effectiveness was enhanced by increasing its inclination from the vertical from 15° to 19°, while the deck armor performance was improved by concentrating more of the total plating thickness in one deck.

The hull form of the *South Dakota* was wall-sided, the result of relocating the inclined side armor inboard from the shell of the ships. This change added to the stability of the ships in a listing condition, as compared to the hull form of the *North Carolina*, by increasing the effective waterplane area.

The potential performance of the side protective system was augmented by a change in the designed liquid-loading scheme. Whereas the outboard layer on the *North Carolina* had been designed to be kept void, the outboard layer of the side protective system of the *South Dakota* was intended to be kept liquid loaded, thereby lessening the listing effects of flooding within the system after torpedo damage.

The armament was only slightly modified. The dual-purpose guns were arranged a deck higher than in the *North Carolina*, giving better arcs of fire and better potential performance during operations in heavy seas. The *South Dakota* had only sixteen 5-inch guns (the other three ships had twenty each), as she was designed for service as a flagship and required added superstructure volume.

All-in-all, with their 27-knot speed, improved protection, powerful armament, and considerable endurance, the *South Dakota*-class battleships were unquestionably the best of the first generation of battleships designed under the limitations of the Washington Treaty.

Iowa-class ships. When the standard displacement was increased to a more workable 45,000 tons, the U.S. Navy was finally able to design a fast battleship with suitable protection and armament. The classic *Iowa*-class ships were essentially an adaptation and refinement of the *South Dakota* design. The added displacement permitted an added 82,000 shaft horsepower and an increase in the waterline length of some 180 feet. These changes, coupled with the necessary added fuel capacity, accounted for most of the increase in displacement. To all intents and purposes, the *Iowa* was a 33-knot version of the *South Dakota*. Armament and protection were improved in only relatively minor details—most notably by the adoption of a 16-inch/50 caliber gun in place of the 16-inch/45 caliber gun of the earlier ships.

The *Iowa*-class ships featured a remarkable combination of attributes:

- Main-battery firepower at least the equal of that of any other battleship ever built.
- Superb antiaircraft gunnery capability, certainly unmatched by any foreign capital ship to enter service during World War II.
- Excellent armor protection, exceeded only by that of the much heavier *Yamato*.
- The most efficient side protective system ever to be given an American capital ship.
- Maximum speed exceeded by no other battleship.
- Cruising range exceeded by no foreign capital ship that ever entered service.
- Good but not outstanding seakeeping characteristics.
- Excellent maneuverability.

As a consequence, it is reasonable to consider the *Iowa, New Jersey, Missouri,* and *Wisconsin* the best battleships ever built.

Montana-class ships. The *Montana*-class battleships were a manifestation of the traditional U.S. Navy emphasis on capital-ship gunnery and protection. Despite an increase of well

The battleship Arkansas was still burning coal in the early 1920s when this torpedo practice was conducted (top). The pilot of the seaplane observing the run rode out in the open cockpit of his craft, but the hot straight run of the torpedo was indicative of things to come—powerful airborne weapons and highly maneuverable aircraft against which slow-moving battleships were nearly defenseless.

A deckload of 14" projectiles aboard a battleship prior to the 1944 invasion of Guam pointed out one fault in the use of major caliber guns: after about 300 rounds were fired by such a gun, it had to be relined in a time-consuming navy yard overhaul. A carrier delivered bombs to a target by aircraft, and a whole shipload of new aircraft could be flown aboard in a few hours. (Bottom)

200

The main battery fire of battleships was highly
effective in shore bombardment, in World War II,
and the Korean and Vietnam actions, because
of the great accuracy possible through radar fire-
control and air spotting. Long-range gunfire
could be concentrated on a small area, as
shown by the splashes of a broadside fired by the
New Jersey during a practice run.

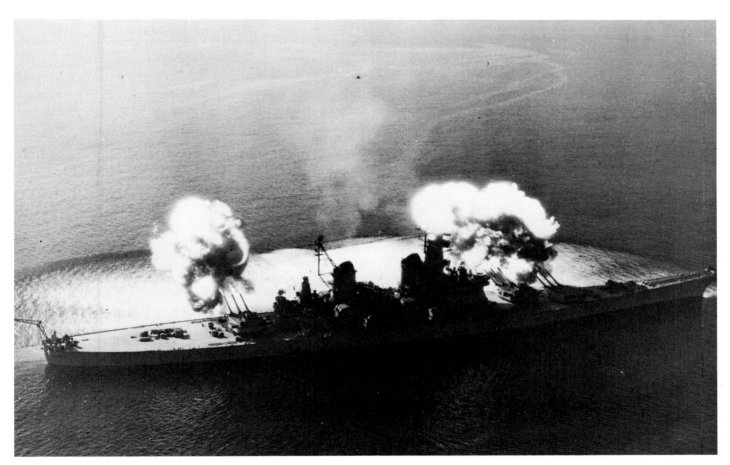

over 10,000 tons in displacement as compared to the *Iowa*, length was only slightly increased and shaft horsepower was actually reduced by 40,000. The result was a marvelously well-protected design with a full dozen of the superb 16-inch/50 caliber guns first given to the *Iowa* class. The *Montana* was the first U.S. Navy warship design to be given a beam barring transit of the Panama Canal. With an excellent main battery, improved antiaircraft armament, and truly outstanding protection and compartmentation, the *Montana* was the most powerful battleship design ever seriously projected for construction. The later German *"H"*-class design studies and the Japanese super-*Yamato* designs were never specifically scheduled for construction. The ships of the *Montana* class were projected for construction, and contract plans were in preparation when the ships were cancelled.

Alaska-class ships. The *Alaska*-class "large cruisers" were, in every sense of the word, battlecruisers, with all the vulnerabilities characteristic of the type but lacking the advantage of superior speed as compared to contemporary battleships. The *Alaska*-class ships could not withstand battleship shellfire at any range and they lacked adequate protection against torpedo attack. At best, these ships could outfight only heavy cruisers. Inspired by President Roosevelt's fascination with naval matters, the *Alaska* and *Guam* were supposedly to provide an "answer" to the raider potential of the German *Gneisenau* and *Scharnhorst.*

By the time the *Alaska* was completed in 1944, both German ships had been destroyed, and the "modern" capital ship was valued as much for its antiaircraft gunnery capability as for its heavy guns. In this respect, the *Alaska*-class ships were very much a liability, as they had only slightly more antiaircraft capability than American heavy cruisers of half the displacement. Hence, the two ships of the class that were completed served for less than three years before they were placed in reserve.

Armament.
The United States Navy initially planned to arm the *North Carolina* with new 14-inch/50 caliber guns, believing the performance of these guns was adequate and opting for a more numerous main battery (twelve guns in three quadruple turrets) on a well-balanced design. The insistence of the Bureau of Ordnance and a growing awareness of the near-universal adoption of either 15-inch or 16-inch guns finally led to the 1938 decision to give the *North Carolina* an armament of nine 16-inch/45 caliber guns.

16-inch/45 caliber. The U.S. Navy has had relatively few guns with truly excellent ballistic performance, apparently in part a result of the emphasis on longer barrel life and mechanical reliability. Certainly, the new 16-inch/45 caliber gun, Mark 6, on the *North Carolina* and *Washington* had only fair ballistic performance. This was a result of the extremely low muzzle velocity (only 2,300 feet per second) when firing the new 2,700-pound armor-piercing shell. Only in the predreadnought era did battleship main-battery guns have such low muzzle velocity.

16-inch/50 caliber. On the other hand, the new 16-inch/50 caliber gun, Mark 7, given the *Iowa* and the *Montana*, with a muzzle velocity of 2,500 feet per second, was one of the truly outstanding battleship guns. To all intents and purposes, the 2,700-pound shell from this gun could match the penetration performance of the 3,220-pound shell fired by the Japanese 18.1-inch/45 caliber gun. This apparent anomaly (for the Japanese shell was heavier and had higher muzzle velocity) was caused by the much greater relative frontal density, in terms of the average weight per unit cross-sectional area, of the American shell.

12-inch/50 caliber. Similarly, the 12-inch/50 caliber gun, Mark 8, on the *Alaska* was the most powerful 12-inch naval gun ever to enter service, again featuring a rather heavy projectile with modest muzzle velocity.

5-inch/38 caliber. The United States Navy consistently favored a dual-purpose armament for its capital ships, cruisers, and destroyers—a decision eased by the availability of a reliable 5-inch/38 caliber dual-purpose gun. Although its ballistics were not outstanding, this gun was service-tested, proven reliable, and provided with excellent fire-control systems. The wartime development of radar fire-control systems and the evolution of the proximity (VT) fuze accentuated the considerable utility of this 5-inch gun.

6-inch/47 caliber. In an effort to further improve the heavy antiaircraft gunnery capabilities of the fleet, the Navy had initiated development of a twin antiaircraft turret installation for the 6-inch/47 caliber rapid-fire gun in September of 1937. Because of the weight penalties and reduced rates of fire characteristic of this heavier installation, as well as its early state of development, the Navy decided to defer the service introduction of this turret. The *Worcester*-class light cruisers finally introduced it into service in 1949.

5-inch/54 caliber. The 5-inch/54 caliber gun, of the type projected for the *Montana* class, first entered service in April of 1945 on the *Midway*-class aircraft carriers. It represented a considerable improvement in performance over earlier U.S. Navy antiaircraft guns, having a much heavier shell with an improved charge, as well as substantially increased range. Unquestionably, the battery of such guns projected for the *Montana* would have been markedly superior in effectiveness to the 5-inch/38 caliber batteries given earlier battleships.

1.1-inch and .50 caliber. The exigencies of the war forced the U.S. Navy to acknowledge the inadequacies of American-developed antiaircraft machine guns. Although the 1.1-inch quadruple machine gun mount had adequate ballistic performance, the weapon was mechanically unreliable and overly complex. The older ".50 caliber" (0.50-inch) machine gun was mechanically sound, but the gun was simply too light to adequately cope with modern aircraft at acceptable ranges. Hence, in the summer of 1940, the Navy started exhaustive investigation of possible alternatives to both guns.

Bofors and Oerlikon. During 1941, the Navy finally obtained licenses for the domestic manufacture of the Swedish 40mm Bofors machine gun and the Swiss 20mm Oerlikon machine gun. Wartime production of the Navy adaptations of these machine guns was truly remarkable:

40mm/56 Bofors	about 39,200 guns
20mm/70 Oerlikon	124,735 guns

The heavy armor of a battleship is seldom apparent in the usual photographs of hulls and turrets. Here, the open door to the New Jersey's conning tower shows the 17.5-inch armor (444mm) protecting that vital area.

The combination of the 40mm Bofors and the 20mm Oerlikon provided indispensible close-in augmentation of the 5-inch dual-purpose batteries on American capital ships. The available close-range antiaircraft firepower was immense.

3-inch/50 caliber. Near the end of the war, it was realized that the performance of the fleet's machine gun batteries was at best marginal against Japanese suicide attacks. As a result, the substitution of the 3-inch/50 caliber twin gun mount for quadruple 40mm machine gun mounts was proposed. The 3-inch rapid fire gun was available, and plans were actually developed for the rearmament of the *Iowa*-class ships, but cost considerations ultimately forced abandonment of the project.

Armor. Traditionally, U.S. Navy battleships have been characterized by very good armor protection. Improvements in gun performance in the decades preceding World War II were such that it was extremely difficult if not impossible to adhere to the traditional requirement that battleship armor be sufficient to withstand guns equivalent to the main battery. As designed, the *North Carolina* did have an adequate immunity zone against the originally proposed armament of 14"/50 guns, but no U.S. battleships armed with the new 16-inch guns were capable of adequate resistance against their main-battery armament.

The armor systems of new U.S. battleships were adequate to withstand the guns listed below:

Ship	Gun		
North Carolina	14"/50	1,500 lb. AP shell	2,800 fps
South Dakota	16"/45	2,240 lb. AP shell	2,520 fps
Iowa	16"/45	2,240 lb. AP shell	2,520 fps
Montana	16"/45	2,700 lb. AP shell	2,300 fps

The following tabulation summarizes the immunity zones (in yards) for BB-55 through BB-71:

Gun Class	14"/50 1,500 lb.	16"/45 2,240 lb.	16"/45 2,700 lb.
North Carolina (BB-55/56)	19,000-30,000 11,000 wide	21,300-27,800 6,500 wide	. . .
South Dakota (BB-57/58/59/60)	. . .	17,700-30,900 13,200 wide	20,500-26,400 5,900 wide
Iowa (BB-61/62/62/64/65/66)	. . .	17,600-31,200 13,600 wide	20,400-26,700 6,300 wide
Montana (BB-67/68/69/70/71)	. . .	16,500-34,500 18,000 wide	18,000-31,000 13,000 wide

Side armor. The side armor systems were inclined outboard from the vertical in an effort to improve the effective resistance of the plating. On the *North Carolina*, this plating was external, as the ship had the belt armor plating attached to the side shell plating above the prominent blister characteristic of the side protective system. Later ships of the *South Dakota* and *Iowa* classes had a wall-sided hull form, with the inclined armor system attached to a bulkhead within the side protective system. The *Montana*, on the other hand, was a composite of the two schemes, with an inclined external main side belt combined with an inclined internal lower side belt system within the side protective system. However, the most prominent protective feature of the *Montana* was the reversion to the blister concept, which provided added support for the main side belt armor and improved resistance to torpedo attack.

Deck armor. Deck armor on all the battleships was substantial, although the details of the arrangement were improved in later designs. Deck armor in the *Montana* was considerably heavier than that of earlier designs. In all cases, the deck armor systems could not withstand direct hits from heavy armor-piercing bombs dropped from high altitudes.

Conning tower. Although the conning tower structures were consistently well protected, stability considerations forced all battleship designers to accept only minimal fragmentation or strafing protection for most other vital spaces in the superstructure. This was a crucial weakness in all battleships, particularly with the progressive adoption of sophisticated electronic systems as the war progressed. In many actions, such as the sinking of the *Bismarck* and the *South Dakota*'s participation in the Naval Battle of Guadalcanal, key fire-control systems were disabled relatively early by enemy gunfire, thus severely reducing or eliminating the ship's ability to effectively defend itself.

Underwater Protection. Except for belt armor location, the structural arrangements of the side protective systems in all modern U. S. Navy battleships were generally similar, featuring a multiple-layer system with varying liquid-loading arrangements, depending on the ship in question. The systems were systematically improved in detail, giving superior resistance to underwater detonations because of refined liquid-load schemes and improved structural arrangements.

Underbottom protection. A double-layer underbottom system was used in all new battleships; the intent was more to restrict and confine damage and flooding than to totally absorb and dissipate the effects of an underbottom detonation. There was no feasible system for restricting the effects of an underbottom detonation within the confines of the protective system.

The *Alaska*-class ships were notable exceptions to the general rule regarding the protection of American capital ships. Their armor was only marginally capable of withstanding even 12-inch shellfire, and their double-layer side protective system was ineffective against the relatively low-powered detonation of an aerial torpedo. The *Alaska* was decidedly vulnerable to all forms of heavy ordnance, far more so than were the battleships.

Stability and subdivision. Stability of all the ships was good and considerably increased resistance to battle damage. In the case of the *Montana*, the designers were so confident in the stability and the side protective system of the ships that they elected to accept longitudinal subdivision of the main machinery spaces, with the attendant implications of off-center flooding.

Propulsion Plants.

The United States Navy was far ahead of most foreign navies in the adoption of modern steam turbine propulsion systems operating at relatively high pressures and temperatures. The Navy's success in solving the technical problems associated with such propulsion systems conferred an enormous advantage on the designers of American warships. The relative advantages are vividly demonstrated by the following comparison of machinery plants of the *Iowa* class and the *Yamato*:

	Iowa	Yamato
Steam pressure (PSI)	565	355.6
Steam temperature (°F.)	850	618
Shaft horsepower	212,000	147,948
Machinery weight (tons)*	5,980	6,599
SHP/ton	35.4	22.4

Although detailed variations occurring between the weight classification systems employed by the two navies prevent an exact comparison of such weights as those given, the SHP/ton ratios effectively demonstrate the advantages resulting from the superior technology available to the U. S. Navy.

Electrical systems. The U. S. Navy had decided before World War II to adopt alternating current for shipboard electrical installations, in preference to the older direct current systems in general use on most foreign warships. Again, a major technological breakthrough resulted in weight and operational advantages. Far more so than with most foreign ships, key auxiliary installations on American capital ships were electric-powered rather than steam- or diesel-driven.

Displacement.

The Washington Treaty defined the standard displacement of a warship as being equal to the full-load displacement less the reserve feed water and the maximum fuel capacity. In a naval architectural sense, the standard displacement is a meaningless number—more pertinent from the technical standpoint are the light ship (total displacement less all stores, fuels, personnel, and other movables), the designed water line (an estimated "average" condition for the ship), and the full load (maximum) displacement.

---

*Including propulsion machinery and liquids therein, auxiliary equipment, and electrical installation.

Critical factors in battleship design were their beam and draft, which affected their ability to enter U. S. ports and drydocks, as well as passage through the Panama Canal. Displacement could also be a problem; in order to dock the old battleship Mississippi *in this floating repair dock in the Philippines in World War II, some 700,000 gallons of fuel had first to be off-loaded.*

Politically, of course, the standard displacement was of considerable importance, as it set the norm against which compliance with the Washington and London Treaties could be measured.

Throughout World War II, there was increasing use of welding in warship construction. This trend was characteristic of American capital ship construction, although key structural and protective system components were riveted throughout the war.

As completed, all American battleships substantially exceeded treaty displacement limits:

Ship Class	Nominal Standard Displacement	Actual Standard Displacement
North Carolina	35,000 tons	38,005 tons [1]
South Dakota	35,000 tons	38,664 tons [2]
Iowa	45,000 tons	49,657 tons [3]

Note: [1] USS *Washington* weight summary, 1941
[2] USS *South Dakota* weight summary, 1942
[3] USS *New Jersey* weight summary, 1943

All U. S. battleships prior to the North Carolina*-class ships were technically obsolete before World War II began. Modernization merely postponed their eventual retirement and scrapping. Some ships were expended in the atomic bomb tests at Bikini. The* New York *(top) and* Pennsylvania *(bottom) survived the bombs, but were later disposed of in tests with conventional weapons.*

208

The second atomic bomb exploded at Bikini Atoll, in July 1946, was detonated under water. The explosion, which lifted the old battleship **Arkansas** *out of the water, demonstrated a new order of power far beyond that inherent in the great guns of the battleships.*

In fairness, one must acknowledge that the displacement limitations were no longer in effect when the ships were completed, but they would have somewhat exceeded the limitations anyway, to some degree. This was true for *all* World War II capital ships supposedly designed and built in conformance with the requirements of the Washington Treaty.

Perhaps the most useful displacement value, in terms of comparing ships, is the fully loaded displacement. As various navies differently define the intermediate loading conditions used in establishing the "designed" displacement used for detailed naval architectural calculations, this data is important in only a general sense.

Summary.

The battleship era of naval history has apparently ended, although four *Iowa*-class ships remain in reserve, theoretically available for reactivation.

The *New Jersey* was reactivated in 1968-69 for service in Vietnam, and provided effective gunfire support before being returned to the reserve fleet. A few years later her firepower and relative invulnerability would unquestionably have saved numerous aircraft and lives, had she still been in service. Too many pilots and costly aircraft were lost during raids near the coast of Vietnam, in areas within reach of the *New Jersey*'s 16-inch guns. This is hindsight, but the fact remains that such a bombardment capability is a vital necessity in many limited war situations.

Practically, it is highly unlikely that reactivation will ever occur, because of the logistic and engineering difficulties of operating warships that are over thirty years old.

This is singularly unfortunate, for in this era of "smart bombs" and guided missiles it seems that the most useful surface warships are either the very large capital ship (such as the carrier or the battleship) or the very small, mobile craft such as high-speed missile boats. Intermediate-sized ships—cruisers and destroyers—are simply incapable of withstanding the explosions of heavy modern ordnance.

An *Iowa*-class battleship could be a most formidable, extremely well-protected adversary for a conventional warfare role in the mid-1970s, given such improvements as the following:

- Refined gunfire control systems.
- Rocket-assisted projectiles for main-battery guns, preferably with some form of terminal guidance. These should at least double the range of the guns.
- Guided missiles for antiaircraft defense.
- Improved electronic systems for communications and for electronic countermeasures (ECM).
- Thorough auxiliary and machinery systems rehabilitation and overhaul.

The World War II operations of American battleships demonstrated that the U. S. Navy had produced a remarkable series of capital ships. The unprecedented offensive power and operational mobility of these ships were of great value in combat operations. Of those U. S. battleships that served in World War II, the *Iowa*-class ships stand out as the best battleships ever built.

From start to finish, the battleship era in the U. S. Navy extended over some half-century of time. Modern battleships were powerful and impressive machines, but the technological advances of the period between two world wars doomed them to obsolescence while they were still on the drawing boards. Scenes such as this have now become history.

The Tosa Experiments

In the decades following the end of World War I, the great naval powers conducted systematic full-scale ordnance trials in efforts to improve their understanding of the complex phenomena involved in the detonation of large explosive charges against the sides of ships, as well as the performance of armor systems in resisting shellfire.

These trials frequently involved former German capital ships, such as the American trials involving the *Ostfriesland*. In some cases, former active service capital ships of the Navy conducting tests were used, such as in the Royal Navy experiment with the *Marlborough*. There were also trials on the incomplete hulks of new construction warships, such as the U. S. Navy's trials on the *Washington* (BB-47).

The Imperial Japanese Navy's *Tosa* experiments, conducted in 1924, are representative of the full-scale tests just mentioned. Although these empirical experiments led to differing conclusions, in general they contributed appreciably to an upgrading of the standard of protection given modern capital ships.

The *Tosa* was laid down by Mitsubishi at Nagasaki, on 16 February 1920, and launched on 18 December 1921. As a consequence of Japanese acceptance of the Washington Treaty, all work on the ship ceased, and eventually it was decided to utilize the hulk in a systematic series of ordnance tests.

The *Tosa* was one of two *Kaga*-class fast battleships. The *Kaga* was ultimately converted into an aircraft carrier and was sunk during the World War II Battle of Midway. These ships were part of the Japanese "Eight-Eight Fleet" building program begun near the end of World War I. The designed characteristics of the *Kaga*-class were as follows:

Displacement	38,500 tons (39,118 m.t.) Standard
	39,900 tons (40,541 m.t.) Normal
Length overall	768' 0" (234.086 m.)
Waterline length	760' 0" (231.648 m.)
Beam	100' 0" (30.480 m.)
Mean draft	30' 9" (9.373 m.)
Armament	10 — 16"/45 (406mm) paired
	20 — 5.5"/50 (140mm) casemated
	4 — 3"/40 (75mm) single
	8 — 24" (610mm) torpedo tubes
Belt armor	11.0" (280mm)
Deck armor	4.0" (102mm)
Shaft horsepower	91,000 (92,262 mph)
Maximum speed	26.5 knots

Japanese experiments with the battleship Tosa *were veiled in secrecy. Similar tests conducted by the U. S. Navy were given ample publicity, although the exact findings were not always released. The battleship* Washington *(BB47), an uncompleted unit of the* Colorado *class, was cancelled on 8 February 1922 when 75 per cent complete, and sunk under the provisions of the Washington Treaty, as a gunnery target, on 25 November 1924.*

During the summer of 1924, the hulk of the *Tosa*, essentially complete up to the main deck, was expended in a series of ordnance tests that had major influences on Japanese capital ship design philosophy. Refer to Figure A-1 for a representation of the internal arrangements of the ship, including transverse sections in way of the contact explosions. Table A-1 gives details on the conditions applying at the time of the five contact explosions, as well as the results of the trials.

Test One confirmed the extreme vulnerability of the bow structure, as a relatively small charge of only 220 pounds caused considerable flooding and extensive local structure damage. The damage was considered sufficient to have prevented the battleship from continuing operations at high speeds.

Tests Two and Five were conducted in way of the forward main battery magazines. Larger charges, of 441 and 331 pounds, respectively, succeeded in defeating the side protective system and causing some flooding beyond the holding bulkhead. The standard Japanese three-compartment, all-void arrangement of the side protective system was shown to be vulnerable to contact detonations of 331 or more pounds of TNT.

Tests Three and Four were conducted slightly aft of amidships in way of the two forward engine rooms. The heavier charges, of 661 and 772 pounds, respectively, succeeded in causing massive flooding and list changes in excess of 6 degrees each, despite the improved resistance of the side protective system amidships.

Despite these four instances of failure of the standard all-void side protective system, the Japanese analysts persisted in employing all-void systems in the design of future capital ships, ultimately including the giants of the *Yamato* class. As will be described later in this discussion, arrangements refinements were adopted as a result of the *Tosa* trials that were believed by the Japanese to provide for considerably improved resistance to torpedo contact detonations.

The *Tosa* was provided with a torpedo magazine in the forecastle. Such magazines had always been considered a grave point of vulnerability in the protection of capital ships, and the Japanese examined this question by causing the detonation of several torpedo warheads within this torpedo room. This trial caused extreme structural damage above the waterline, confirming the menace of torpedo magazine detonations to the safety of capital ships.

Naturally, as a result of this experiment, the Japanese were convinced of the necessity of adequate armor protection over torpedo magazines. As a decidedly second choice, it was considered advisable to provide the equivalent of blow-out panels on one side of the magazine, to limit the fundamental structural damage resulting from the massive detonation of torpedo warheads. Figure A-2 illustrates the results of this test.

Subsequent to the foregoing tests, an 816-pound TNT charge was detonated at a distance of 16.4 feet from the side of the ship. The results of this test are not known.

In a later test, a 16-inch armor-piercing shell was fired to strike the side of the *Tosa* after a short underwater trajectory. The ship had a 4-degree list to port before the test. The projectile hit the water some 82 feet from the ship and hit about 12 feet below the waterline near Frame 228, between the after two turrets. The shell penetrated the hull just below the lower edge of the main side belt, ripping a large hole, and pierced the holding bulkhead before detonating in a main battery magazine (Figure A-3). This single hit permitted the admission of some 3,000 tons of flooding water, which caused a 6-degree increase in the list to port.

As a result of the *Tosa* experiments, the Japanese Navy was particularly concerned about the danger from shells penetrating the vitals of the ship after falling short and following a brief underwater trajectory. Hence, the design of the *Yamato* featured a relatively heavy lower side belt intended to prevent such shells from rupturing the holding bulkhead.

Despite the extensive flooding experienced during the various *Tosa* trials, the Japanese retained the concept of the all-void side protective system, relying on the added lower side belt armor to improve resistance. This practice was at variance with accepted design practice in Western navies, which incorporated both void and liquid-loaded compartments in attempting to maximize the resistance of side protective systems to torpedo attack. Incidentally, such systems were known to the Japanese, for such a relatively modern system as that of the *Maryland*-class battleships of the United States Navy had been publicly described in detail.

The hulk of the *Tosa*, relegated to use as a target for the Hiroshima gunnery school after the systematic trials discussed above, sank in the Bungo Straits on 9 February 1925.

TABLE A-1

Tosa Contact Explosion Trials, June 1924

Test number	One	Two	Three	Four	Five
Date	6 June	8 June	8 June	12 June	13 June
Test charge (lb.)	220.462	440.924	661.386	771.617	330.693
(kg)	(100)	(200)	(300)	(350)	(150)
Position	Frame 57 Stbd.	Frame 87 Port	Frame 192 Stbd.	Frame 192 Port	Frame 87 Stbd.
Depth below	12' 0"	13' 3"	13' 3¼"	16' 0"	20' 9¼"
waterline (m)	(3.658)	(4.039)	(4.045)	(4.877)	(6.097)
Area damaged:					
Ruptured (sq. ft.)	240	240	160	280	190
	(22.297)	(22.297)	(14.864)	(26.013)	(17.652)
Plating dished	750	1400	1700	1200	1300
(m²)	(69.677)	(130.06)	(157.94)	(111.48)	(120.77)
Compartments flooded:					
Rapidly	17	19	26	15	10
Slowly	5	9	1	11	10
Flooding water (tons)	995	1008	1203	1160	726
(m.t.)	(1010.97)	(1024.18)	(1222.35)	(1178.66)	(737.65)
List					
Prior to test	0° 14' Port	1° 40' Stbd.	2° 51' Port	1° 0' Stbd.	3° 50' Port
After test	1° 40' Stbd.	4° 36' Port	5° 22' Stbd.	5° 20' Port	0° 48' Stbd.
Change	1° 54'	6° 16'	8° 13'	6° 20'	4° 38'

216

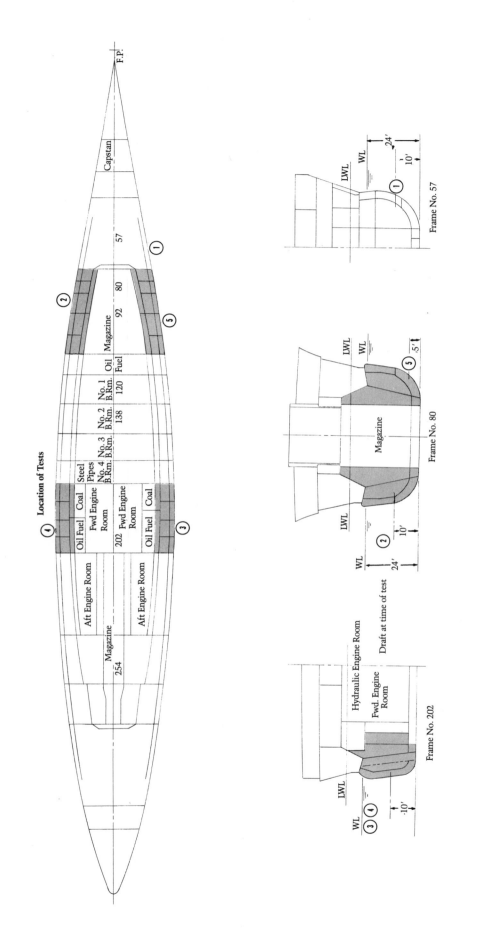

Figure A-1

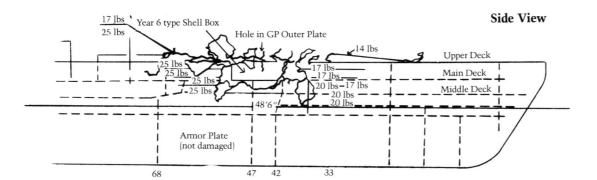

Side View

17 lbs
25 lbs

Year 6 type Shell Box

Hole in GP Outer Plate

14 lbs

Upper Deck

25 lbs
25 lbs

17 lbs
17 lbs
20 lbs — 17 lbs

Main Deck

25 lbs

Middle Deck

25 lbs

20 lbs

48'6"

20 lbs

Armor Plate
(not damaged)

68   47 42   33

**Results of Tests in
Torpedo Tube Room**

Figure A-2

Deck Plan

40 lbs

Upper Deck Side Line
Main Deck Side Line

30 lbs

14 lbs 20 lbs

10 lbs

#1 Turret

10 lbs

10 lbs

64

20 lbs

33

20 lbs

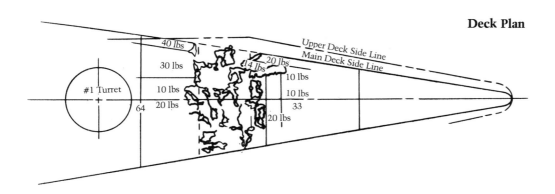

A.

25 meters

16" Shell

17°

WL

11'8"

**Tosa Experiments,
June 1924**

16-inch Shell Test

Figure A-3

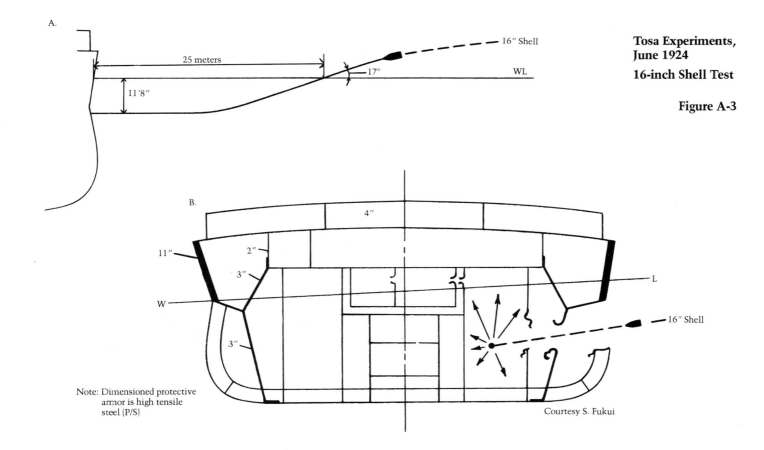

B.

4"

11"

2"

3"

L

W

3"

16" Shell

Note: Dimensioned protective
armor is high tensile
steel (P/S)

Courtesy S. Fukui

Ordance and Fire Control

1 Main battery director
2 Secondary gun director
3 Antiaircraft gun director†
4 Turret officer's booth
5 Optical workshop
6 Turret
7 Sixteen-inch guns
8 Gun chamber
9 Barbette
10 Ammunition hoist
11 Powder hoist
12 Shell hoist
13 Powder magazine
14 Shell magazine
15 Powder magazine, 5" guns
16 Shell magazine, 5" guns
17 Handling room
18 40mm ready service
19 40mm AA gun*
20 40mm magazines†
21 20mm magazines†
22 Chemical warfare material†
23 Magazine lighting control booth
24 Small arms magazine
25 Landing force equipment
26 Small arms magazine†
27 Marine stores
28 Ordnance stores
29 Fire control spare parts†
30 Conning tower tube
31 Fire control station
32 Armory
33 Director tube
33A Sky lookout station
33B After surface lookout station

Ship Control

34 Pilot house
35 Ship conning station
36 Flag conning station
37 Chart room
38 Flag plot
39 Flag plotting room
39A Compass room

Outfit

40 Steering gear room
41 Windlass room
42 Anchor*
43 Rudders*
44 Steering machinery room
45 Boatswain's stores
46 Chain locker
47 Air conditioning machinery†
48 After gyro and compass†
49 Fan room
49A Compressor and air conditioning room
50 Canvas and awning stores and workshop
51 Supply department stores
52 Inflammable liquid stowage
53 Spare parts storeroom
54 Pipe, bar, & plate stowage†
55 Construction and repair stowage†
56 Ship's service stores
57 Miscellaneous stores
58 Repair station†
59 Electrical shop
60 Sand locker
61 Carpenter-shipfitter shop†
62 Blacksmith-coppersmith shop†

63 General workshop†
64 Photo laboratory†
65 Trash burner†
66 Main issue room
67 Tool issue room†
68 Emergency diesel generator room
69 Pump room
70 Boat engine, electrical repair
70A Navigator's storeroom†
70B Paint mixing room†

Offices

71 Captain, navigator's office†
72 Supply office†
73 Gunnery, aviation office†
74 Log room†
75 Engineer's office†
76 Master-at-arms shack†
77 Deck office†
78 Operations office†

Personnel

78A Admiral's cabin
79 Officer staterooms
80 Captain's sea cabin
81 Junior officers†
82 JO bunkrooms
83 CPO quarters
84 Master-at-arms†
85 Mess attendants berthing
86 Crew living space
86A Marines
87 Officers' WR & WC
88 CPO WR & WC†
89 Mess attendant WR & WC†
90 Crew WR & WC
91 Showers†
92 Wardroom messroom
93 CPO messroom
94 Crew messroom
95 Officers' galley†
96 CPO pantry
97 Crew galley
98 Scullery
99 Garbage disposal room†
100 Bakery†
101 Bakery stores†
102 Bread room†
103 Vegetable preparation room
104 Butcher shop†
105 Fruit and vegetable storeroom
106 Meat storeroom†
107 Butter & egg storeroom†
108 Ice machine room
109 Ships store†
110 Barber shop†
111 Post office†

112 Laundry†
113 Laundry stores
114 Laundry receiving room
115 Tailor shop†
116 Cobbler shop†
116A Hospital ward†
117 Sick bay
118 Sick bay bath†
119 Surgical dressing room†
120 Operating room†
121 Dental office†
122 X-Ray darkroom†
123 Alcohol locker†
124 Medical inflammable liquids†
125 Medical stores†
126 Quiet room†
127 Doctors office†
128 Clerical office, medical†
129 Bacteriology laboratory†
130 Dispensary†
131 Treatment room†
131A Sterilizing room†
131B Diet kitchen†
132 Detention cell†
133 Prisoners cell†
134 Athletic gear locker†
135 Provisions issue room†
135A Provisions
136 Ships store†
136A Ships store stores†
137 Wardroom stores†
138 Clothing and small stores store room†
139 CPO storeroom
140 Lucky bag†
141 Battle dressing station†
141A RCM room

Damage control

142 DC central†
143 Repair lockers
144 Repair stations†

Miscellaneous

145 Passages
146 Trunks†

Electrical plant

147 Electrical stores†
148 Transformer room†
149 Forward distribution room†
150 After distribution room
151 Electrical load center†
151A Wiring trunk

Propulsion plant

152 Machinery room
153 Shaft alley†

154 Uptakes
154A Air intakes
155 Boilers**
156 Turbines**
156A Reduction gears**
157 Shafts**
158 Propellers**
159 Evaporators, distillers, emergency diesel room**
159A Engineers stores†

Electronics

160 Radar room
161 Telephone exchange†
162 TBK equipment room†
163 Plotting room†
164 Interior communications room†
165 Emergency radio station†
166 Combat information center†
167 Main communications room
168 Radio central
169 Radio transmitter room†
170 Radar transmitter room†
171 Flag radio room†
172 Radar and radio

Aircraft

173 Bomb magazine†
174 Catapult*
175 Airplane crane*
176 Aviation stores
177 Catapult charge magazine†
178 Airplane crane machinery room

Minesweeping

179 Paravane†
180 Spare & working paravanes†
181 Paravane storeroom

Tanks

182 Fuel oil
183 Fuel oil and salt water ballast†
184 Salt water ballast†
185 Lube oil†
186 Potable water†
187 Reserve feed water†
188 Gasoline tank
189 Void
190 Cofferdam†
191 Overflow tank†
192 Peak tanks
193 Fuel oil service tanks†

*See plan and outboard profile, *South Dakota* class
**See machinery schematic, *South Dakota* class

Representative Battleship Arrangement

In order to provide a better understanding of the internal arrangement of a new construction battleship serving in the U. S. Navy during World War II, an inboard profile of a *South Dakota*-class ship is reproduced here, with a numerical key to indicate the functions of the various compartments and spaces.

The key to the plans is categorized as follows:

Ordnance and fire control
Ship control
Outfit
Offices
Personnel
Damage control
Miscellaneous

Electrical plant
Propulsion plant
Electronics
Aircraft
Minesweeping
Tanks

Note that many of the external features of the ship are also depicted on plan and outboard profiles, and that some elements of the propulsion plant are shown in the machinery schematic. Note also that as the inboard profile depicts a centerline view of the ship, many offices, shops, medical facilities, and storerooms in outboard areas are not keyed to the profile. Such features in the following list are identified with a dagger.

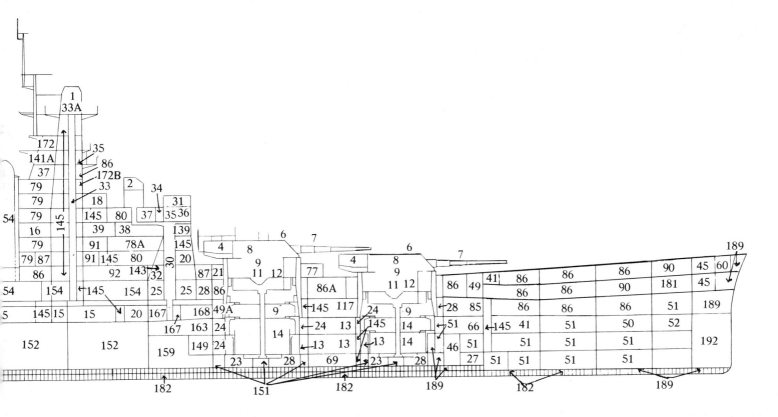

Battleship and Battlecruiser Guns

Battleships and battlecruisers in general have been perhaps the world's most popular warships, in terms of public interest in the ships, their characteristics, and careers. As conventional capital ships served primarily as gun platforms, naturally their big guns were a major factor in their potential combat effectiveness. All other attributes were intended only to allow the ship to determine the time and place of engagement, function effectively in combat, and withstand the destructive efforts of the enemy.

The primary weapons of battleships and battlecruisers, their guns, have been perhaps the subject of the greatest interest and speculation. Unfortunately, as is usually the case in such technical matters, one cannot merely assume that because one ship has 16-inch guns, it is necessarily more powerfully armed than another ship with 15-inch guns. Additionally, despite the potential destructive effects of a given gun, as measured by ballistics and penetration performance, such capabilities are totally wasted if the fire control equipment is unable to accurately direct the gunfire against the enemy.

In order to furnish a better insight into the gunnery capabilities of United States Navy capital ships, and to compare the main battery guns of these ships with those of contemporary foreign ships, this appendix is designed to first discuss in general various aspects pertinent to the question of the effectiveness of capital ship guns in combat, and then provide added comments by way of explaining the detailed gun data tables which follow.

General discussion. Capital ship main battery guns were primarily intended to engage and disable enemy surface ships, and particularly capital ships. For this purpose, the most important performance characteristic was the ability to penetrate the armor protecting the enemy ship. The armor-piercing shells fired by heavy naval guns relied exclusively on kinetic energy to force their way through the armor. The ability of a shell to penetrate armor is a function of a series of factors interrelated in a complex way not thoroughly understood even today (the best formulations for estimating armor penetration are totally empirical as opposed to being derived from theoretical considerations). These basic factors include the following:

- Diameter of the shell.
- Weight of the shell. The greater the specific frontal density—the weight per unit frontal cross section area—the better.
- Striking velocity. The greater the velocity, the greater the kinetic energy and the better the chances of penetration.
- Angle of impact. The more nearly perpendicular the angle of impact of the shell against the armor, the greater the thickness penetrated. If the angle is excessively oblique, the shell may ricochet from the armor.
- Characteristics of the armor. This is the most difficult factor to evaluate when comparing penetration tables for guns of different navies. Differing penetrations may be as much a function of varying qualities of armor as of the basic performance of the gun.

Battleships were designed for one purpose—to serve as mobile, floating platforms on which guns could be mounted. The 16″ guns pictured here comprised the main battery of modern U. S. battleships, but many other types of guns were carried. They are described in the following pages.

- Structural adequacy of the projectile. If the shell breaks up on striking the armor, or the fuze is rendered inert, then the projectile has been defeated by the armor and the armor has accomplished its purpose. As a result, heavy-gun armor-piercing shells are massively constructed, with the explosive charge always comprising less than ten per cent of the total weight of the shell.
- Shape of the projectile. This affects the ballistic performance of the shell, and the penetrative performance is affected by the shape of the shell. Similarly, the adequacy of the cap, which is designed to lessen the tendency of the shell to ricochet, fundamentally influences the ability of the shell to penetrate armor.

The tendency in modern heavy naval guns has been to accentuate penetrative performance by employing as heavy a shell as is possible. This is a compromise judgment, partially sacrificing close-range performance in order to maximize the likelihood of penetration at longer ranges. The high-velocity, lightweight shell (tank guns are classic examples of this approach to armor penetration) is outstanding at the closer ranges, but performance deteriorates severely as range is increased. This is a consequence of the fact that the velocity is such a major factor in the kinetic energy of the projectile, and this deteriorates much more rapidly in the case of lightweight projectiles as compared to the heavier naval armor-piercing shells.

Capital ship main battery guns are also employed against lighter ships and shore targets, where some form of high-explosive shell is more suited to the target than the armor-piercing shell, which has at best a modest lethal radius—the distance in which any exposed personnel and unprotected equipment are subject to almost certain destruction. As a matter of fact, during the course of World War II, bombardment became of such importance to U. S. Navy capital ships that often reduced charges were used to reduce barrel wear. Barrel wear is a fundamental consideration in the performance of heavy guns. Literally, the bore erosion is so significant that the muzzle velocity and accuracy deteriorates with every round that is fired. The reduced velocity was not a particular concern with high-explosive shells—assuming the available ballistic range was adequate—as the striking energy is not at all a factor in the destructive effects of the projectile.

The U. S. Navy adopted the concept of the dual-purpose gun for new construction capital ships, employing the 5-inch/38 caliber gun in all ships actually completed. Antiaircraft defense requires a gun large enough to fire a projectile with sufficient destructive effect, while at the same time demanding a gun small enough to have a higher rate of fire to cope with high-speed targets. The result of the compromises required for the dual-purpose gun was a gun with good effectiveness against air targets and fair effectiveness at best against cruiser- and destroyer-sized surface targets.

Antiaircraft projectiles are only as effective as their fuzes. For the heavier guns, such as the 5-inch, a direct hit on an aircraft is highly unlikely. As a result, the mechanical time fuze provides for a delay in detonation of the shell until it reaches the predicted location of the aircraft. The inevitable time lag inherent in firing at ranges of several thousands of yards makes this prediction evolution a chancy process at best. Hence, the U. S. development of the variable time (proximity) fuze, which utilized a small radio transceiver inside the projectile to sense the proximity of the target and activate the fuze, was a major breakthrough in antiaircraft gunnery, considerably enhancing the effectiveness of the 5-inch guns against air targets.

At times, the proximity or the mechanical time fuze might be used against surface targets, but normally the point-detonating fuze was employed against "soft" targets, while projectiles with a base-detonating fuze were used against armored or reinforced structures.

Antiaircraft machine guns, such as the 40mm and the 20mm, relied on high volumes of fire to contend with high-speed targets. Normally, such machine gun projectiles had only a primitive contact fuze at best, and the smaller-bore weapons, such as the 0.50-caliber, did not have explosive shells.

The great intangible in evaluating gunnery systems is the relative capabilities of the fire control systems of the various navies. This is extremely difficult to quantify, and this study will limit itself to a few most superficial observations. In general, early in the war, the Axis ships had somewhat of an advantage, because of their superb optical range-finding systems. Midway through the war the Allies overcame this advantage with the development of radar gunfire control systems. The Germans did have similar systems but they did not approach the operational effectiveness of U. S. and Royal Navy systems.

In general, U. S. Navy guns can be characterized as quite reliable from a functional standpoint, with generally excellent projectiles and fuzes, although normally American naval guns at best have mediocre ballistic performance. The 16-inch/50 caliber gun on the *Iowa* class is a brilliant exception to this general rule—it was clearly the best battleship gun to enter service, including the 460mm giants carried by the Japanese *Yamato* and *Musashi*.

Discussion of Gun Data Tables. Tables C-1 through C-10 present data on contemporary foreign capital ship main battery guns. Tables C-11 through C-21 present similar information on U. S. Navy capital ship main battery, secondary battery, and antiaircraft machine guns. These tables are intended to give a detailed comparison of the relative characteristics of capital ship main battery guns, with a secondary detailing of U. S. Navy dual-purpose and antiaircraft machine gun characteristics. They are organized as follows:

- Projectiles. Types of shells, their weights, and the weights of the bursting charges.
- Range Table Data. Shell weight, muzzle velocity, and ranges for various firing elevations. Wherever possible, new gun muzzle velocities are given.
- Armor penetration. For a given shell weight, data for penetration of vertical and horizontal plates is given, for specified ranges, striking velocities, and angles of fall. To permit comparisons, wherever ballistic data permits, calculated penetrations using a detailed U. S. Navy empirical equation are given. This means such data may not be precisely correct, but it should give a very accurate measure of relative gun performance.
- Mount/Turret Data. Details pertinent physical characteristics and performance data.
- Gun Data. Detailed physical and descriptive characteristics, including propelling charge.
- Interior Ballistics. Muzzle energy, maximum pressure, and approximate barrel life.

U. S. Navy data is exclusively from official sources, while the information for foreign guns is from a variety of official and unofficial but authoritative sources.

TABLE C-1
15"/45 (380mm) Gun

Nation:	France			
Ships Mounting:	*Richelieu, Jean Bart*	Designation:	380 Mle 1935	
Nominal Caliber:	380mm /45	Year of Design:	1935	
Actual Bore:	14.96" (380mm)	Entered Service:	1940	

Projectiles:	O.Pf(RC) KMle 36	O.Pf(RC) KMle 43	O.E.A. Mle 1945	O.E.A. Mle 1949
Type shell	AP	AP	HE	HE
Shell weight	1,948.888 (884)	1,948.888 (884)	1,948.888 (884)	1,937.86 (879)
Charge	47.840 (21.7)	44.092 (20)	136.687 (62)	136.687 (62)

Range Table Data:

Shell weight	1,948.888 (884)
Muzzle velocity	2,575 (785)
Range @ 45°	—
Range @ 40°	43,099 (39,410)
Range @ 35°	41,065 (37,550)
Range @ 30°	38,058 (34,800)
Range @ 25°	34,361 (31,420)
Range @ 20°	29,910 (27,350)
Range @ 15°	24,716 (22,600)
Range @ 10°	18,373 (16,800)

Armor Penetration:

A.P. Shell Weight	Range	Side Plates	Deck Plates	Striking Velocity	Angle of Fall
1,948.888 (844)	0	*29.43 (748)		2,575 (785)	0°
	24,060 (22,000)	*15.49 14.76 (393) (375)	* 4.15 (105)	1,644 (501)	19.33°
	29,528 (27,000)	*13.12 12.80 (331) (325)	* 5.44 (138)	1,555 (474)	26.83°
	38,277 (35,000)	*10.29 11.02 (261) (280)	* 8.31 (211)	1,552 (473)	40.42°
	41,557 (38,000)	* 9.79 (249)	* 9.27 10.63 (235) (270)	1,585 (483)	43.83°
	43,088 (39,400)	* 8.82 (224)	*10.98 11.81 (279) (300)	1,637 (499)	49.67°

*Calculated penetration, using USN empirical equation. Other data official.

Mount/Turret Data:

Designation	Tourelle quadruple Mle 1936 de 380			
Elevation	35° max.	− 5° min.	5.5°/sec	
Train	5°/sec		Gun recoil	Max. 4.347′ (1.325) Min. 4.101′ (1.250)

Gun Data:

Gun weight	207,522 (94,130) 195,947 (88,880)	(including breech mechanism) (without breech mechanism)	
Gun length	56.617′ (17.257) 58.668′ (17.882)	(breech face to muzzle) (overall)	
Type of breech	Interrupted-thread		
Number of grooves	80	Twist	1/25.57
Length of rifling	557.36″ (14.157)	Length of chamber	122.052″ (3.100)
Chamber volume	27,216 cu. in. (446 cu. dm.)	Powder container	4 bags
Powder charge	564.39 lb. (256) of SD_{19} 610.68 lb. (277) of SD_{21}		

Interior Ballistics:

Muzzle energy	90,002 foot-tons (27,750 ton-meters)
Maximum pressure	19.2 tons/sq. in. (2,940 atmospheres)
Approximate barrel life	200 rounds

Miscellaneous:

Data provided by French naval attache, August 1971.

TABLE C-2
13″/52 (330mm) Gun

Nation:	France		
Ships Mounting:	*Dunkerque, Strasbourg*	Designation:	330 Mle 1931
Nominal Caliber:	330mm/52	Year of Design:	1931
Actual Bore:	12.99″ (330mm)		

Projectiles:	O.Pf(RC) KMle 35	O.E.A. Mle 35
Type shell	AP	HE
Shell weight	1,234.59 (560)	1,150.81 (522)
Charge	44.753 (20.30)	132.277 (60)

Range Table Data:

Shell weight	1,234.59 (560)	1,150.81 (522)
Muzzle velocity	2,854 (870)	2,904 (885)
Range @ 45°	50,142 (45,850)	48,906 (44,720)
Range @ 40°	48,338 (44,200)	47,572 (43,050)
Range @ 35°	45,604 (41,700)	44,401 (40,600)
Range @ 30°	42,104 (38,500)	41,032 (37,520)
Range @ 25°	37,992 (34,740)	37,073 (33,900)
Range @ 20°	33,191 (30,350)	32,524 (29,740)
Range @ 15°	27,603 (25,240)	27,231 (24,900)
Range @ 10°	20,888 (19,100)	20,779 (19,000)

Armor Penetration:

A.P. Shell Weight	Range	Side Plates		Deck Plates		Striking Velocity	Angle of Fall
1,234.59 (560)	0	*28.08 (713)				2,854 (870)	0°
	25,153 (23,000)	*13.46 (342)	12.60 (320)	* 3.42 (87)		1,660 (506)	18.5°
	30,114 (27,500)	*11.48 (292)	9.45 (240)	* 4.32 (110)		1,558 (475)	25.0°
	38,277 (35,000)	* 9.11 (231)	6.30 (160)	* 6.22 (158)		1,512 (461)	36.83°
	44,291 (40,500)	* 8.07 (205)		* 7.95 (202)	4.53 (115)	1,568 (478)	44.67°
	49,759 (45,500)	* 7.08 (180)		*10.75 (273)	6.69 (170)	1,716 (523)	53.83°

*Calculated penetration, using USN empirical equation. Other data official.

Mount/Turret Data:

Designation	Tourelle quadruple Mle 1933 de 330		
Elevation	35° max.	−5° min.	6°/sec.
Train	5°/sec.		
Rate of fire	2.73 rounds/minute	Gun recoil	Max. 3.773′ (1.150) Min. 3.609′ (1.100)

Gun data:

Gun weight	155,503 (70,535) 148,889 (67,535)	(including breech mechanism) (without breech mechanism)	
Gun length	54.609′ (16.645) 56.332′ (17.170)	(breech face to muzzle) (overall)	
Type of construction	Autofrettage		
Type of breech	Interrupted-thread		
Number of grooves	80	Twist	1/25.6
Length of rifling	548.820″ (13.940)	Length of chamber	106.500″ (2.705)
Chamber of volume	17,880 cu. in. (293 cu. dm.)	Powder container	4 bags
Powder charge	423.29 lb. (192) SD$_{19}$		

Interior Ballistics:

Muzzle energy	69,746 foot-tons (21,600 ton-meters)
Maximum pressure	19.84 tons/sq. in. (3.040 atmospheres)
Approximate barrel life	250 rounds

Miscellaneous:

Data provided by French naval attache, August 1971.

TABLE C-3
16″/52 (406mm) Gun

Nation:	Germany			
Ships Mounting:	"H"-class (design)		Designation:	SKC/34
Nominal Caliber:	40.6 cm./		Year of Design:	1934

Projectiles:

Type shell	AP	SAP	HE
Shell weight	2,271.759 (1030)	2,271.759 (1030)	2,271.759 (1030)
Charge			102.295 (46.4)

Range Table Data:

Shell weight	2,271,759 (1030)
Muzzle velocity	2,657 (810)
Range @ 52°	47,025 (43,000)
Range @ 30°	40,245 (36,800)

Armor Penetration:

A.P. Shell Weight	Range	Side Plates	Deck Plates	Striking Velocity	Angle of Fall
2271.759	0	31.72 (806)		2,657 (810)	0°
(1030)	5,000 (4,572)	28.50 (724)	0.53 (13)	*2,418 (737)	* 2.2°
	10,000 (9,144)	25.12 (638)	1.39 (35)	*2,179 (664)	* 5°
	15,000 (13,716)	21.61 (549)	2.07 (55)	*1,940 (604)	* 8°
	20,000 (18,288)	18.84 (479)	3.15 (80)	*1,780 (543)	* 13°
	25,000 (22,860)	15.93 (405)	4.06 (103)	*1,621 (494)	*18.5°
	30,000 (27,432)	13.60 (345)	4.99 (127)	*1,514 (461)	*24.5°
	35,000 (32,004)	11.88 (302)	6.44 (164)	*1,488 (453)	* 32°
	40,000 (36,576)	10.24 (260)	8.51 (216)	*1,514 (461)	* 41°

Calculated, using USN empirical equation. *Estimated value.

Mount/Turret Data:

Designation	40.6 cm. Drh.L. C/?	Weight	1,451.715 (1,475 mt)
Elevation	30° max.		
Rate of fire	1.93 rounds/minute		
Roller path diameter	36.645' (11.2 m.)		

Gun Data:

Gun weight	352,740 (160,000)	(including breech mechanism)
Gun length	64.797' (19.750)	(breech face to muzzle)
	72.835' (21.120)	(overall)
Powder charge	577.609 (262) or	
	771.62 (350) a later, cooler-burning powder, giving same muzzle velocity.	

Interior Ballistics:

Maximum pressure	20.992 tons/sq. in. (33,062 kg/sq. mm)
Approximate barrel life	210 rounds

Miscellaneous:

Oversized liner provided to permit ultimate conversion to 16.65" (420mm) bore. Turrets never completed; completed guns put into service by German army at original 406mm caliber.

TABLE C-4
15"/52 (380mm) Gun

Nation:	Germany		
Ships Mounting:	*Bismarck, Tirpitz*	Designation:	SKC/34
Nominal Caliber:	38 cm.	Year of Design:	1934
Actual Bore:	14.96" (380mm)	Entered Service:	1940

Projectiles:

Type shell	AP	SAP	HE
Shell weight	1,763.70 (800)	1,763.70 (800)	1,763.70 (800)
Charge	41.447 (18.3)	71.871 (32.6)	141.647 (64.25)

Range Table Data:

Shell weight	1,763.70 (800)
Muzzle velocity	2,690 (820)
Range @ 52°	45,932 (42,000)
Range @ 30°	39,589 (36,200)

Armor Penetration:

A.P. Shell Weight	Range	Side Plates	Deck Plates	Striking Velocity	Angle of Fall
1,763.70 (800)	0	29.17 (741)		2,690 (820)	0°
	7,765 (7,100)	24.26 (616)	1.02 (26)	2,297 (700)	4°
	19,685 (18,000)	17.31 (440)	2.89 (73)	1,804 (550)	13°

Note: Penetrations calculated, using USN empirical equation with estimated angles of fall.

Mount/Turret Data:

Designation	38 cm. Drh.L. C/34	Weight	1053.104 (1070)
Elevation	30° max. −5.5° min.	6°/sec	
Train	5.5°/sec		
Rate of fire	2.33 rounds/minute	Gun recoil	3.445′ (1.050m)
Roller path diameter	28.806′ (8.78m)		

Gun Data:

Gun Weight	244,713 (111,000)	(including breech mechanism)	
	60.384′ (18.405)	(breech face to muzzle)	
Gun length	64.433′ (19.63)	(overall)	
Type of construction	Loose liner, built-up		
Number of grooves	90	Twist	1/36 increasing to 1/30
Chamber volume	22,073 cu. in. (361.7 liters)		
Length of rifling	724.596″ (18.405)	Powder container	Case
Powder charge	452.4 (205.2) OR 575.4 (261)*		

*a later, cool-burning powder, giving same muzzle velocity

Interior Ballistics:

Maximum Pressure	20.992 tons/sq. in. (33,062 kg/sq. mm)
Approximate barrel life	240 rounds

TABLE C-5
11.1″/54 (283mm) Gun

Nation:	Germany		
Ships Mounting:	*Scharnhorst, Gneisenau*	Designation:	SKC/34
Nominal Caliber:	28 cm.	Year of Design:	1934
Actual Bore:	11.14″ (283mm)	Entered Service:	1938

Projectiles:

Type shell	AP	SAP	HE
Shell weight	727.53 (330)	694.45 (315)	694.45 (315)
Charge	14.551 (6.6)	35.274 (16)	48.061 (21.8)

Range Table Data:

Shell weight	727.53 (330)	694.45 (315)
Muzzle velocity	2,920 (890)	2,953 (900)
Range @ 40°	45,822 (41,900)	46,479 (42,500)

Armor Penetration:

A.P. Shell Weight	Range	Side Plates	Deck Plates	Striking Velocity	Angle of Fall
727.53 (330)	0	23.79 (604)		2,920 (890)	0°
	5,000 (4,572)	20.46 (520)	0.34 (7)	*2,550 (777)	* 2°
	8,640 (7,900)	18.09 (459)	0.76 (19)	2,297 (700)	* 4°
	10,000 (9,144)	17.15 (436)	0.95 (24)	*2,200 (671)	* 5°
	15,000 (13,716)	14.21 (341)	1.36 (35)	*1,900 (579)	* 8°
	16,514 (15,100)	13.18 (335)	1.63 (41)	1,804 (550)	* 10°
	20,000 (18,288)	11.47 (291)	1.87 (48)	1,640 (500)	*12.7°
	25,000 (22,860)	9.55 (243)	2.37 (60)	*1,475 (450)	* 18°
	30,000 (27,432)	8.08 (205)	2.99 (76)	*1,375 (419)	*24.5°
	35,000 (32,004)	7.12 (181)	3.79 (96)	*1,350 (412)	*31.5°
	40,000 (36,576)	6.50 (165)	4.71 (120)	*1,375 (419)	* 38°
	45,000 (41,148)	5.19 (132)	6.54 (166)	*1,425 (434)	* 50°

Calculated, using USN empirical equation. *Estimated value.

Mount/Turret Data:

Designation	28 cm. Drh.L. C/28	Weight	738.15 (750)
Elevation	40° max. A −8°/B −9°/C −8° min	7.2°/Sec.	
Train		8°/Sec.	
Rate of fire	3.53 rounds/minute	Gun recoil	3.937' (1.200)
Roller path diameter	29.528' (9.0)		

Gun Data:

Gun weight	117,396 (53,520)	(including breech mechanism)
Gun length	47.589' (14.505)	(breech face to muzzle)
	50.574' (15.415)	(overall)
Type of construction	Built-up; loose liner	
Number of grooves	80	Twist 1/50 increasing to 1/35
Length of rifling	461.604″ (11.725)	Length of chamber 103.116″ (2.619 m.)
Chamber volume	10,984 cu. in. (180 liters)	Powder container Cartridge
Powder charge	255.52 (115.9) OR 260.81 (118.3) OR 264.55 (120)	

Interior Ballistics:

Muzzle energy	not available
Maximum pressure	20.992 tons/sq. in. (33.062 kg./sq. mm)
Approximate barrel life	300 rounds

Miscellaneous:

The armored ships preceding *Gneisenau* and *Scharnhorst* were armed with the 28 cm. SKC/28.

TABLE C-6
15"/50 (381mm) Gun

Nation:	Italy		
Ships Mounting:	*Vittorio Veneto* class	Designation:	Model 1934
Nominal Caliber:	381mm/50	Year of Design:	1934
Actual Bore:	15.00" (381mm)	Entered Service:	1940

Projectiles:

Type shell	AP	Common
Shell weight	1,951.09 (885)	1,816.61 (824)
Charge	23.237 (10.540)	66.602 (30.210)

Range Table Data:

	AP	Common
Shell weight	1,951.09 (885)	1,816.61 (824)
Muzzle velocity	2,789 (850)	2,854 (870)
Range @ 45°	50,612 (46,280)	52,788 (48,259)
Range @ 40°	48,884 (44,699)	50,889 (46,533)
Range @ 35°	46,216 (42,260)	47,977 (43,870)
Range @ 30°	42,738 (39,080)	44,222 (40,437)
Range @ 25°	38,572 (35,270)	39,790 (36,384)
Range @ 20°	33,701 (30,816)	34,668 (31,700)
Range @ 15°	27,996 (25,600)	28,675 (26,220)
Range @ 10°	21,019 (19,220)	21,462 (19,625)

Armor Penetration:

A.P. Shell Weight	Range	Side Plates	Deck Plates	Striking Velocity	Angle of Fall
1,951.09 (885)	0	*32.07 (814)		2,789 (850)	0°
	10,936 (10,000)	*25.08 (637)	*1.41 (36)	2,254 (687)	5°
	15,311 (14,000)	*22.58 (574)	*2.12 (54)	2,080 (634)	7.83°
	17,498 (16,000)	*21.25 (540)	*2.48 (63)	1,991 (607)	9.5°
	19,685 (18,000)	*20.06 (510)	*2.86 (73)	1,916 (584)	11.33°
	21,872 (20,000)	*18.89 (480)	*3.26 (83)	1,847 (563)	13.4°
	24,080 (22,000)	*17.84 (453)	*3.69 (92)	1,791 (546)	15.65°
	26,000 (23,774)	13.7 (348)			
	26,247 (24,000)	*16.80 (427)	*4.13 (105)	1,739 (530)	18.05°
	28,434 (26,000)	*15.36 (403)	*4.61 (117)	1,699 (518)	20.67°
	30,621 (28,000)	*14.93 (380)	*5.11 (130)	1,663 (507)	32.4°
	32,808 (30,000)	*14.08 (358)	*5.59 (148)	1,634 (498)	26.1°
	37,183 (34,000)	*11.92 (303)	*7.20 (183)	1,591 (485)	34.33°

*Calculated, using USN empirical equation. Other data official.

Mount/Turret Data:

Designation			Weight	1,570 (1,595.20)	
Elevation	35° max.	6°/Sec.			
Train		6°/Sec.			
Rate of fire	3 rounds/minute		Gun recoil	3.281′ (1.000)	
Roller path diameter	38.7′ (11.896)				

Gun Data:

Gun weight	260,145 (118,000)	(including breech mechanism)
Gun length	64′ 10″ (19,781)	(breech face to muzzle)
Type of construction	Built-up; loose liner	
Type of breech	Interrupted-screw	
Number of grooves	96	Twist 1/30
Length of rifling	624.048″ (15.850)	Length of chamber 120.9″ (3.071)
Chamber volume	27,840.4 cu. in. (456.216 cu. dm.)	Powder container Bag
Powder charge	AP Shell 599 (271.702)	
	COM Shell 608 (275.790)	

Interior Ballistics:

	AP Shell	COM Shell
Muzzle energy	105,252 (32,595)	102,724 foot-tons (31,813 ton-m.)
Maximum pressure	21 tons/sq. in. (3,201 atmospheres)	20 tons/sq. in. (3,049 atmospheres)
Approximate barrel life	110-130 rounds	

Miscellaneous:

Official data provided by Italian Navy using *English* units, vice metric measurements.

TABLE C-7
18.1″/45 (460mm) Gun

Nation:	Japan
Ships Mounting:	*Yamato* class
Nominal Caliber:	406mm
Actual Bore:	18.11″ (460mm)

Designation:	Type 94
Year of Design:	1939
Entered Service:	1941

Projectiles:

	AP	AAC	IS
	Type 91	Type 0	Type 3
Type shell			
Shell weight	3,218.777 (1,460)	2,998.277 (1,360)	2,998.277 (1,360)
Charge	52.6 (23.86)	136 (61.688)	

Note: AAC = Antiaircraft Common
 IS = Incendiary Shrapnel (used for AA)

Range Table Data:

	AP	AAC
Shell weight	3,218.777 (1,460)	2,998.277 (1,360)
Muzzle velocity	2,559 (780)	2,640 (805)
Range @ 45°	45,276 (41,400)	45,600 (41,696)

AA Ceiling: 32,820′ (10,004 m.)

Armor Penetration:

A.P. Shell Weight	Range	Side Plates	Deck Plates	Striking Velocity	Angle of Fall
3,218.777 (1,460)	0	34.00 (864)		2,559 (780)	0°
	5,468 (5,000)	30.03 (763)	0.86 (22)	*2,300 (701)	* 3°
	10,936 (10,000)	26.56 (675)	2.01 (51)	*2,090 (637)	* 6.5°
	16,404 (15,000)	22.77 (578)	3.07 (78)	*1,875 (572)	* 10.8°
	21,872 (20,000)	19.43 (494)	4.30 (109)	1,713 (522)	16.52°
	27,430 (25,000)	16.63 (422)	5.63 (143)	*1,605 (451)	*23.125°
	32,808 (30,000)	14.19 (360)	7.43 (189)	1,558 (475)	31.35°
	38,277 (35,000)	11.95 (303)	9.92 (252)	*1,570 (479)	* 41°

Calculated, using USN empirical equation. *Estimated value.

Mount/Turret Data:

Designation	Triple Turret		Weight	2,730.231 (2,774 m.t.)
Elevation	45° max.	−5° min.	10°/Sec.	
Train			2°/Sec.	
Rate of fire	1.5 rounds/minute		Gun recoil	4.692′ (1.430)
Roller path diameter	40.269′ (12.274 m.)			

Gun Data:

Gun weight	363,762 (165,000)	(including breech mechanism)
	352,739 (160,000)	(without breech mechanism)
Gun length	69,882′ (21.300)	(overall)
Type of construction	Wire-wound and radially expanded; built-up	
Type of breech	Screw	
Number of grooves	72	Twist 1/28
Chamber volume	29,292 cu. in. (480 liters)	Powder container 6 bags
Powder charge	727.53 lb. (330) Cordite	
	6.614 (3) Black Powder ignition charges	

Interior Ballistics:

Muzzle energy	not available
Maximum pressure	20.32 tons/sq. in. (32 kg/sq. mm.)
Approximate barrel life	200-250 rounds

Miscellaneous:

A total of twenty-seven 460mm guns were built, including the nine slated for the *Shinano*. Official Japanese data on penetration of Vickers Hardened (VH) armor:

@ 21,872 yd. 22.3″ (565mm) side
(20,000 m.) 6.6″ (168mm) deck

@ 32,808 yd. 16.4″ (417mm) side
(30,000 m.) 9.1″ (231mm) deck

TABLE C-8
14″/45 (356mm) Gun

Nation:	United Kingdom		
Ships Mounting:	*King George V* class	Designation:	Mark 7
Nominal Caliber:	14″/45	Year of Design:	1936-41
Actual Bore:	14″ (356mm)	Entered Service:	1941

Projectiles:

Type shell	AP HE
Shell weight	1,590 (721.218)
Charge	not available

Range Table Data:

Shell weight	1,590 (721.218)	1,590 (721.218)
Muzzle velocity	(New) 2,475 (754)	(Avg.) 2,400 (732)
Range @ 45°		37,100 (33,924)
Range @ 40°		36,300 (33,193)
Range @ 35°		34,600 (31,638)
Range @ 30°		32,300 (29,535)
Range @ 25°		29,200 (26,700)
Range @ 20°		25,600 (23,409)
Range @ 15°		21,300 (19,477)
Range @ 10°		15,900 (14,539)

Armor Penetration:

A.P. Shell Weight	Range	Side Plates	Deck Plates	Striking Velocity	Angle of Fall
1,590 (721.218)	0			2,400 (732)	0°
	10,000 (9,144)	15.6" (396)	1.15" (29)		
	15,000 (13,716)	13.2" (335)	1.95" (50)		
	20,000 (18,288)	11.2" (285)	2.85" (72)		
	25,000 (22,860)	9.5" (241)	4.0 " (102)		

Mount/Turret Data:

Designation	14-inch Quad Turret 14-inch Twin Turret	Weight	1,582 (1,607.416) 915 (929.68)
Elevation	40° max. −3° min.	8°/Sec.	
Train		2°/Sec.	
Rate of fire	2 rounds/minute/gun	Gun recoil	45" (1.143)
Roller path diameter	35' 4"	(quadruple turret)	

Gun Data:

Gun weight*	207,200 (93,986) 197,688 (89,667)	(including breech mechanism) (without breech mechanism)
Gun length	52' 6" (16.002) (54' 2.8" (16.530)	(breech face to muzzle) (overall)
Type of construction	Inner "A" tube, "A" tube, breech bush, jacket, thrust collar, and breech ring	
Number of grooves	72	Twist RH 1/30
Length of rifling	515.68" (13.098)	Length of chamber 108.54" (2.756)
Chamber volume	22,000 cu. in. (360.515 cu. dm)	Powder container Bag
Powder charge	338.25 lb. (153.43 kg.)	

*Note: Gun weight includes 11.5 ton (11.685 m.t. balance weight)

Interior Ballistics:

Muzzle energy	not available
Maximum pressure	20.5 tons/sq. in. (3,125 atmospheres)
Approximate barrel life	375 rounds

TABLE C-9
15″/42 (381mm) Gun

Nation:	United Kingdom			
Ships Mounting:	*Vanguard*		Designation:	Mark 1
Nominal Caliber:	15″/42		Year of Design:	1912
Actual Bore:	15″ (381mm)		Entered Service:	1914

Projectiles:

Type shell	AP	COMMON	HE
Shell weight	1,938 (879.04)	1,938 (879.04)	1,938 (879.04)
Charge			107 (48.534)

Range Table Data:

	Service (Average)	Supercharge (New)	Supercharge (Average)
Shell weight	1,938 (879.04)	1,938 (879.04)	1,938 (879.04)
Muzzle velocity	2,400 (732)	2,640 (805)	2,575 (785)
Range @ 45°	36,700 (33,558)		
Range @ 40°	35,900 (32,827)		
Range @ 35°	34,300 (31,364)		
Range @ 30°	32,100 (29,352)		
Range @ 25°	29,300 (28,792)		
Range @ 20°	25,900 (23,683)		28,700 (26,243)
Range @ 15°	21,800 (19,934)		
Range @ 10°	16,700 (15,270)		

Armor Penetration:

A.P. Shell Weight	Range	Side Plates	Deck Plates	Striking Velocity	Angle of Fall
1,938 (879.037)	0	*27.07 (687)		2,400 (732)	0°
	10,000 (9,144)	16.6 (422)	1.25 (32)		
	15,000 (13,716)	13.9 (353)	1.95 (50)		
	20,000 (18,288)	11.7 (297)	3.1 (79)		
	25,000 (22,860)	10.2 (259)	4.3 (109)		
	30,000 (27,432)	9.0 (229)	5.7 (145)		
	35,000 (32,004)	8.8 (224)	7.3 (185)		
	0	*29.28 (744)		2,575 (785)	0°
	0	*30.10 (765)		2,640 (805)	0°

*Calculated, using USN empirical equation. Other data official.

Mount/Turret Data:

Designation	Mark I/N		Weight	904 (918.50)
Elevation	30° max.	−4° min.	5°/Sec.	
Train	150° max.	150° min.	2°/Sec.	
Rate of fire	2 rounds/minute/gun		Gun recoil	3′ 10′′ (1.168)
Roller path diameter	27′ 0′′ (8.230)			

Gun Data:

Gun weight	224,000 (101,605)	(including breech mechanism)
	217,616 (98,708)	(without breech mechanism)
Gun length	54′ 2.4′′ (16.520)	(overall)
Type of construction	Built-up; wire-wound	
Type of breech	Welin	
Number of grooves	76	Twist 1/30
Length of rifling	516.33′′ (13.122)	Length of chamber 107.68′′ (2.735)
Chamber volume	30,658 cu. in. (502.395 liters)	Powder container 4 bags
Powder charge	Service 430 lb. (195.04 kg.)	
	Supercharge 490 lb. (222.26 kg.)	

Interior Ballistics:

Muzzle energy	76,000 foot-tons (23,722 ton-meters)
Maximum pressure	19.5 tons/sq. in. (30.71 kg./sq. mm.)
Approximate barrel life	AP 335 rounds
	HE 260 rounds

Miscellaneous:

The obsolescent World War I projectile weighed 1,920 lb. (870.87 kg.). Maximum range with service charge was 30,300 yards (27,706 m.) when fired at 30° elevation.

Supercharge normally was used in ships having turrets with maximum elevation of only 20°.

Same gun was carried in numerous battleships, battlecruisers, and monitors.

Data collated from contributions of Mr. Ian L. Buxton as well as official sources.

TABLE C-10
16″/45 (406mm) Gun

Nation:	United Kingdom			
Ships Mounting:	*Lion* class (design)	Designation:	Mark 2/Mark 3	
Nominal Caliber:	16″/45	Year of Design:	1940-44	
Actual Bore:	16″ (406mm)	Entered Service:	never	

Projectiles:

Type shell	AP
Shell weight	2,375 (1,077.32)

Range Table Data:

Shell weight	2,375 (1,077.32)	2,375 (1,077.32)	
Muzzle velocity	(New) 2,475 (754)	(Avg.) 2,400 (732)	
Range @ 40°		38,200 (34,766)	

Armor Penetration:

A.P. Shell Weight	Range	Side Plates	Deck Plates	Striking Velocity	Angle of Fall
2,375 (1,077.32)	0	*29.03 (737)		2,400 (732)	0°
	10,000 (9,144)	21.0 (533)	1.30 (33)		
	15,000 (13,716)	17.7 (450)	2.22 (56)		
	20,000 (18,288)	15.3 (389)	3.24 (82)		
	25,000 (22,860)	13.2 (335)	4.41 (112)		
	30,000 (27,432)	11.5 (292)	5.73 (146)		
	35,000 (32,004)	10.1 (257)	7.25 (184)		

*Calculated, using USN empirical equation. Other data official.

Mount/Turret Data:

Elevation	40° max.	

Gun Data:

Gun weight	266,000	(including breech mechanism)
	293,000	(including breech mechanism and balance weight)
	260,064	(without breech mechanism)
Gun length	61′ 11.3″	(overall)
Powder container	Bag	
Powder charge	516 (234.052)	

Interior Ballistics:

Muzzle energy	Not available
Maximum pressure	19.5 tons/m²

Miscellaneous:

Both Mark 2 and Mark 3 are similar
Enlarged 14″ (Mark VII)

Some data contributed by John Campbell

TABLE C-11
16″/45 (406mm) Gun

Nation:	U.S.A.		
Ships Mounting:	*Maryland* class	Designation:	Mark 5
Nominal Caliber:	16″/45		
Actual Bore:	16″ (406mm)		

Projectiles:

Type shell	AP Mark 5	AP Mark 3	HC Mark 13	
Shell weight	2,240 (1,016.06)	2,110 (957.10)	1,900 (861.84)	
Charge	33.57 (15,227)		153.58 (69.662)	

Range Table Data: — *Reduced Charge*

	AP Mark 5	AP Mark 3	HC Mark 13	Reduced Charge
Shell weight	2,240 (1,016.06)	2,110 (957.10)	1,900 (861.84)	2,240 (1,016.06)
Muzzle velocity	2,520 (768)	2,600 (792)	2,635 (803)	1,935 (590)
Range @ 45°	40,200 (36,759)	39,700 (36,302)	37,084 (33,910)	25,315 (23,148)
Range @ 40°	39,300 (35,936)	38,600 (35,296)		
Range @ 35°	37,500 (34,290)	36,800 (33,650)		23,900 (21,854)
Range @ 30°	35,000 (32,004)	34,000 (31,090)	35,000 (32,004)	22,500 (20,574)
Range @ 25°	31,900 (29,169)	31,200 (28,529)		20,600 (18,837)
Range @ 20°	27,900 (25,512)	27,400 (25,055)		18,000 (16,459)
Range @ 15°	23,000 (21,031)	22,900 (20,940)		15,000 (13,716)

A.P. Shell Weight	Range	Side Plates	Deck Plates	Striking Velocity	Angle of Fall (°)
2,110 (957.10)	0	29.72 (755)		2,600 (792)	0
2,240 (1016.064)	0	29.68 (754)		2,520 (768)	0
	5,000 (4,572)	26.04 (661)	0.75 (19)	2,253 (687)	3.03
	10,000 (9,144)	22.53 (572)	1.52 (39)	2,007 (612)	5.92
	15,000 (13,716)	19.22 (488)	2.51 (64)	1,796 (547)	10.5
	20,000 (18,288)	16.24 (412)	3.56 (90)	1,629 (497)	16.33
	25,000 (22,860)	13.74 (349)	4.78 (121)	1,522 (464)	23.55
	30,000 (27,432)	11.68 (297)	6.24 (158)	1,472 (449)	31.68
	35,000 (32,004)	10.02 (254)	8.15 (207)	1,486 (453)	49.47
	40,000 (36,576)	8.27 (210)	11.39 (289)	1,586 (483)	51.86

Mount/Turret Data:

Designation	16-inch/45 caliber 2-gun turret, BB-45 class	Weight	880-920 tons (894.08-934.72 m.t.)
Elevation	30° max. −4° min.		
Train	306° max. 279° min.		
Rate of fire		Gun recoil	4′0″ (1.219 m.)
Roller path diameter	27′ 7.25″ (8.414 m.)		

Gun Data:

Gun weight	235,796 (106,959)	(including breech mechanism)
	230,948 (104,757)	(without breech mechanism)
Gun length	—	(breech face to muzzle)
	61' 4" (18.694)	(overall)
Type of construction	Built-up	
Type of breech	Down-swing carrier type	

Number of grooves	not available	Twist	RH 1/50 to 1/32
Length of rifling	616.86" (15.668)	Length of chamber	not available
Chamber volume	23,506 cu. in. (385,263 liters)	Powder container	5 bags

Powder charge	charge 540 lb. (244.94 kg.)
	Ignition charge 4.63 lb. (2.24 kg.)

Interior Ballistics:

Muzzle energy	Not available
Maximum pressure	18 tons/sq. in. (28.35 kg./sq. mm.)
Approximate barrel life	395 rounds

Miscellaneous:

Data specifically for 16"/45 Mark 5 Modification 1. This was relined, slightly different version of the Mark 5 Modification 0, which was a relined version of the 16"/45 Mark 1 Modification 2, which, in turn, was a relined slightly different version of the 16"/45 Mark 1 Modification 0.

In other words, the 16"/45 series (Mark 1, 5, 8) was in reality a progression of relinings of the same basic gun.

TABLE C-12
16"/50 (406mm) Gun

Nation:	U.S.A.		
Ships Mounting:	*Iowa* class, *Montana* class	Designation:	Mark 7
Nominal Caliber:	16"/50	Year of Design:	about 1939
Actual Bore:	16" (406mm)	Entered Service:	1943

Projectiles:

Type shell	AP Mark 8	HC Mark 14 HC Mark 13
Shell weight	2,700 (1,224.7)	1,900 (861.8)
Charge	40.47 (18.357)	153.58 (69.662)

Range Table Data:

		Postwar	Reduced charge			Reduced charge
Shell weight	2,700 (1,224.7)	2,700 (1,224.7)	2,700 (1,224.7)	1,900 (861.8)		1,900 (861.8)
Muzzle velocity	2,500 (762)	2,425 (1,739)	1,800 (549)	2,690 (820)		2,075 (632)
Range @ 45°	42,345 (38,720)		24,181 (22,111)	41,622 (38,059)		27,350 (25,009)
Range @ 40°	41,430 (37,884)	40,185 (36,745)		40,600 (37,163)		
Range @ 35°	39,500 (36,119)			38,650 (35,342)		
Range @ 30°	36,700 (33,558)			36,000 (32,918)		
Range @ 25°	33,300 (30,450)			32,700 (29,901)		
Range @ 20°	29,000 (26,518)			28,800 (26,335)		
Range @ 15°	23,900 (21,854)			24,100 (22,037)		
Range @ 10°	17,650 (16,139)			18,200 (16,642)		

Armor Penetration:

A.P. Shell Weight	Range	Side Plates	Deck	Striking Velocity	Angle of Fall
2,700 (1,224.7)	0	32.62 (829)		2,500 (762)	0°
	5,000 (4,572)	29.39 (747)	.67 (17)	2,280 (695)	2.5°
	10,000 (9,144)	26.16 (664)	1.71 (43)	2,074 (632)	5.7°
	15,000 (13,716)	23.04 (585)	2.79 (71)	1,893 (577)	9.8°
	20,000 (18,288)	20.04 (509)	3.90 (99)	1,740 (530)	14.9°
	25,000 (22,860)	17.36 (441)	5.17 (131)	1,632 (497)	21.1°
	30,000 (27,432)	14.97 (380)	6.65 (169)	1,567 (478)	28.25°
	35,000 (32,004)	12.97 (329)	8.48 (215)	1,555 (474)	36.0°
	40,000 (36,576)	11.02 (280)	11.26 (286)	1,607 (490)	45.47°
	42,345 (38,720)	9.51 (241)	14.05 (357)	1,686 (514)	53.25°

Mount/Turret Data:

Designation	16-inch/50-caliber 3-gun turret, BB-61 class	Weight	1,701-1,708 (1,728.4-1,735.4)
Elevation	45° max. −5° min.	12°/Sec.	
Train	+150° max. −150° min.	4°/Sec.	
Rate of fire	2 rounds/minute	Gun recoil	4'0" (1.219)
Roller path diameter	34'7" (10.541)		

Gun Data:

Gun weight	267,904 (121,515)	(including breech mechanism)
	239,156 (108,483)	(without breech mechanism)
Gun length	—	(breech face to muzzle)
	68'0" (20.726)	(overall)
Type of construction	Built-up	
Type of breech	Down-swing carrier type	
Number of grooves	not available	Twist RH 1/25
Length of rifling	682.46" (17.344)	Length of chamber not available
Chamber volume	27,000 cu. in. (442.451 liters)	Powder container 6 bags

Powder charge	W.W. II:	Service	660 + 4.63 (299.37 + 2.100)
		Reduced	315 + 4.63 (142.884 + 2.100)
	Postwar:	Service	655 + 4.63 (297.108 + 2.100)

Interior Ballistics:

Muzzle energy	Not available
Maximum pressure	18.5 tons/sq. in. (29.137 kg./sq. mm.)
Approximate barrel life	290 rounds

Miscellaneous:

Data from official USN documents.

After World War II, a cooler-burning powder was adopted in order to prolong barrel life.

TABLE C-13
16"/45 (406mm) Gun

Nation:	U.S.A.		
Ships Mounting:	*North Carolina* class *South Dakota* class	Designation:	Mark 6
Nominal Caliber:	16"/45	Year of Design:	about 1936
Actual Bore:	16" (406mm)	Entered Service:	1941

Projectiles:

Type shell	AP Mark 5	AP Mark 8	HC Mark 13 HC Mark 14	
Shell weight	2,240 (1,016.064)	2,700 (1,224.7)	1,900 (861.8)	
Charge	33.57 (15.228)	40.47 (18.357)	153.58 (69.662)	

Range Table Data:

		AP Mark 8	AP Mark 5	HC Mark 13/14
Shell weight		2,700 (1,224.7)	2,240 (1,016.064)	1,900 (861.8)
Muzzle velocity		2,300 (701)	2,520 (768)	2,635 (803)
Range @ 45°		36,900 (33,741)	40,200 (36,759)	40,180 (36,741)
Range @ 40°		36,100 (33,010)	39,300 (35,936)	39,200 (35,844)
Range @ 35°		34,500 (31,547)	37,500 (34,290)	37,400 (34,219)
Range @ 30°		32,200 (29,444)	35,000 (32,004)	34,900 (31,913)
Range @ 25°		29,500 (26,975)	31,900 (29,169)	31,700 (28,986)
Range @ 20°		25,500 (23,317)	27,900 (25,512)	27,950 (25,568)
Range @ 15°		21,000 (19,202)	23,000 (21,031)	23,400 (21,397)
Range @ 10°		15,900 (14,539)	17,500 (16,002)	17,700 (16,185)

Armor Penetration: Calculated, using USN empirical data.

A.P. Shell Weight	Range	Side Plates	Deck Plates	Striking Velocity	Angle of Fall
2,700 (1,224.7)	0	29.74 (755)		2,300 (701)	0°
	5,000 (4,572)	26.60 (676)	0.76 (19)	2,090 (637)	2.98°
	10,000 (9,144)	23.51 (597)	1.87 (28)	1,900 (579)	6.8°
	15,000 (13,716)	20.47 (520)	3.04 (77)	1,734 (529)	11.73°
	20,000 (18,288)	17.62 (448)	4.29 (109)	1,604 (489)	17.93°
	25,000 (22,860)	15.05 (382)	5.76 (146)	1,521 (463)	25.4°
	30,000 (27,432)	12.77 (324)	7.62 (194)	1,490 (454)	34.063°
	35,000 (32,004)	10.49 (266)	10.57 (268)	1,531 (488)	45.16°
2,240 (1,016.064)	0	29.68 (754)		2,520 (768)	0°
	5,000 (4,572)	26.04 (661)	0.75 (19)	2,253 (687)	3.03°
	10,000 (9,144)	22.53 (572)	1.52 (39)	2,007 (612)	5.92°
	15,000 (13,716)	19.22 (488)	2.51 (64)	1,796 (547)	10.5°
	20,000 (18,288)	16.24 (412)	3.56 (90)	1,629 (497)	16.33°
	25,000 (22,860)	13.74 (349)	4.78 (121)	1,522 (464)	23.55°
	30,000 (27,432)	11.68 (297)	6.24 (158)	1,472 (449)	31.68°
	35,000 (32,004)	10.02 (254)	8.15 (207)	1,486 (453)	39.47°
	40,000 (36,576)	8.27 (210)	11.39 (289)	1,586 (483)	51.86°

Mount/Turret Data:

Designation	16-inch/45-caliber 3-gun turret, BB-55/BB-57 class	Weight	1,403-1,437 (1,425.548-1,460.094)
Elevation	45° max. −2° min.	12°/Sec.	
Train	150° max. −150° min.	4°/Sec.	
Rate of fire	2 rounds/minute	Gun recoil	4' 0" (1.219)
Roller path diameter	34' 5" (10.490)		

Gun Data:

Gun weight	—	(including breech mechanism)
	192,310 (87,231)	(without breech mechanism)
Gun length	—	(breech face to muzzle)
	736.0" (18.694)	(overall)
Type of construction	Built-up	
Type of breech	Down-swing carrier	
Number of grooves	not available	Twist 1/50 increasing to 1/32 or 1/25
Length of rifling	616.86" (15.668)	Length of chamber not available
Chamber volume	23,195 cu. in. (380.097 liters)	Powder container 6 bags
Powder charge	Charge 540 lb. (244.95 kg.) Ignition charge 4.63 lb. (2.24 kg.)	

Interior Ballistics:

Muzzle energy	not available
Maximum pressure	18 tons/sq. in. (28.35 kg./sq. mm.)
Approximate barrel life	395 rounds

TABLE C-14
14"/50 (356mm) Gun

Nation:	U.S.A.
Ships Mounting:	*New Mexico* class, *Tennessee* class Designation: Mark 11
Nominal Caliber:	14"/50
Actual Bore:	14" (356mm)

Projectiles:

Type shell	AP Mark 16	HC Mark 22	HC Mark 19
Shell weight	1,500 (680.40)	1,275 (578.34)	1,275 (578.34)
Charge	22.83 (10.356)	104.21 (47.270)	104.21 (47.270)

Range Table Data:

			Reduced Charge Firing	
	New	*New*	*New*	*Avg.*
Shell weight	1,500 (680.40)	1,275 (578.34)	1,500 (680.40)	1,500 (680.40)
Muzzle velocity	2,700 (823)	2,825 (861)	1,935 (590)	1,860 (567)
Range @ 45°	43,200 (39,502)	42,585 (38,940)		
Range @ 40°	42,100 (38,496)	41,500 (37,948)		
Range @ 35°	39,800 (36,393)	39,500 (36,119)		
Range @ 30°	36,800 (33,650)	36,600 (33,467)		20,200 (18,471)
Range @ 25°		33,500 (30,632)		18,500 (16,916)
Range @ 20°		29,500 (26,975)		16,300 (14,905)
Range @ 15°		25,000 (22,860)		13,500 (12,344)
Range @ 10°		19,000 (17,374)		10,000 (9,144)

Armor Penetration: Calculated, using USN empirical data.

A.P. Shell Weight	Range	Side Plates	Deck Plates	Striking Velocity	Angle of Fall (°)
1,500 (680.40)	0	28.03 (712)		2,700 (823)	0
		27.17 (690)		2,625 (800)	0
	5,000 (4,572)	23.66 (601)	0.48 (12)	2,326 (709)	2.36
	10,000 (9,144)	20.12 (511)	1.27 (32)	2,040 (622)	5.61
	15,000 (13,716)	16.76 (426)	2.13 (54)	1,789 (545)	10.23
	20,000 (18,288)	13.75 (349)	3.02 (77)	1,588 (484)	16.33
	25,000 (22,860)	11.27 (286)	4.05 (103)	1,455 (443)	24.08
	30,000 (27,432)	9.29 (236)	5.31 (135)	1,390 (424)	33.0
	35,000 (32,004)	7.82 (199)	6.97 (177)	1,402 (427)	42.5

Mount/Turret Data:

Designation:	14-inch/50 caliber 3-gun turret, BB-40/BB-43 class	Weight	897/958 tons (911.35-973.21 m.t.)
Elevation	30° max. −5° min.	−°/Sec.	
Train	300° max. 280° min.	−°/Sec.	
Rate of fire	not available	Gun recoil	3' 8" (1.117 m.)
Roller path diameter	28' 1.25" (8.567 m.)		

Gun Data:

Gun weight	179,614 (81,473) 177,440 (80,487)	(including breech mechanism) (without breech mechanism)	
Gun length	— 59' 6" (18.136)	(breech face to muzzle) (overall)	
Type of construction	Built-up		
Type of breech	Down-swing carrier type		
Number of grooves	not available	Twist	RH 1/25
Length of rifling	607.358" (15.427)	Length of chamber	not available
Chamber volume	16,982 cu. in. (278,335 liters)	Powder container	4 bags
Powder charge	Service 420 + 2.65 (190.512 + 1.202) Reduced 200 + 2.65 (90.72 + 1.202)		

Interior Ballistics:

Muzzle energy	not available
Maximum pressure	18 tons/sq. in. (28.35 kg./sq. mm.)
Approximate barrel life	250 rounds

Miscellaneous:

Data specifically for 14"/50 Mark 11 Modification 5.
Gun weight varied slightly for other Mods.

TABLE C-15
12"/50 (305mm) Gun

Nation:	U.S.A.		
Ships Mounting:	*Alaska* class	Designation:	Mark 8
Nominal Caliber:	12"/50	Year of Design:	1939
Actual Bore:	12" (305mm)	Entered Service:	1944

Projectiles:

Type shell	AP Mark 18	HC Mark 17 HC Mark 22
Shell weight	1,140 (517.093)	940 (426.38)
Charge	17.44 (7.911)	79.44 (36.034)

Range Table Data:

	New	Reduced charge	New	Reduced charge
Shell weight	1,140 (517.093)	1,140 (517.093)	940 (426.38)	940 (426.38)
Muzzle velocity	2,500 (762)	1,800 (549)	2,650 (808)	1,965 (599)
Range @ 45°	38,573 (35,271)	22,604 (20,669)	38,021 (34,766)	23,800 (21,763)
Range @ 40°	37,800 (34,564)	22,100 (20,208)	37,250 (34,061)	23,200 (21,214)
Range @ 35°	36,000 (32,918)	21,200 (18,151)	35,550 (32,507)	22,200 (20,300)
Range @ 30°	33,600 (30,724)	19,850 (18,151)	33,200 (30,358)	20,900 (19,111)
Range @ 25°	30,450 (27,843)	18,000 (16,459)	30,100 (27,523)	19,000 (17,374)
Range @ 20°	26,600 (24,323)	15,850 (14,493)	26,500 (24,232)	17,000 (15,545)
Range @ 15°	22,200 (20,300)	12,950 (11,841)	22,200 (20,300)	14,000 (12,802)
Range @ 10°	16,700 (15,270)	9,500 (8,687)	17,000 (15,545)	10,500 (9,601)

Armor Penetration: Calculated, using USN empirical data.

A.P. Shell Weight	Range	Side Plates	Deck Plates	Striking Velocity	Angle of Fall
1,140 (517.093)	0	24.48 (622)		2,500 (762)	0°
	5,000 (4,572)	21.34 (542)	0.51 (13)	2,215 (675)	2.6°
	10,000 (9,144)	18.23 (463)	1.26 (32)	1,948 (594)	6°
	15,000 (13,716)	15.56 (395)	2.14 (54)	1,745 (532)	11°
	20,000 (18,288)	12.73 (323)	3.02 (77)	1,550 (472)	17.5°
	25,000 (22,860)	10.52 (267)	4.02 (102)	1,435 (437)	25.3°
	30,000 (27,432)	9.08 (231)	5.11 (130)	1,400 (427)	32.8°
	35,000 (32,004)	7.35 (187)	7.18 (182)	1,427 (435)	44.5°

Mount/Turret Data:

Designation	12″/50 3-gun turret, CB-1 class	Weight	922-934 tons (936.792-948.984)
Elevation	45° max. −3° min.	11.97°/Sec.	
Train	150° max. 150° min.	5 °/Sec.	
Rate of fire	not available	Gun recoil	3′ 0″ (0.9144)
Roller path diameter	26′ 10.984″ (8.204 m.)		

Gun Data:

Gun weight	121,856 (55,262)	(including breech mechanism)
	108,800 (49,351)	(without breech mechanism)
Gun length	—	(breech face to muzzle)
	51′ 0″ (15.545)	(overall)
Type of construction	Built-up	
Type of breech	Down-swing carrier	
Number of grooves	not available	Twist 1/25
Length of rifling	511.96″ (13.004)	Length of chamber not available

Chamber volume	11,863 cu. in. (194.400 liters)	Powder container	4 bags

Powder charge   Service 270 + 2.65 (122.47 + 1.202)
Reduced 132 + 2.65 (59.874 + 1,202)

Interior Ballistics:

Muzzle energy	not available
Maximum pressure	19 tons/sq. in. (29.92 kg./sq. mm.)
Approximate barrel life	344 rounds

TABLE C-16
12"/50 (305mm) Gun

Nation:	U.S.A.		
Ships Mounting:	*Arkansas* class	Designation:	Mark 7
Nominal Caliber:	12"/50		
Actual Bore:	12" (305mm)	Entered Service:	1912

Projectiles:

Type shell	AP Mark 15	HC Mark 16
Shell weight	870 (394.63)	740 (335.66)
Charge	—	—

Range Table Data:

Shell weight	870 (394.63)	740 (335.66)
Muzzle velocity	2,900 (884)	3,000 (914)
Range @ 15°	23,500 (21,488)	23,900 (21,854)

Armor Penetration:

A. P. Shell Weight	Range	Side Plates	Deck Plates	Striking Velocity	Angle of Fall
870 (394.63)	0	*25.30 (643)		2,900 (884)	0°
	14,000 (12,802)	13.0 (330)			
	17,500 (16,002)	11.0 (279)			
	34,000 (31,090)	6.0 (152)			
	28,000 (25,603)		3.9 (99)		
	30,700 (28,072)		4.75 (121)		

* Calculated, using USN empirical data.

Mount/Turret Data:

Designation	12-inch/50-caliber 2-gun turret, BB-32 class	Weight	491 tons (498.86 m.t.)
Elevation	15° max. −5° min.	____°/Sec.	
Train	____ max. ____ min.	____°/Sec.	
Rate of fire	not available	Gun recoil	3' 2" (0.965 m.)
Roller path diameter	24' 11" (7.595 m.)		

Gun Data:

Gun weight	124,140 (56,310) 121,905 (55,296)	(including breech mechanism) (without breech mechanism)	
Gun length	— 607.25" (15.424)	(breech face to muzzle) (overall)	
Type of construction	Built-up		
Type of breech	Smith-Asbury side-swing		
Number of grooves	not available	Twist	RH 1/50 to 1/32
Length of rifling	500.925" (12.724)	Length of chamber	not available
Chamber volume	14,871 cu. in. (243.736 cu. dm.)	Powder container	4 bags
Powder charge	337 lb. (152.863 kg.)		

Interior Ballistics:

Muzzle energy	51,644 foot-tons (15,994 ton-meters)
Maximum pressure	17.5 tons/sq. in. (27.56 kg./mm²)
Approximate barrel life	not available

Miscellaneous:

Above data for 12-inch Mark 7 Mod. 19

TABLE C-17
5"/54 (127mm) Gun

Nation:	U.S.A.			
Ships Mounting:	*Montana* class	Designation:	Mark 16	
Nominal Caliber:	5"/54	Year of Design:	about 1939	
Actual Bore:	5.0" (127mm)	Entered Service:	1945	

Projectiles:

	AAC	HC	ILLUM	COM	VT
Type shell	Mark 41	Mark 41	Mark 48	Mark 42	Mark 41
Shell weight	69.45 (31.502)	69.33 (31.448)	69.2 (31.389)	70.00 (31.751)	69.19 (31.384)
Charge	7.75 (3.515)	7.75 (3.515)	0	2.14 (0.971)	7.87 (3.570)

Range Table Data: *New*

Shell weight	70.00 (31.751)
Muzzle velocity	2,650 (808)
Range @ 45°	25,909 (23,691)
Range @ 40°	—
Range @ 35°	24,100 (22,860)
Range @ 30°	22,500 (20,574)
Range @ 25°	—
Range @ 20°	19,000 (17,374)
Range @ 15°	16,300 (14,905)
Range @ 10°	13,000 (11,887)
AA Ceiling:	51,600′ (15,728 m.)

Armor Penetration: not available

Mount/Turret Data:

Designation	5″ Twin Mount	Weight	not available
Elevation	85° max. −10° min.	15°/Sec.	
Train	____ max. ____ min.	30°/Sec.	
Rate of fire	not available	Gun recoil	1′ 7″ (0.483)
Roller path diameter	not available		

Gun Data:

Gun weight	—	(including breech mechanism)
	5,361 (2,432)	(without breech mechanism)
Gun length	—	(breech face to muzzle)
	22′ 6″ (6.858)	(overall)
Type of construction	Monobloc	
Type of breech	Semi-automatic, vertical sliding wedge	
Number of grooves	not available	Twist 1/25
Length of rifling	229.07″ (5.820)	Length of chamber not available
Chamber volume	825.38 cu. in. (13.525 liters)	Powder container Cartridge 34.14 (15.486)
Powder charge	18.5 (8.188)	

Interior Ballistics:

Muzzle energy	not available
Maximum pressure	18.5 tons/sq. in. (29.137 kg/sq. mm.)
Approximate barrel life	3,070 rounds

TABLE C-18
5"/38 (127mm) Gun

Nation:	U.S.A.				
Ships Mounting:	*Alaska* class, *South Dakota* class *Iowa* class, *North Carolina* class		Designation:	Mark 12	
Nominal Caliber:	5"/38				
Actual Bore:	5" (127mm)		Entered Service:	1934	

Projectiles:

Type shell	VT Mk. 35 VT Mk. 49	AAC Mk. 35 AAC Mk. 49	HC Mk. 35 HC Mk. 49	WP WP	COM Mk. 38 COM Mk. 46
Shell weight	54.61 (24.771)	55.18 (25.030)	54.3 (24.630)	54.39 (24.671)	55.18 (25.030)
Charge	7.86 (3.565)	7.55 (3.424)	7.55 (3.424)	0	

Range Table Data:

		AAC Mk. 49 New	AAC Mk. 49 Avg		WP New
Shell weight		55.18 (25.030)	55.18 (25.030)		53 (24.040)
Muzzle velocity		2,600 (792)	2,500 (762)		2,600 (792)
Range @ 45°		18,200 (16,642)	17,392 (15,903)		17,575 (16,071)
Range @ 40°			17,240 (15,764)		17,450 (15,956)
Range @ 35°			16,739 (15,298)		17,050 (15,591)
Range @ 30°			15,919 (14,556)		16,200 (14,813)
Range @ 25°			14,804 (13,537)		15,050 (13,762)
Range @ 20°			13,395 (12,248)		13,650 (12,482)
Range @ 15°			11,663 (10,665)		11,900 (10,881)
Range @ 10°			9,506 (8,692)		9,800 (8,961)
	AA Ceiling:		37,200' (11,887 m.)		

Armor Penetration: Not available

Mount/Turret Data:

Designation	5" Mount Mk. 28 Mod. 0			156,295 (70,893)	
	5" Mount Mk. 28 Mod. 2			170,635 (77,398)	
	5" Mount Mk. 32 Mod. 4		Weight	120,369 (54,598)	
Elevation	85° max.	−15° min.	15°/Sec.		
Train	____ max.	____ min.	25°/Sec.		
Rate of fire	not available		Gun recoil	1' 7" (0.473) max.	
Roller path diameter	not available				

Gun Data:

Gun weight	—	(including breech mechanism)
	3,990 (1,810)	(without breech mechanism)
Gun length	—	(breech face to muzzle)
	15' 10" (4.826)	(overall)
Type of construction	Monobloc	
Type of breech	Semi-automatic, vertical sliding wedge	

Number of grooves	not available	Twist	RH 1/30
Length of rifling	157.225" (3.994 m.)	Length of chamber	not available
Chamber volume	650 cu. in. (10.652 liters)	Powder container	Cartridge 27 (12.247)

Powder charge   Flashless 15.5 lb. (7.031 kg.)
                    Nonflashless 15.4 lb. (6.986 kg.)

Interior Ballistics:

Muzzle energy	not available
Maximum pressure	18 tons/sq. in. (28.35 kg/sq. mm.)
Approximate barrel life	4,600 rounds

Miscellaneous:

Above-listed mounts all twin mounts
   5" Mount Mk. 28 Mod. 0   BB 55-60
   5" Mount Mk. 28 Mod. 2   BB 61-66
   5" Mount Mk. 32 Mod. 4   CB   1- 6

TABLE C-19
1.57"/56 (40mm) Gun

Nation:	U.S.A.			
Ships Mounting:	Numerous		Designation:	Mark 2
				Mark 1
Nominal Caliber:	40mm/56.3		Year of Design:	1941
Actual Bore:	.575" (40mm)			

Projectiles:	*HE*	*HE*	*AP*	*AP-T*
Type shell	Mark 1	Mark 2	M81A1	Mark 4
Shell weight	1.985 (0.900)	1.985 (0.900)	1.96 (0.889)	
Charge	0.148 (0.067)	0.150 (0.068)	none	none

Range Table Data:	New	New
Shell weight	1.985 (0.900)	1.96 (0.889)
Muzzle velocity	2,890 (881)	2,890 (881)
Range @ 45°	11,133 (10,180)	9,492 (8,679)
Range @ 40°	11,208 (10,249)	9,618 (8,795)
Range @ 35°	11,057 (10,111)	9,568 (8,749)
Range @ 30°	10,691 (9,776)	9,358 (8,557)
Range @ 25°	10,103 (9,238)	8,959 (8,192)
Range @ 20°	9,295 (8,499)	8,389 (7,671)
Range @ 15°	8,227 (7,523)	7,580 (6,931)
Range @ 10°	6,844 (6,258)	6,466 (5,913)
AA Ceiling:	22,299	(6,797 m.)

Armor Penetration: Estimated, for "Class B" (homogeneous) armor

A. P. Shell Weight	Range	Side Plates	Deck Plates	Striking Velocity	Angle of Fall
1.96 (0.899)	0	2.7" (69)		2,890 (881)	
	2,000 (1,829)	1.2" (30)			
	4,000 (3,658)	0.6" (15)			
	6,000 (5,486)	0.45" (11)			

Mount/Turret Data: not available

Gun Data:

Gun weight	—	(including breech mechanism)
	202 (91.63)	(without breech mechanism)
Gun length	—	(breech face to muzzle)
	8′ 2.373" (2.499)	(overall)
Type of construction	Monobloc	
Type of breech	Vertical sliding wedge	
Number of grooves	not available	Twist 1/45 to 1/30
Length of rifling	75.85" (1.927) 28.3 cu. in.	Length of chamber not available
Chamber volume	(0.464 liter)	Powder container Cartridge
Powder charge	0.694 lb. (0.314 kg.)	

Interior Ballistics:

Muzzle energy	not available
Maximum pressure	19.5 tons/sq. in. (30.707 kg./sq. mm.)
Approximate barrel life	9500 rounds

Miscellaneous:

40mm Mounts	Mark 1 Twin	Mark 2 Quad	Mark 4 Quad
Elev. limits	+90° − 15°	+90° − 15°	+90° − 15°
Elev. rates	24°/sec.	24°/sec.	55°/sec.
Train limits	−360°	−360°	−360°
Train rates	26°/sec.	26°/sec.	50°/sec.
Weight—no shield	9,800-13,000 (4445-5897)	23,200-23,800 (10,524-10,796	22,795-24,553 10,340-11,137)
Weight—shield 0.375″ (10mm)		24,900-25,500 (11,294-11,567	25,140-26,623 11,404-12,076)

TABLE C-20
1.1″/75 (28mm) Gun

Nation:	U.S.A.		
Ships Mounting:	*North Carolina* class *South Dakota* class	Designation:	Mark 1
Nominal Caliber:	1.1″/75	Year of Design:	about 1934
Actual Bore:	1.1″ (28mm)	Entered Service:	about 1936

Projectiles:

Type shell	AA Mark I	AA Mark 2
Shell weight	0.917 (0.416)	0.917 (0.416)
Charge	not available	

Range Table Data:	New	Average
Shell weight	0.917 (0.416)	0.917 (0.416)
Muzzle velocity	2,700 (823)	2,600 (792)
Range @ 45°		
Range @ 40° 53′		7,400 (6,767)
Range @ 35°		
Range @ 30°		
Range @ 25°		6,900 (6,309)
Range @ 20°		6,600 (6,035)
Range @ 15°		6,100 (5,578)
Range @ 10°		5,300 (4,846)
AA Ceiling:		19,000′ (5,791 m.)

Armor Penetration: not available

Mount/Turret Data:

Designation	1.10-inch Mount Mark 2 Mod. 2 (quadruple)	Weight	10,500 (4,763)
Elevation	110° Max. −15° Min.	24°/Sec.	
Train	360° Max. 360° Min.	30°/Sec.	
Rate of fire	150 rounds/minute/gun	Gun recoil	3.25″ (0.0825)
Roller path diameter	not available		

Gun Data:

Gun weight	—	(including breech mechanism)	
	556 (252)	(without breech mechanism)	
Gun length	not available	(breech face to muzzle)	
	not available	(overall)	
Type of construction	Monobloc		
Type of breech	Horizontal sliding		
Number of grooves	not available	Twist	not available
Length of rifling	not available	Length of chamber	not available
Chamber volume	not available	Powder container	Cartridge 0.688 (0.312)
Powder charge	0.265 lb. (0.120 kg.)		

Interior Ballistics:

Muzzle energy	not available
Maximum pressure	18 tons/sq. in. (28.35 kg./sq. mm.)
Approximate barrel life	not available

TABLE C-21
0.79/72 (20mm) Gun

Nation:	U.S.A.		Designation:	Mark 4
				Mark 3
				Mark 2

Ships Mounting: Numerous
Nominal Caliber: 20mm/72
Actual Bore: 0.7898″ (20mm)

Projectiles:	*HE*	*HE-I*	*HE-T*	*HE-T*	*AP-T*
Type shell	Mark 3	Mark 3	Mark 4	Mark 7	Mark 9
Shell weight	0.2714 (0.1231)	0.2714 (0.1231)	0.2621 (0.1169)	0.2714 (0.1231)	0.2686 (0.1218)
Charge	0.0243 (0.0110)	0.0171 (0.0077)	0.0099 (0.0045)	0.0099 (0.0045)	none

Range Table Data:	*New Gun*	*HE Mk. 3 Average*	*HE-I Mk. 3 Average*	*AP-T Mk. 9 Average*
Shell weight	0.2714 (0.1231)	0.2714 (0.1231)	0.2714 (0.1231)	0.2686 (0.1218)
Muzzle velocity	2,770 (844)	2,740 (835)	2,725 (831)	2,740 (835)
Range @ 45°			4,800 (4,389)	
Range @ 40°			4,775 (4,366)	
Range @ 35°			4,725 (4,320)	
Range @ 30°			4,650 (4,252)	
Range @ 25°			4,525 (4,138)	
Range @ 20°			4,275 (3,909)	
Range @ 15°			3,950 (3,612)	
Range @ 10°			3,450 (3,154)	

AA Ceiling: 10,000′   (3,048 m.)

Armor Penetration: Not available

Mount/Turret Data:

Weight Mk. 6   1,691 (767.0)
       Mk. 5/4 1,394 (632.3)
       Mk. 5/3 1,538 (697.6)
       Mk. 4   (1,695)
       Mk. 2   (768.8)

Designation Mounts Mark 2, 4, 5, 6, and 10 Single
                 Mount Mark 24 Twin

Elevation   87/90/85 max. −5/−15/−15 min.   −°/sec.
Train   180° max.   −180° min.   −°/sec.
Rate of fire   450 rounds/minute/gun   Note: Manual train & elevation *only*

Gun Data:

Gun weight   150 (68.04)   (including breech mechanism)
                     46 (20.865)   (without breech mechanism)
Gun length   not available   (breech face to muzzle)
                    4′ 9.172″ (1.452)   (overall)
Type of construction   Monoblock
Type of breech   Horizontal sliding
Number of grooves   9   Twist   RH 1/36
Length of rifling   not available   Length of chamber   not available
Chamber volume   not available   Powder container   Cartridge
Powder charge   0.061 lb. (0.0277 kg.)
                   FHN type nitrocellulose

Interior Ballistics:

Muzzle energy	not available
Maximum pressure	not available
Approximate barrel life	9,000 rounds

Miscellaneous:

Mounts Mark 2 and 4 had provision for mechanical trunnion height adjustment for ease of gunner.
Mount Mark 6 had hydraulic trunnion height adjustment.
Mounts Mark 5, 10, and 24 had fixed trunnion heights.

Bibliography

he technical details in this work are based principally on official United States Navy documents, primarily those in the detailed design archives, supplemented by official reports. The authors were allowed access to the classified ship design files in the Preliminary Design Branch of the Bureau of Ships (now the Naval Sea Systems Command). The materials examined included:

- Design histories
- Internal correspondence regarding alternative design concepts
- Minutes of Ship Characteristics Board meetings
- Detailed engineering analyses and calculations (stability, weight, propulsion, protection, etc.)
- Battle damage reports

Such material was of fundamental importance, as it was this largely unpublished data that permitted a systematic analysis of the design evolution of the various classes, including a detailed study of the ships as completed.

This technical data was supplemented by various battle damage reports, special incident reports, and other operational reports made available by the Operational Archives Branch of the Naval Historical Center. In addition, the Naval Historical Center's ship histories provided a useful starting point for the narratives of the ship operational careers.

The actual characteristics of the ships as built were obtained from such official sources as the Ship's Data Book for each U. S. naval ship, numerous official plans, and the General Information Book, which gives general physical characteristics as well as detailed system descriptions for each U. S. naval ship.

The authors were given further insight into the design of American capital ships through the kindness and consideration of Rear Admiral C. D. Wheelock, a naval constructor in the Bureau of Ships who was personally involved in the design of the ships, and Mr. George Sieker, a civilian naval architect whose 50-year career spanned most of the era of the modern battleship in the U. S. Navy. Both men were helpful in offering comments on the Capital ship design process in the U. S. Navy.

Certain private firms were also helpful in providing technical background data for this book.

Technical background data for this book was provided by the firms of Foster Wheeler, Babock & Wilcox, General Electric Corporation, Westinghouse Electric Corporation, New York Shipbuilding Corporation, and Gibbs & Cox, Inc. Published works consulted included the *History of United States Naval Operations in World War II*, by Samuel Eliot Morison, *Jane's Fighting Ships*, *Ships and Aircraft of the U. S. Fleet*, and *Warships of the World*.

Finally, an expression of appreciation is due to Mr. Richard L. Welch, of the Office of the Chief of Naval Operations, for his review and security clearance of the manuscript.

The authors and illustrator are fully responsible for the accuracy of this book. All opinions and conclusions, unless specifically identified otherwise, are theirs, and are not to be construed as official, or necessarily reflecting the views of the Navy Department.

BOOKS

Babcock and Wilcox. *Steam—Its Generation and Use.* 37th ed. New York: 1963.
Bowen, Harold G. *Ship Machinery and Mossbacks.* Princeton: Princeton University Press.
Breyer, Siegfried. *Battleships and BattleCruisers, 1905—1970.* Garden City, N.Y.: Doubleday, 1973.
Clagat, John. *The United States Navy in Action.* Derby, Conn.: Monarch, 1963.
Cole, Robert H. *Underwater Explosions.* Princeton: Princeton University Press, 1948.
Field, James A. *History of United States Naval Operations, Korea.* Washington, D. C.: Government Printing Office, 1962.
Halsey, William, and Bryan, J. *Admiral Halsey's Story.* Hightstown, N.J.: McGraw-Hill: 1947.
Hovgaard, William. *Structural Design of Warships.* Annapolis: Naval Institute Press, 1940.
Jane's Fighting Ships. London: Sampson Low, 1939, 1944-45, 1950-51, 1968-69.
Kafka, Roger, and Pepperburg, Roy L. *Warships of the World.* New York: Cornell Maritime Press, 1946.
Korotkin, I. M. *Battle Damage to Surface Ships during World War II.* Leningrad: Sudpromgiz, 1960.
Lord, Walter. *Day of Infamy.* New York: Harper and Row, 1957.
Manning, G. C., and Schumacher, T. L. *Principles of Naval Architecture and Warship Construction.* Annapolis: Naval Institute Press, 1928.
Matsumoto, Kitaro. *Design and Construction of the Battleships Yamato and Musashi.* Tokyo: Haga, 1961.
Morison, Samuel E. *History of United States Naval Operations in World War II.* Vols. 1-14. Boston: Little, Brown, 1947-1960.
Potter, E. B., and Nimitz, Chester W., eds. *Sea Power, A Naval History.* Englewood Cliffs: Prentice-Hall, 1960.
Rigdon, William. *White House Sailor.* Garden City: Doubleday, 1962.
Rowe, John S., and Morison, Samuel L., comp. *Ships and Aircraft of the U. S. Fleet.* 9th ed. Annapolis: Naval Institute Press, 1972.
Rowland, Buford, and Boyd, William. *U. S. Navy Bureau of Ordnance in World War II.* Washington, D. C.: Government Printing Office, 1953.
U. S. Department of the Navy. Office of the Chief of Naval Operations, Naval History Division. *Dictionary of American Naval Fighting Ships.* Vols. 1-4. Washington, D. C.: Government Printing Office, 1959-1969.

PERIODICALS

Boatwright, G. M., Hauschildt, M. R., and Welling, M. "Naval Propulsion Machinery." *Journal of the American Society of Naval Engineers.* Vol. 57, no. 4, pt. 2.
Holtzworth, E. C. "U. S. Navy Battle Damage Pictures from World War II." *Journal of the American Society of Naval Engineers.* Vols. 57, no. 4, pt. 1; and 58, no. 1, pt. 2; no. 2, pt. 3; no. 3, pt. 4.

NEWSPAPERS

"Big Battlewagons Primed for Comeback in Brushfire War Arenas," *New York Journal American,* 10 November 1962.
"Navy Hopes to Reactivate its Four Old Battlewagons," *Christian Science Monitor,* 12 November 1962.
"New Jersey's Big Guns Bite Deep," *Pacific Stars & Stripes,* 27 January 1969.
"Use of Battleships in War Considered by McNamara," *New York Times,* 9 April 1967.

PROCEEDINGS—PUBLISHED

Gisserot, P. "Batiments de Ligne Modernes." *Bulletin de l'Association Technique Maritime et Aeronautique.* Vol. 49. Paris: 1950.

Keil, A. H. "The Response of Ships to Underwater Explosions." *Transactions of the Society of Naval Architects and Marine Engineers.* Vol. 69. New York: 1961.

Sherwin, Rodney, and Miller, Richards T. "Impact of Electronics on Warship Design." *Transactions of the Society of Naval Architects and Marine Engineers.* Vol. 70. New York: 1962.

Strope, Walter, and Dwyer, Stanley. "The Small Displacement Capital Ship." *Transactions of the Society of Naval Architects and Marine Engineers.* Vol. 50. New York: 1942.

UNITED STATES GOVERNMENT DOCUMENTS

U. S. Congress. Senate. Committee on Naval Affairs. *Construction of Certain Naval Vessels. Hearing before the Committee on Naval Affairs* on H. R. 6604, 73rd Cong., 2nd sess., 1934.

U. S. Congress. Senate. Committee on Naval Affairs. *Construction of Certain Naval Vessels at the Limits Prescribed by the Treaties Signed at Washington and London. Hearing before the Committee on Naval Affairs* on S. 2493, 73rd Cong., 2nd sess., 1934.

U. S. Department of the Navy. Bureau of Ships. *General Information Book—USS Massachusetts (BB-59).* 1942.

_____. _____. *General Information Book—USS North Carolina (BB-55).* 1945.

_____. _____. *Ships' Data, U. S. Navy Vessels.* Vol. 2. 1949.

_____. Division of Naval History. *History of Ships Named Iowa.* November 1962.

_____. _____. *History of Ships Named New Jersey.* August 1969.

_____. _____. *History of USS Alabama (BB-60).* April 1957

_____. _____. *History of USS Massachusetts (BB-59).* April 1947.

_____. _____. *History of USS Missouri (BB-63).* October 1956.

_____. _____. *History of USS North Carolina (BB-55).*

_____. _____. *History of USS Washington (BB-56).* January 1957.

_____. _____. *History of USS Wisconsin (BB-64).* March 1958.

_____. Ordnance Systems Command. *Abridged Range Tables for U. S. Naval Guns.* Nav Ord OP 1188, 1st rev. (1947).

_____. _____. *Gun Mount and Turret Catalog.* Nav Ord OP 1112, 2nd rev. (1945).

_____. _____. *Gun Mounts and Turrets.* Nav Ord OP 1112, change 1 to 3rd rev. (1968).

_____. _____. *Service Life of U. S. Naval Gun Barrels.* Nav Ord OP 1549, 3rd rev.

_____. _____. *16-Inch Three Gun Turrets BB-61 Class.* Nav Ord OP 769. 1968.

_____. _____. *United States Naval Guns, Marks and Modifications, Obsolete Guns.* Nav Ord OP 127, Vol. 2, 4th rev. (1956).

UNPUBLISHED MATERIAL

U. S. Department of the Navy. Bureau of Construction and Repair. *Battleship 1935—Spring Styles.* September 25, 1935.

_____. Bureau of Ordnance. *Armament Summary, BB-55–BB-64, CB1-CB2.* 1941-1945.

_____. _____. *Bulletin 1-53.*

_____. Bureau of Ships. *Salvage of USS Missouri (BB-63).* BuShips 250-694-3. June 1, 1950.

_____. _____. *USS South Dakota, Gunfire Damage, Battle of Guadalcanal, 14-15 November 1942.* War Damage Report #57.

_____. _____. Preliminary Design Branch. *Study of Bismarck.* December 1941.

_____. Commanding Officer, USS Indiana (BB-58). *Report of Collision.* Letter of February 3, 1944.

_____. Commanding Officer, USS Iowa. *Action Report—Bombardment of Mille—18 March 1944.* Letter serial #033 of March 28, 1944.

_____. _____. *Circumstances Attending the Grounding of USS Iowa (BB-61).* Letter serial #007 of July 18, 1943.

_____. _____. *Damage Report—USS Iowa.* Letter serial #007 of July 31, 1943.

_____. _____. *Grounding and Salvage of USS Iowa.* Letter serial #3197 of July 31, 1943.

_____. _____. *Special Employment of Task Group 27.5 during the Period October 24, 1943 to December 16, 1943.* December 1943.

_____. Commanding Officer, *USS North Carolina. Action Damage Report of 6 April 1945.* Letter serial #005 of April 11, 1945.

_____. _____. *Torpedo Damage Report.* Letter serial #1028 of September 26, 1942.

_____. Commanding Officer, *USS South Dakota. Action Report October 26, 1942 off Santa Cruz Islands.* Letter serial #0154 of November 2, 1942.

_____. _____. *Report of Structural Damage Occasioned by Collision with USS Mahan.* Letter serial #0151 of November 2, 1942.

_____. Commanding Officer, *USS Washington. Report of Collision between USS Washington and USS Indiana.* Letter serial #0012 of February 8, 1944.

_____. Commanding Officer, *USS Wisconsin. Action Report for 15-19 March 1952.* Letter serial #043 of 29 March 1952.

_____. Office of Chief of Naval Operations. *Combat Narratives—Miscellaneous Actions in the South Pacific, 8 August 1942 to 22 January 1943.*

_____. *USS Massachusetts (BB-59) Ships Log, November 7-8, 1942.*

PAMPHLETS

Gorrell, Dick, and Roberts, Bruce. *USS North Carolina, the "Showboat."* Charlotte, N.C.: Heritage, 1961.

The Missouri, the Mighty Man O' War on Which Japan Surrendered. Laurel Process Co.: 1945.

Stillwell, Paul. *USS South Dakota—The Story of Battleship X.* Sioux Falls, S.D: 1972.

Thomte, Theodore. *The Battleship USS Massachusetts.* Boston: Burdette, 1965.

INTERVIEWS & LETTERS

Maxwell, William, RADM, USN (Ret.). *USS North Carolina* Memorial, Wilmington, North Carolina. Interview. October 1961.

Meirat, Jean. Letters to William Garzke. 1966-1969.

Sieker, George. Bureau of Ships, Washington, D. C. Interview. 1965.

Wheelock, Charles, RADM, USN (Ret.). Society of Naval Architects and Engineers, New York. Interview. November 1965.

PLANS & ENGINEERING CALCULATIONS

U. S. Department of the Navy. Bureau of Ordnance. *Penetration Chart for Projectiles with Major Caliber Characteristics.* Bu Ord no. 78841. 25 March 1936.

_____. Bureau of Ships. *USS North Carolina (BB-55) Battleship 1937 Scheme XVI, Inboard Profile and Deck Plan.* C & R no. 012835-A.

_____. _____. *Weight Summary—USS New Jersey (BB-62).* 1943.

_____. _____. *Weight Summary—USS South Dakota (BB-57).* 1942.

_____. _____. *Weight Summary—USS Washington (BB-56).* 1941.

For USS *North Carolina* (BB-55), BuShips Plan Numbers 303627 (Plates 2-13), dated 15 May 1946, and 303688 (Plates 1-3); BuC&R Plan Numbers 267729, 267730, and 267731, dated August 1941.

For USS *Washington* (BB-56), BuShips Plan Number 303693 (Plates 2-15), dated September 1945.

For USS *South Dakota* (BB-57), BuShips Plan Number 460648 (Plates 2-19), dated 10 April 1946.

For USS *Alabama* (BB-60), BuShips Plan Number 524264 (Plates 1, 3-14, 16, 17), revised 25 March 1953, and BuShips Plan Number 337244 (Plate 4).

For USS *Iowa* (BB-61), BuShips Plan Number 578106 (Plates 2-15) dated 29 June 1945; BuC&R Plan Numbers 353188, 353189, and 353190, dated November 1940.

For USS *New Jersey* (BB-62), BuShips Plan Number 578273 (Plates 1-4).

For USS *Alaska* (CB-1), BuShips, Plan Number CB-1-50103-437333 (Plates 2-17), dated 19 June 1946; and BuShips Sketch 435-203-0A.

Index